Paul Ibbotson
What it Takes to Talk

Cognitive Linguistics Research

Editors
Dirk Geeraerts
Dagmar Divjak

Honorary editors
René Dirven
Ronald W. Langacker

Volume 64

Paul Ibbotson

What it Takes to Talk

Exploring Developmental Cognitive Linguistics

DE GRUYTER
MOUTON

ISBN 978-3-11-099203-8
e-ISBN (PDF) 978-3-11-064791-4
e-ISBN (EPUB) 978-3-11-064450-0
ISSN 1861-4132

Library of Congress Control Number: 2020940474

Bibliographic information published by the Deutsche Nationalbibliothek
The Deutsche Nationalbibliothek lists this publication in the Deutsche Nationalbibliografie;
detailed bibliographic data are available on the Internet at http://dnb.dnb.de.

© 2022 Walter de Gruyter GmbH, Berlin/Boston
This volume is text- and page-identical with the hardback published in 2020.
Typesetting: Integra Software Services Pvt. Ltd.|
Printing and binding: CPI books GmbH, Leck

www.degruyter.com

Summary

This book puts cognition back at the heart of the language learning process and challenges the idea that language acquisition can be meaningfully understood as a purely linguistic phenomenon. Summarizing decades of important research on the topic, it outlines the contribution that psychology has made to understanding the mechanisms driving language development. For each domain-general capacity placed under the spotlight – memory, attention, inhibition, categorization, analogy and social cognition – we establish the extent to which they shape the acquisition of sounds, words and grammar. *Developmental Cognitive Linguistics* explores how the unfolding cognitive and social world of the child interacts with, constrains, and predicts language use. Linguists have often drawn attention to the expressive power and combinatorial possibilities of grammar and asked why certain generalizations are possible but not entertained by the child – typically proposing language-internal solutions. Here is where a developmental perspective really matters: without it, it is difficult to make sense of what kind of thing language is, because learning constrains and shapes what kind of thing language can be. As a cultural tool, linguistic knowledge has to pass through the bottleneck of what cognition can do, and allow, at any stage in development, and these self-imposed constraints can be adaptive for learning because they further dampen the degrees of freedom available for linguistic generalizations. Much of the energy in language acquisition research has been expended in pursuit of developmental mechanisms that are both able to generate abstractions and constrain generalizations. And it is that balance between creativity and conformity in language that this book aims to address too, evaluating the contribution cognition can make to answering these long-standing questions. The implications of this are that the traditional linguistic-internal analysis is no longer an adequate theoretical framework for studying language acquisition, and a more integrative approach offered by developmental cognitive linguistics is what is needed. Language is special not because of some encapsulated module separate from the rest of cognition. It is special because of the forms it can take rather than the parts it is made of and because it could be nature's finest example of cognitive recycling and reuse.

Preface

For the past 10 years my own research has focused on the relationship between language and cognition, trying to understand what the value is of integrating memory, inhibition, attention, categorization and so on, into a theory of acquisition. That work has often concluded with a statement along the lines of . . . *thus this provides further evidence that domain-general processes can help narrow the degrees of freedom on language learning*. It has become increasingly clear that to really make good on this claim requires setting out the evidence in a way that no one paper could achieve by itself – evidence that spans neuroscience, animal cognition, evolution, artificial intelligence, developmental psychology and of course linguistics itself. So, while my work and original ideas appear in this book, the general argument has been immeasurably enhanced, and indeed made possible, by the thousands of linguists and psychologists who have all been, in one way or another, interested in the same questions as I have. Their work makes up the majority of the book's content and I am indebted to the contribution they have made. The story that research tells, in my opinion, should be of interest to scholars of linguistics and psychology alike, and more generally those seeking to understand the complex developmental relationship between language and cognition.

Thank you to all those who have offered comments on or else have provided information for this book, including Adele Goldberg, Morten Christiansen, Nick Chater, Michael Tomasello, John Oates, Kieron Sheehy, Jeff Zachs, David Messer, Ernesto Roque-Gutierrez, Tess Millar and Eva van Lier. I am grateful to Birgit Sievert and Kirstin Boergen at *DeGruyter Mouton* and to an anonymous reviewer who helpfully pointed out omissions and connections to more recent theoretical developments I had overlooked. A special thanks to Elena Lieven who read the penultimate manuscript in its entirety and provided many insightful comments that strengthened the argument.

The book is organized into three parts. Part I of the book briefly reviews how we got here, presents the case why anyone would *want* to integrate language and cognition in the first place, and why reunification might be a project worth pursuing, even if it turns out to be the wrong one. Part II zooms in on a number of domain-general capacities – memory, attention, inhibition, categorization, analogy and social cognition – and asks to what extent they shape the developmental trajectory of language. Part III focuses on the theoretical fall-out of adopting a developmental cognitive approach, how one might do research in this spirit, and pulls together some of the more important recurring themes that have emerged over the course of the book. The hope is that ideas presented here are stimulus enough for others to disprove, advance, refine and get us closer to the true nature of our language and cognition.

Contents

Summary —— V

Preface —— VII

Part I

Chapter 1
Talking of cognition —— 3
- 1.1 The (re)unification of language and cognition —— 3
- 1.2 Why integrate language and cognition? —— 6
- 1.3 Arguments from genetics, atypical populations and neuroscience —— 7
- 1.4 Arguments from human evolution, comparative psychology and typology —— 12
- 1.5 Arguments from computational modelling, artificial intelligence and robotics —— 16
- 1.6 Summary —— 20

Part II

Chapter 2
Memory —— 25
- 2.1 The development of memory —— 25
- 2.2 Working memory and language development —— 28
- 2.3 Long-term memory and language development —— 35
- 2.4 Computational modelling of memory and language —— 39
- 2.5 Summary —— 43

Chapter 3
Categorization and analogy —— 45
- 3.1 The development of pre-verbal categorization —— 48
- 3.2 Prototypicality and item weight in categories —— 50
- 3.3 Event cognition and mapping verbs —— 58
- 3.4 Lumping and splitting —— 70
- 3.5 Summary —— 72

Chapter 4
Attention and inhibition —— 76
    4.1   The development of attention and inhibition —— 76
    4.2   What attention can do for language and language acquisition —— 81
    4.3   What inhibition can do for language and language acquisition —— 89
    4.4   Summary —— 93

Chapter 5
Social cognition —— 94
    5.1   The development of social cognition —— 96
    5.2   Social cognition, cooperative action and language —— 99
    5.3   Social cognition and language development —— 103
    5.4   Normative reasoning – we say things this way —— 105
    5.5   Discourse and narrative —— 113
    5.6   Summary —— 115

Part III

Chapter 6
Developmental cognitive linguistics —— 121
    6.1   Dynamic systems theory and developmental cognitive linguistics —— 124
    6.2   A dynamic network analysis of emergent grammar —— 131
    6.3   Developmental cognitive linguistics, language differences and similarities —— 144
    6.4   'Doing' developmental cognitive linguistics —— 147
    6.5   Language constraining the degrees of freedom on cognition —— 156
    6.6   A test of the directionality of cognitive transfer —— 158
    6.7   Conclusions —— 160

About the Author —— 165

References —— 167

Index —— 223

Part I

Chapter 1
Talking of cognition

1.1 The (re)unification of language and cognition

> It would surprising indeed if we were to find that the principles governing [linguistic] phenomena are operative in other cognitive systems, although there might be certain loose analogies, perhaps in terms of figure and ground, or properties of memory, as we see when the relevant principles are made explicit. Such examples illustrate . . . that there is good reason to suppose that the functioning of the language faculty is guided by special principles specific to this domain . . . (Chomsky, 1980, p.44)

In the same year that these words were published, Jerry Fodor was teaching a graduate cognitive psychology course with Noam Chomsky at MIT. The notes for those lectures evolved into his book-length essay *Modularity of Mind*, a broad ranging philosophical and scientific work that made strong claims about the way the mind was organized into independent units, or modules. The work had implications for all of areas of psychology, but the way in which Fodor talked of a "language-recognition module" in particular, picked up where Chomsky's "language faculty" and "mental organ" had left off:

> All the available evidence suggests that the computations which sentence recognizers perform must be closely tuned to a complex of stimulus properties that is quite specific to sentences. Roughly, the idea is that the structure of the sentence recognition system is responsive to universal properties of language and hence that the system works only in domains which exhibit these properties (Fodor, 1983, p.50)

The claim was that language gets its own ring-fenced mental processor, areas of which cannot be accessed by other cognitive systems such as movement or vision. Furthermore, this area comes with content organized in advance of experience, designed to work exclusively on linguistic input. Both works went on to have huge influence in the field of language and cognition being citied more than 22-thousand times between them. As it turned out, *Modularity of Mind* represented something of a high-water mark for the conceptual unity of the language module, after which it fragmented into ever-smaller sub-modules. Pinker, (1994), argued that general cognition operated independently from the language module, which itself could be subdivided into lexical and syntactic components (Pinker, 1999). Others went further and specified modules for verbs and nouns, with nouns subcategorized into modules for tool use and utensil use (Tranel et al. 1997), until ultimately, modules were atomized at the size of a single concept (Sperber, 2002).

Then, in a 2002 *Science* article co-authored by Chomsky – the principle architect of the language-as-a-module view – there appeared a softening of the stance, allowing for both a Narrow Language Faculty containing aspects of language unique to language, and a Broad Language Faculty, which had some overlap with other cognitive functions (Hauser, Chomsky & Fitch 2002). To say the least, not everyone agreed about *what* went into the language-unique part of the faculty, but some still held on to the idea that it was "conceptually useful to distinguish between the language faculty in its broad and narrow sense" (e.g., Pinker & Jackendoff, 2005, p.205). The journey of fragmentation that the language module had taken, partly reflected the slipperiness of pinning modules to the evidence: when an existing module cannot accommodate the behavioral data, a new one is suggested, wherein the existence of the behavioral data is then used to justify the necessity of the module. The morphing of what the language module could be and the retreat of its scope, also, I think, reflects that the metaphor of an encapsulated system for language is fundamentally the wrong one. Over fifty years of research now demonstrates how this modular view vastly underestimates both the breadth and depth with which cognition interacts with, constrains, and predicts language use. For example, domain-general processes have been shown to penetrate so deep into the linguistic system that they interact with very basic 'core' grammatical processes, once thought to be isolated from the rest of cognition. If this turns about to the general picture of how language works, and cognitive processes can do much of the explanatory 'heavy-lifting', then the question arises of what the encapsulated language module is for.

At this point, it's worth briefly reminding ourselves why any of this matters. Scientific claims about what makes *language* special – the content of a language module, for example – are claims about what makes *us* special. Those kinds of statements always tend to catch our attention and invite scrutiny because we all have a vested interest in being human (!) But more than that, they matter because language is a rare thing in nature, and rare things are important and valuable. Of course we are not alone in being special. To paraphrase the quip, our species is unique, just like every other one. While that is true, here we selfishly focus on the linguistic niche we have created for ourselves, whereas others choose to shine the light on no less remarkable non-human feats, such as migration, echolocation and metamorphosis. Something in our human nature allows language to happen and whatever that turns out to be, it is of significance because it answers two of the most stubborn and non-trivial problems in developmental science. First, children have syntax but they don't hear it, what they hear are utterances, so the question it begs is one of process; how to do children get the former from the latter? Second, whatever process governs this transition, in theory it is also possible for it to generate a grammar that sprawls beyond what it should. Thus much of the energy in language acquisition research has been expended in pursuit of developmental mechanisms that are both able to generate abstractions and constrain generalizations. And it is that balance between creativity and conformity in language that this book aims to address too, evaluating the contribution cognition can make to answering these long-standing questions.

This introductory section is called the *re*-unification of language and cognition, because, before Chomsky took linguistics down the modular path, language was not always thought of as so separate from domain-general processes. Sapir talked of language as a system that "gets what service it can out of nervous tissues that have come into being and are maintained for very different ends than its own" (adapted from Sapir, 1921). Piaget's mechanisms of assimilation, accommodation and equilibrium were indiscriminate as to whether they were operating on spatial input, numbers, social cognition or language (Piaget 2007). Likewise for the conditioned stimulus-responses that were basically the same whether they were recruited for verbal behavior or non-verbal behavior (Skinner 1957). And so too for modern-day statistical approaches to learning that are equally suited to visual or auditory input (Aslin, Saffran, & Newport, 1998; Fiser & Aslin, 2002; Gebhart, Newport, & Aslin, 2009; Kirkham, Slemmer, & Johnson, 2002). For what insight these domain-general approaches brought to language learning, none of them gave a proposal as definitive as Chomsky's to the question "what makes the difference?" that is, why are we the ones speaking. For Chomsky, it was clear and it was the content of the Narrow Language Faculty. However, no-one seriously proposed that equipping chimpanzees or computers with more assimilation, statistical learning or operant conditioning would make them talk. In that respect, Chomsky's proposal got to the heart of the matter on human uniqueness.

There has, of course, been a sustained and comprehensive theoretical attempt to reunify language and cognition under the *Cognitive Linguistics* banner. This however, has traditionally focused on end-state adult language, with less interest in the dynamic systems that enabled learners to reach that capability. By contrast, language acquisition research has naturally taken a developmental perspective but, in the main, sought to explain language development with respect to other language-internal factors – the effect of word frequency on word age-of-acquisition to give one example. Here we try to blend elements of the two fields in an approach that could be called *Developmental Cognitive Linguistics*. "Linguistics" because our primary goal is to understand how language – any language – works. "Cognitive" because it understands language with respect to what has been independently understood in other areas of cognition, and, finally, "development" because we are interested in the mechanisms by which language structure is acquired and knowledge becomes organized. In fact, the inclusion of a developmental perspective goes beyond a mere interest in "how we got here"; without such a perspective it is difficult to make sense of what kind of thing language *is*, because learning constrains and shapes what kind of thing language can *be*.

One of our goals is to understand language with respect to what has been independently understood in other areas of cognition, but what does it mean to say a cognitive faculty operates independent of language? To take the relatively uncontroversial example of memory first, independence, as used here, has three main senses. First, human infants show that they have memory before they develop language. Second, memory can operate independently of language once language is acquired. Third, memory is present in non-human species that never develop language. Even in 1980, pre-Narrow Language Faculty, Chomsky appeared comfortable with the idea that "properties of memory" might be relevant to language processing, as the first quote showed. What the intervening years have demonstrated is how deep the relationship persists not just for memory but for attention, categorization, inhibition, social cognition and many other domains. The main body of this book is devoted to making the case that the developmental trajectory of language is in some important sense contingent on the development of other non-linguistic abilities. Along with others, I suggest that the conclusion that follows from this is that language is constructed using species-general cognitive mechanisms (e.g., categorization, inhibition, memory, attention) and constrained by a species-unique set of social skills (e.g., cooperative action). The scope of the book allows a 'deep dive' into each of these areas to explore the mechanisms by which they dampen the degrees of freedom on linguistic generalizations. Most recently, Chomsky still maintains that modules (of which language is one) have "enough internal integrity so that it makes good sense to study each in abstraction from the others" (Chomsky, 2011, p.264). This book is essentially a systematic evaluation of whether that claim makes sense for language.

1.2 Why integrate language and cognition?

We have briefly reviewed how we got here, what is at stake, and where we are going with this line of reasoning. But before we launch into the main section of the book, which is orientated towards the developmental psychology literature, we might reasonably ask why anyone would *want* to integrate language and cognition in the first place. For example, it might seem that inhibition and grammar are fundamentally very different players on the psychological stage, with not much to say to one another. Below is an outline of some reasons, independent of developmental psychology, that suggests why the reunification of language and cognition might be a project worth pursuing.

1.3 Arguments from genetics, atypical populations and neuroscience

A tenet of contemporary genetics is that the brain structure that supports complex cognitive functions like language, is built from thousands of DNA differences of very, very small effect size, typically explaining around 0.01% of the variance, for example (Plomin 2018). Furthermore, each DNA difference affects many, many different traits. As Plomin summarizes "generalist genes imply that individual differences in brain structure and function are largely caused by diffuse effects that affect many regions and functions . . . it seems likely that generalist genes result in generalist brains" (2018, p.70). The many-to-many model of genes-to-function predicts a continuum of linguistic function and dysfunction. A potential counter-example to this view is the classic double dissociation which seems to provide a clean-cut division of the kind an encapsulated modular view of language would predict. Person A has function X but not Y. Person B has function Y, but not X. With respect to language, it has been argued we see this dissociation most clearly between Williams Syndrome (WS); where language abilities (X) are relatively intact but general cognitive abilities (Y) are impaired; and Developmental Language Disorder or DLD (previously known as Specific Language Impairment); where cognitive ability (Y) is preserved and language capacity (X) is impaired. It is interesting to note that this pattern has been variously interpreted as evidence for a syntactic module (Pinker 1994; Pinker 1999), a social reasoning module (Baron-Cohen 1998; Tager-Flusberg, Boshart & Baron-Cohen 1998) and a music module (Levitin & Bellugi 1998), in part, reflecting the problems with the module methodology we encountered earlier. More importantly, careful research into the profiles of these individuals reveal the real story is more nuanced and complex than the pioneering early work by Bellugi and her colleagues originally suggested (Bellugi, Wang & Jernigan 1994; Stojanovik, Perkins & Howard 2001; Stojanovik, Perkins & Howard 2004; Brock 2007; Stojanovik & van Ewijk 2008; Parsell 2010).

On closer inspection, language comprehension, phrase repetition, mean length of utterance and object categorization are all delayed in the WS population, and phonological processing and morphology follow an atypical developmental trajectory also (Thomas & Karmiloff-Smith 2003; Martens, Wilson & Reutens 2008).

More complex grammatical skills such as gender agreement, pragmatics and semantic fluency seem to be both delayed and developmentally atypical for individuals with WS (Martens, Wilson & Reutens 2008). Their pragmatic problems appear more rooted in a failure to read the communicative intentions of others and a lack of social motivation to coordinate mutual topics of interest in a conversation (Laws & Bishop 2004; Stojanovik 2006). Thus, when compared with typically developing individuals, those with WS are more likely to misinterpret the literal or metaphorical meanings of phrases while conversations remain typically confined to their own specialisms (Stojanovik 2006).

The conclusion from this work is that the WS arm of the WS-DLD comparison does not provide a very good case for a clean-cut dissociation, at least not of the type that would suggest linguistic, modular-encapsulation of some sort. Rather, the behavioral data points to deeply overlapping bell-curves of WS and DLD language performance, as one would expect if the many-to-many view of gene-to-functions is on the right lines. This kind of overlap is exactly what Stojanovik et al. (2004) found in the behavioral data: on an individual level, some DLD individuals actually performed *better* than the WS participants, but at a group level, there were no statistically significant results between the WS and DLD populations on standardized language tests. Prefacing some of the evidence reviewed in Part II, Robinson, Mervis, & Robinson (2003) found the acquisition of grammar in children with WS is more closely correlated with their working memory ability. As Parsell (2010) notes, this kind of "interaction between language and other preserved domains [in WS] is indicative of a highly interactive mind in which 'language abilities cannot develop separately from other cognitive skills (Stojanovik, 2006, p.168)'".

More generally, the developmental neurolinguistic evidence is telling a similar story of complex interdependent relationships between language and cognition that defy a simple dissociative logic. For example, some agrammatic patients show weak preservation of grammatical judgment whereas agrammatic symptoms can be caused by damage to areas other than Broca's (Dick et al., 2001; Wulfeck & Bates, 1991). Indeed the whole Classic Model of Neurolinguistics, whereby the two interconnected "language epicenters" (Papathanassiou et al. 2000) of "Broca's" and "Wernicke's" represent a high degree of functional modularity, is proving difficult to sustain in light of the overwhelming evidence that language functions are supported by vastly distributed networks across the brain (Crosson, 2013; Hebb & Ojemann, 2013; Mariën et al., 2014; Price, 2010).

For areas like Wernicke's and Broca's that are defined by their anatomical function, there is surprisingly little agreement, 150 years after they were first described, about what either their anatomy or function *is* (Pascale, Tremblay & Dick, 2016). For example, ever since Wernicke's located his area of interest, almost every other part of the perisylvian temporal and inferior parietal cortex has been implicated as the locus of his eponymous region (Bogen & Bogen 1976). Binder notes (2015, p.5) "speech comprehension is a highly distributed function, involving a bi-hemispheric phoneme perception system and a widely distributed semantic network. To refer to all of these regions as the Wernicke area seems to sacrifice any utility that the term might have . . . ". But in a move familiar to the modularity approach, ultimately Binder takes this as evidence that the function of Wernicke's area needs to be redefined rather than conceding that a language epicenter might not be on the right lines. Though this poor anatomical resolution is not unique to neurobiological models of language per se, the general problem it creates is that it is difficult to test specific hypothesis about brain/language relationships and confuses functional definitions with anatomical ones.

As well as language epicenters, the Classic Model also describes a single fiber pathway – the *arcuate fasciculus* – that has a crucial role in linking the speech and language hubs. Recent evidence suggests this too vastly underestimates the interconnectivity of language in the brain, with significant linguistic pathways and cross-talk between fronto-temporal, parieto-temporal, occipito-temporal, and fronto-frontal regions, as well as thalamic radiations, and cortico-subcortical loops connecting the cortex to the basal ganglia, cerebellum, midbrain and pontine nuclei (Axer, Klingner, & Prescher, 2013; Dick, Bernal, & Tremblay, 2014; Dick & Tremblay, 2012; Gierhan, 2013; Saur et al., 2008; Weiller, Bormann, Saur, Musso, & Rijntjes, 2011). Even if a single pathway did exist, anatomical connectivity imposes only a loose constraint on functional connectivity or on the domain-specificity of any network. And our estimates of interconnectivity are only likely to increase, as our understanding of long-distant region-to-region and lobe-to-lobe connectivity advances with the technology that allows us to detect them with accuracy.

The contemporary neurolinguistics view is that language, like other cognitive functions, depend on distributed computations with dynamic networks built out of domain-general neural resources (Rijntjes et al. 2012; Bornkessel-Schlesewsky et al. 2015; Friederici & Singer 2015). For example, activity in the anterior part of the right temporal cortex differentiates between predictable and unpredictable sequences for both auditory and visual inputs (Nastase, Iacovella & Hasson 2014). Tremblay, Baroni, & Hasson, (2013) found that these lateral temporal regions were also equally sensitive to the predictability of auditory input streams, regardless of whether they were examples of speech or non-speech, and importantly, no temporal regions showed sensitivity to predictability in speech series alone. It seems certain brain networks have the capacity to generate predictions in an abstract, domain-general manner and may generate prediction in both linguistic and non-linguistic domains (Hasson et al. 2018). Forecasting the way the world works is one of the big benefits of having a brain which costs so much to run (2% by weight, 25% of the calories). So, it seems to make good economics for different domains to capitalize on the benefits that prediction can bring wherever they can; whether that is modelling the future trajectory of objects from visual input or predicting upcoming words in dialogue (Adams, Friston, & Bastos, 2015; Bar, 2007).

This level of interconnectivity of brain systems would suggest a reason why damage to Broca's or Wernike's areas is neither necessary nor sufficient to produce the classic aphasiac symptoms (Goodglass 1993; Dronkers 2000). And also why Broca's area has been implicated in a number of non-linguistic processes including musical syntax (Maess et al. 2001), executive functions (Kan & Thompson-Schill 2004) and imitation (Heiser et al. 2003). Most modern and integrative models of the neurobiology of language now acknowledge a much greater role for regions that had never before been considered to support language functions.

There are well understood developmental neurological processes that lead to a perceptual narrowing of what the child attends to, can process efficiently and discriminate between (Nelson 2001; Scott, Pascalis & Nelson 2007; Lewkowicz & Ghazanfar 2009). This functional specialization occurs when the child becomes attuned to processing aspects of their environment they regularly experience (reinforced via Hebbian learning (Hebb 1949)) and progressively worse at those that they do not (deleted via syntactic pruning (Chechik, Meilijson & Ruppin 1998)) underscoring the overall plasticity of neurological development (Kolb & Gibb 2011). For example, Kelly and colleagues (2007) tested 3-, 6-, and 9-month-old infants' ability to discriminate faces within their own ethnic group (Caucasian) versus three other groups (African, Middle Eastern, and Chinese). The 3-month-olds could discriminate faces in all conditions but by 6-months old this had narrowed to just Caucasian and Chinese faces and by 9-months old, successful discrimination was restricted to only their own ethnicity (Caucasian). Of course the clearest example of linguistic fine-tuning comes from the phonemic specialization that occurs somewhere between 6- and 12-months of age (Werker & Tees 2005). During this time period, Werker and Tees found a decline in the ability of English-speaking infants to distinguish Hindi phonemic contrasts (Werker & Tees 1984) – a classic finding that has been replicated across a wide range of languages and with a broader range of phonemic and metrical distinctions (Hannon & Trehub 2005a; Kuhl et al. 2006; Pons et al. 2009). In their paper 'A Domain-General Theory of the Development of Perceptual Discrimination' Scott and colleagues (2007) come to the conclusion there are common principles of perceptual development that operate across phonemic perception

(Kuhl et al. 2006), face perception (Pascalis, De Haan & Nelson 2002; Pascalis et al. 2005), intersensory perception (Lewkowicz & Ghazanfar 2006), visual language discrimination (Weikum et al. 2007) and the discrimination of culturally specific musical rhythms (Hannon & Trehub 2005b; Hannon & Trehub 2005a).

Note how the list of domains over which perceptual narrowing takes place – native languages, faces, vocalizations, and music – are all examples of what might be called socio-ecologically-relevant multisensory signals (Lewkowicz & Ghazanfar 2009). The infant learns to progressively narrow their perceptual attention and processing to best match their native perceptual ecology, in a process that could be thought of as cultural bet-hedging: precisely because a child does not know which culture it is going to be born into, nor does a culture know which child will try to learn it, these capabilities need to be defined at quite a general level (more on this in section 1.3 below). What this means for the encapsulated module debate is (a) there are domain-general perceptual narrowing processes operating across language and cognition (Scott, Pascalis & Nelson 2007) and (b) noting adult Japanese-speakers have an inability to discriminate /r/ and /l/s, for example, is very different to the claim that domain-general cognitive processes do not act on the linguistic /r/ and /l/ categories or were not available at the time they were constructed. The claim of this book is that, by the time *content* is canalized, domain-general *processes*, cognitive *architecture* and *representations* have been acting and continue to act across linguistic and domain-general boundaries.

Note also that many authors (Werker & Tees 2005; Lewkowicz & Ghazanfar 2009; Pons et al. 2009) are keen to point out perceptual narrowing does not entail a complete loss of perceptual sensitivity to non-native inputs, rather it reflects a reorganization of perceptual mechanisms that leads to a change in sensitivity. This suggests some information transfer between domains is still possible beyond 'critical periods' and may not entail irreversible encapsulation of content either. We will return to some of these concepts of canalization with discussion of Dynamic Systems Theory in the final part of this book.

The most recent neuroscience suggests language acquires Fodorian-like qualities of being processed fast and automatically over the course of many years of development, but, these two modular criteria in isolation have almost nothing to say about (a) what the content of language module would be in advance of experience or as a result of experience (b) what is unique to language. More likely is that language emerges via a coordination of anatomically distributed resources by breaking the modularity of more basic processing systems, in an architecture that connects hierarchically nested networks (Dehaene, Kerszberg, & Changeux, 1998). In sum, there is no clear evidence that the neurobiological bases of language are domain-specific (and neither should we expect there to be if the arguments from comparative and evolutionary psychology are persuasive, in the next section).

Finally, humans show relatively more cortical complexity than non-human primates, who show relatively more complexity than their nearest relatives (Markov & Kennedy 2013). Complexity is a measure of how much information can be supported in the network and analyses suggest that the human brain is close to the functional and structural optimum (Tononi, Edelman & Sporns 1998; Sporns 2002). This optimum is achieved where connectivity is somewhere between completely random and completely regular. Relevant for the argument here is the fact that human cortical networks seems to possess a disproportionate number of strategic hubs. These hubs have an exceptionally high degree of neural connectivity with other nodes in the network, and occur wherever the network supports the integration of high-level cognitive functions, such as that between hearing and vision or sound and meaning in language. Friederici and Singer, (2015, p. 335) conclude "This emergence of highly interconnected hubs may be intimately related to the evolution of language competence. As these motifs of the connectome show little inter-individual variability within a given species, it must be assumed that they are genetically specified" (2015, p. 335). Thus it seems human brains appear particularly well suited to distribute language processing across multiple cortical regions and to integrate and coordinate language with other cognitive functions. Of course the DNA that builds brains with a preference for treating language in this way, was itself shaped by the forces of natural selection, a source of evidence considered next.

1.4 Arguments from human evolution, comparative psychology and typology

Studying human cognition from an evolutionary and comparative psychology perspective can give us a sense of not only *why* we might want to integrate language but *what* we should be integrating it with. The argument is as follows. The later a species diverged from the human lineage the more similar our DNA will be to theirs, and the more likely that the DNA will build similar brains whose job it is to do similar things. Our DNA is more similar to a chimpanzee than it is to a gibbon and a gibbon is more similar to a chimpanzee than it is to us. Our closest living evolutionary relatives, chimpanzees, began to separate from our last common ancestor between 4–8 million years ago (Patterson et al. 2006; Langergraber et al. 2012; Steiper & Seiffert 2012; Amster & Sella 2016). Like modern-day humans, chimpanzees share with us many cognitive abilities that we would recognize, like memory (Menzel 1973; Fujita & Matsuzawa 1990), categorization (Spinozzi 1996), attention (Herrmann & Tomasello 2015) and inhibitory control (Beran 2015). Many of these abilities are not unique to primates either (Kuhl & Miller, 1975) and some are not even unique to mammals (Emery & Clayton, 2004). What other species seem to lack is the motivation to convert the basics of cooperative thinking into cooperative behavior. So, there may be many necessary cognitive prerequisites for language – memory, categorization, attention and so on – but without the human motivation to share, inform and request, they may not be sufficient. This idea of *language as intention made public* is explored in much greater depth in the Social Cognition chapter, but for now, all we need to note is that by comparing species that are genetically close to each other at the present-day tip of the evolutionary branches we can infer something about what those species were like in the relatively near past.

Language developed in our species perhaps as recently as 2–300,000 years ago (Henshilwood et al. 2002; Henshilwood & Dubreuil 2009). So, our best guess from using the logic of this comparative psychology approach, is that when language evolved, it is very likely that it must have used pre-existing cognitive mechanisms, the kind we share with our closest evolutionary relatives today. For example, it seems reasonable to suppose that our ancestors were segmenting and organizing motion-perception long before they were using linguistic information structure – given how wide-spread motion-perception is in our phylogenetic neighbourhood. So it also seems reasonable to suggest some of those segmenting and hierarchical cognitive processes employed for motion-perception would have been available to systems performing similar functions and executing similar goals. As Evans and Levinson put it "The null hypothesis here is that all needed brain mechanisms, outside the vocal-tract adaptation for speech, were co-opted from pre-existing adaptations not specific to language" (Evans & Levinson, 2009, p.44). If this turns out to be the way things did unfold for language and cognition, it would be far from a unique example in nature, given how common it is for evolution to recycle and repurpose a trait for a use other than the one natural selection selected it for: limbs evolved from fins; hands and wings evolved from limbs; feathers from scales and so on (Gould & Vrba 1982; Woltering et al. 2014). However, the analogy between these 'exaptations' and language is not perfect. For example, limbs evolving from fins was the result of evolutionary pressure on a population over generations which resulted in a change in the genome, the DNA required to build limbs. The claim with language is similar but different. There is recycling, redeployment and repurposing of existing cognitive structures, but linguistic structure itself is not instantiated into genomic change; it is the result of those cognitive structures which have been acted on by evolutionary pressure and do change the genome:

memory; categorization; attention and linking cooperative cognition with cooperative action.

Unlike humans, chimpanzees obviously do not develop anything like our language capabilities even when born and raised in a rich communicative environment – that's why everybody needs a theory of what makes the difference. As noted, language is a fundamentally unusual thing for an animal (us) to do. But the same can be said of money, government, agriculture, art, technology and music. What these examples have in common, is that they are all cultural innovations that need to pass through the bottleneck of what is learnable, usable and sustainable every single generation, otherwise we would be left having to literally re-invent the wheel every generation (Christiansen & Chater, 2008). Imagine an unborn infant who doesn't know whether they are going to be born into a culture where they will be expected to use the conventions of chopsticks, their hands or knives and forks when eating. It might make sense not for the brain to have encapsulated specialisms for cutlery, but to hedge the bet with the kind of general-purpose intention-reading skills and the sensorimotor capability that can assimilate the variation in the cultural forms. Of course, one particularly amazing feat of cultural learning is language acquisition, whereby a child appears equally equipped to learn anyone (or usually more) of 7000 different systems that structure their thoughts and symbolically manipulate the thoughts of others. By comparison, an unborn infant also doesn't know whether they are going to be born into a culture that requires them to learn the sound systems, words and syntax of *Gujarati*, *Mayan* or *Nyungar*, so they need enough culture-learning firepower, defined at a general-enough level to accommodate the variety. In fact, this puts it slightly backwards, because a language (or chopsticks) wouldn't be there to learn for the second generation if it had not accommodated to the cognitive and social capacities of the first. And so we can state this the other way around. A culture, including language, doesn't know which child it is going to receive, so if it strays beyond what is learnable it will be pruned back for future generations.

A rabbit runs faster than a fox because a fox is running for his dinner and a rabbit is running for his life (Dawkins 1976). The same kind of asymmetric survival pressure is at play in language too because a human can survive without language but a language cannot survive without humans. Thus Christiansen and Chater encourage us to ask not "Why is the brain so well suited to learning language?" but instead "Why is language so well suited to being learned by the brain?" (Christiansen & Chater, 2008 p.490). The struggle for survival that linguistic forms are involved in, both between and within languages, is a point recognized long ago by Darwin himself (1874)

1.4 Arguments from human evolution, comparative psychology and typology — 15

> A language, like a species, when once extinct, never . . . reappears . . . A struggle for life is constantly going on among the words and grammatical forms in each language. The better, the shorter, the easier forms are constantly gaining the upper hand . . . The survival and preservation of certain favored words in the struggle for existence is natural selection. (p. 106)

The Baldwin Effect provides a potential pathway for linguistic-only information to become genetically encoded. This is the process whereby selection reduces the plasticity of traits that initially arose via plasticity and some authors have argued that it played a central role in language evolution (e.g., Pinker, 2003; Pinker & Bloom, 1990). However, the problem is that any bias that helps the learner with a property of particular language is likely to inhibit the learning of another language lacking that property. This problem arises for the same reason of cultural diversity stated above; the child does not know which one of the 7000 languages it is going to be born into. Biases that *would* work have be stated a quite a general level, such as a prosocial motivation to share intentions – a fixed trait which could have indirectly fostered the cultural evolution of language and has the advantage of being a species-specific capacity like language itself. Where the Balwin effect has been demonstrated to play a significant role in language evolution, it has been in these types of cases, where it tends to favor the acquisition of many behaviors, not just language (Christiansen, Reali, & Chater, 2011). Relatedly, Reali and Christiansen (2009) found that Baldwin Effect could be prevented if the resulting changes resulted in cognitive constraints that decreased performance at other tasks. Thus while the role of the Baldwin Effect in the evolution of language is an open field of enquiry, it remains an improbable pathways for encoding language-only information into the genome (Chater, Reali, & Christiansen, 2009; Morgan & Griffiths, 2015). What this means for the discussion at this point, is that we should expect cultural learning mechanisms to interact with the developmental trajectory of other cognitive capacities. That much would seem relatively uncontroversial as all mainstream theories of language acquisition acknowledge that phonological and lexical content is learned.

There is something that needs further explanation at this point. Does talk of "categorization", "attention", "inhibition" and so on, advocate a modular view of these capacities? Care was taken earlier to restrict the claim regarding encapsulation, or the lack of it, to language. There are good reasons to suggest other cognitive systems are not as modular as Fodor originally claimed (Prinz, 2006) but there is an important reason why attention, inhibition and so on may operate differently to language. The target of any would-be language module is a cultural form with incredible diversity (Evans & Levinson 2009). That makes organizing modular content in advance of experience – content that would be useful to learner – very difficult in comparison to organizing the modularization of memory, for example. Part of the difficulty may be that language represents a shifting cultural target that moves quicker than biological evolution can hit (Azumagakito, Suzuki, & Arita, 2018; Chater, Reali, & Christiansen, 2009; Christiansen & Chater, 2008; Számadó & Szathmáry, 2012). But regardless of whether that is true of inter-generational language change, it misses the point made above, that the child does not know which one of thousands of different grammars and phonological communities it is going to born into. This is quite a different situation to the kind of physiological adaptations (e.g., lower placement of the larynx) that has been associated with communicative niche construction in humans (Gintis 2011), where there is no substantive role for cultural variation. This is also why the "organ" metaphor for language fails as physiological organs have no meaningful cultural niche to "grow" into. All of this leads us to the conclusion that the cognitive and social capacities that construct languages must be begin life with a wide-enough scope so as not to prevent learning what are the fine-grained differences between languages.

To summarize, the evolutionary and comparative approach suggests that that modern-day general cognitive capacities of memory, categorization and so on would have been there to be used at the time language evolved, furthermore we should expect these to interact with the species-specific ability of cultural learning.

1.5 Arguments from computational modelling, artificial intelligence and robotics

The collaboration between the cognitive robotics community and language science has served both as a testbed for theories of language evolution, processing and acquisition, and as a driver to build better robots capable of communicating with humans for business, service and entertainment. Whether the motivations have been theoretical or more commercial, decades of trying to equip computers with language has only produced very slow progress towards anything like human performance. A situation that led to an IBM engineer to remark "Every time we fire a linguist, the performance of our system goes up." (Moore, 2005). This situation has persisted even when the conditions for learning are massively, and so unrealistically, simplified to make success more likely. For example, the error feedback is made intensive and explicit; the languages are restricted (usually either English or Japanese); and the pragmatic contexts are tightly regulated. Part of the difficulty is that, from a computational processing perspective, naturalistic discourse is messy. There are different meanings to what someone says; there are different ways for them to say what they mean; different accents and tones of voice in which to say it; dialogue is full of incomplete sentences, overlaps, restarts, abrupt topic shifts, non-sequiturs and so on.

Importantly for the integrationist argument we are pursuing here, more progress has been made recently in tackling these tough problems when language is modelled as a process which dovetails with other cognitive functions such as perception, action and categorization. For example, recent robotic approaches have had more success understanding utterances when the linguistic cues combine with visual ones, such as face recognition (Asoh et al. 2001; Ido et al. 2006) pointing and eye-gaze direction (Hanafiah et al. 2004; Stiefelhagen et al. 2004; Toptsis et al. 2005). Computational word learning models also perform better when they integrate the speakers' intentions and pragmatic context into their learning algorithms than when they use distributed statistical information alone (Frank, Goodman, & Tenenbaum, 2009; Smith, Goodman, & Frank, 2013).

Paralleling psycholinguistic work with adult humans (Pickering & Garrod 2004), robotic simulations have demonstrated how linguistic representations emerge and are coordinated via interactions with other robots, resulting in linguistic meanings that are distributed across a population of like-minded, but differing individuals (Belpaeme & Bleys 2005; Steels & Belpaeme 2005). Key to their success is the idea that embodied action becomes an emergent property of a distributed system composed of brain, body and environment (Lopes & Belpaeme 2008). In this regard the cognitive robotics community have taken the lead from recent advances in our understanding of psycholinguistics, where a similar conclusion has been reached about the embodied nature of cognitive functions (Wilson 2002). For example, Glenberg & Kaschak (2002) asked participants to judge the sensibility of sentences that implied motion toward the body (e.g., *John gave you the notebook*) or away from the body (e.g., *You gave John the notebook*) by pressing a button that was either close to them or far away. When action and language were working together (*John gave you . . . press near button*) participants were quicker to respond, suggesting an integration of language, body and action that facilitates processing speed. Robotic approaches too have had better success when the abstract symbols of language have been grounded in perception, self-generated action and interaction with others (Feldman & Narayanan 2004; Cangelosi, Hourdakis & Tikhanoff 2006). It suggests a robotic implementation of language stands the best chance of moving towards human like performance when language systems mirror the embodied and interconnected nature of the human system. And when robots are allowed to grow, that is, they learn by repeated interaction with other robots, humans and the environment. Then novel problems can be solved by analogy to their experience of the way the world works and means-ends solutions they have been successful in the past. The world is subsequently carved into categories that are meaningful for their experience and these categories can be used as rules-of-thumb to predict behavior in the future. Many of these most-promising approaches are based on neural modelling methodologies, such as connectionist models and dynamic field theory (Perlovsky 2007) which use hierarchically nested networks similar to those attested to in the brain (Dehaene et al., 1998).

At first glance, it might seem that AI models of language should be at an *advantage* to humans in tackling these problems, for example, having access to an almost unlimited memory storage capacity, with superior fidelity in their encoding and retrieval processes. But as we will see, there is good reason to suppose that human maturational constraints, developmental bottlenecks, and biases of cognition are adaptive for learning natural language. That might be because these are the kinds of limitations that the evolution of language has been working with for millennia and the languages that are around to be learned today are the ones that have successfully passed through this bottleneck many times before (Christiansen & Chater, 2008). Moreover, the sequence with which these capacities unfold, and the incremental exposure to data that it creates, is important for dampening the combinatorial possibilities of language, in other words, development matters.

Of particular relevance here are computer models of language evolution showing how seemingly arbitrary properties of language can emerge from constraints on learning and processing (Kirby 1998; Kirby 1999). A good example is the subjacency principle as it is has been argued to be a classic example of an arbitrary linguistic principle, operating with logic internal to the language system (Pinker & Bloom, 1990). Loosely speaking, subjacency states that the interpretation of a phrase crashes when an element has to move across too many significant boundaries in that phrase. It is an attempt to explain why there are restrictions on ordering of words in complex questions, for example, according to subjacency theory (1b) is an acceptable transformation of (1a) because the 'What' element has arrived at its destination to form a question, using landing sites in the phrase (elements underlined) that have not crossed more than one significant boundary in one move. (1d) crosses more than one important boundary in one step and so is not an acceptable transformation of (1c).

1.5 Arguments from computational modelling, artificial intelligence and robotics — 19

1 (a) _[John knows that [everyone hates jazz What

   (b) What did [John know that [everyone hates? What

   (c) _[John knows [the truth that [everybody hates jazz What

   (d) *What did [John know [the truth that [everyone hates? What

Using an artificial language learning experiment with participants and connectionist modelling simulations, Ellefson and Christiansen showed how the same phenomena could be derived from general cognitive limitation on sequential learning, rather than those stipulations internal to the linguistic system alone (Ellefson & Christiansen 2000). Subjacency violations tend to be avoided because they make the sequential structure of language too difficult to learn, and thus make the language as whole more difficult to learn. Any language stipulating element coordination beyond human sequential capacities wouldn't be there to learn for the next generation. More generally, with computer simulations, Kirby (1999) has modelled how many typological universals can be derived from these types of general cognitive and learning constraints (more on this in Section 6.3 Developmental cognitive linguistics, language differences and similarities).

In summary, there has been a convergence between the computational modelling results and the psycholinguistic evidence on the idea that there is rich dialogue between perceptual, sensorimotor, social and internal states such as emotions and motivations. This information-sharing is an aid to language acquisition because the interaction between these elements compels language to face outwards from itself, reduces the degrees of freedom on what language can mean, grounds symbols in experience, and builds structure from patterns of use. 'Degrees of freedom' is a key concept in this argument so it is worth saying exactly what we mean by it. Mathematically it is simply the number of independent values in a calculation that are free to vary. To make things more concrete, imagine a traditional swing-arm desk lamp, that can be swiveled, levered and pitched at various independent points. The degrees of freedom at each point combine to delimit all the coordinates through space that this lamp can move. Now, say somebody were to hold the base of the lamp, preventing it moving in one plane up and down, but it all other respects it could still move as it previously did. The system would have lost a degree of freedom and the coordinates through which the lamp could travel have been reduced. The concept is useful when thinking about any complex dynamic system and the analogy to learning grammar is this. There are infinite degrees of freedom consistent with a finite sample of grammar that a learner is exposed to. For example, (2c-d) are possible coordinates in space generated from the degrees of freedom given by (2a-b) (a domain-general analysis of these sentences is given in Chapter 3).

2   (a) The baby seems to be asleep.
    (b) The baby seems asleep.
    (c) The baby seems to be sleeping.
    (d) *The baby seems sleeping.

What the integration of general-cognition, species-specific cooperative action and developmental processes can do, is in essence hold the base of the lamp, such that the combinatorial possibilities on what words and phrases can mean is massively reduced. A more detailed look at how this works for each cognitive capacity is examined in the next part of the book.

1.6 Summary

We have looked at some reasons why it might make sense to explore the relationship between language and cognition in human development, and that such relationships might be able to get us a long way to understanding the developmental trajectory of language itself. Cognition stands a much better chance of being universalized to all languages because (a) children around the world share a common (but not identical) path of cognitive development and (b) domain-general properties of cognition, for example memory, have not been subject to the same cultural forces of change that act on language. The difference between the standard endowment of French-speakers' memory and Japanese-speakers' memory is less than the difference between French and Japanese. For this reason language is in a worse off position to be universalized than is general cognition because specific linguistic biases that act in favor of learning one language often work against learning the next, or else the specific language structure needs to be stated at such a general level it either is of no advantage to the learner or unlikely to be specific to language anyway.

Many people might already acknowledge the relationship between language and cognition but question whether the weight of evidence is sufficient yet to get language "over the line" in an explanatory satisfactory sort of way.

Rather, they may say, the interaction between language and cognition provides a 'mere' nudge in the right direction towards adult competence. For now, all we can conclude from the arguments above is that there are converging lines of evidence from neuroscience, evolution and artificial intelligence that the reunification of language and cognition is an important enough project to pursue – even if it turns out to be wrong.

Developmental psycholinguistics may already being playing catch-up to those other fields where the tide is now turning against a language-internal analysis of language. After reviewing recent neurobiological studies of language Hasson and colleagues urge that future models "will be less self-referential and increasingly more inclined towards integration of language with other cognitive systems, ultimately doing more justice to the neurobiological organization of language and how it supports language as it is used in everyday life" (2018, p.135). They go on to appeal that:

> linguistic-related constructs such as semantic or syntactic complexity should not constitute the default interpretive framework. Rather, from first principles, such effects should be adopted after considering alternatives that can be formulated in terms of generic predictive and compositional processes not unique to language. Processes that co-occur during naturalistic comprehension, such as memory operations or emotional responses also fall within this category. (2018, p.136)

In a similar way to what is being proposed for neuroscience, Part II of this book tries to show why we should also be shifting the burden of proof: it is incumbent on those wishing to explain the development of a linguistic ability why it cannot (or could not in principle) be explained in terms of the development of deeper, more general cognitive abilities first. The reason to do so is this. If language has a significant relationship to domain-general cognition, then there are behaviors internal to the language system that can never be explained by rules unique to that system. The argument is that language is a permeable system, always losing some information and gaining some information from other mental systems. That means there are going to be a set of language problems that will never fall if a language-internal analysis is the only one that is pursued. The contrast between this cognitive linguistic position and an alternative approach is summarized in Figure 1.

In *Towards an integrated science of language* Christiansen and Chater comment that "the crossword of nature can only be solved by integration and relentless interaction across disciplines. Many mainstream linguists talk of linguistics as part of biology, or draw parallels between theoretical linguistics and theoretical

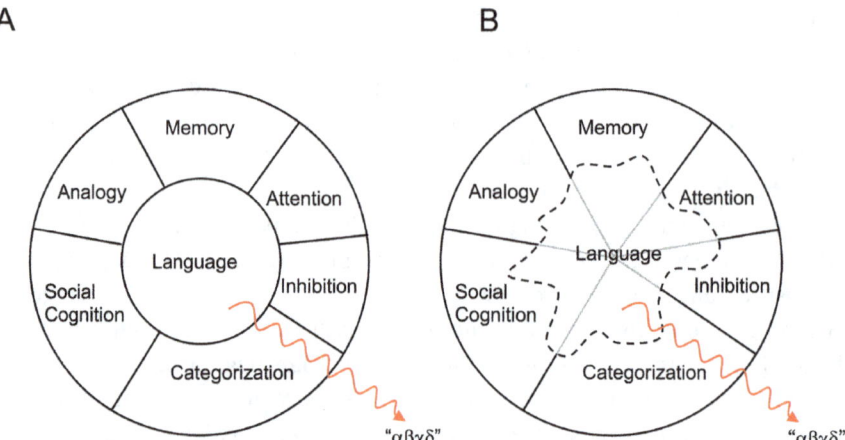

Figure 1: Schematic representation of fully formed language competence as revealed by a developing set of cognitive performance filters (A) and (B) language cognitively recycling domain general functions for its own ends, with cognition penetrating deep into language such that language is built out of those general purpose parts. In both cases a language 'particle' (squiggly red line) emerges as linguistic behavior and detected as "speech" and in both cases is influenced by the cognitive medium it travels through. Thus in practice these conceptualizations have sometimes led to very similar predictions. The deep integrationist account however predicts general cognitive principles should be at work right at the core of linguistic processes, including the very basics of grammar. It also implies a more permeable boundary between language and cognition, higher plasticity (because language function is more substitutable with other cognitive areas) and greater developmental interdependence between these areas. Note the historical reversal in trends: as the content and scope of what is in the language module (A) has diminished, the evidence for the breadth and depth of language interaction in with the rest of cognition has increased (B).

physics – but the reality could not be more different." (Christiansen & Chater, 2017, p.2). The developmental cognitive linguistics approach is an attempt to change that reality with a relentless attempt at integration and interaction across disciplines, in order that we better understand the relentless integration and interaction of cognition and language.

Part II

In this section, for each cognitive and social domain placed under the spotlight, the approach will be as follows. We establish what we know in the non-linguistic domain, establish what we know about the development of these capabilities, then analyze, present and critique the extent to which the developmental trajectory of the domain-general capabilities, confine, predict and explain the developmental trajectory of the linguistic ones, be that phonological, lexical or syntactic. The original intention was treat each domain – memory, attention and so on – as strictly separate chapters. However, that presupposes a kind of clean division that is in reality much fuzzier. Thus the chapters that follow reflect more a way of organizing and presenting a range of topics than a commitment to their mutual independence. Different domain processes therefore are cross-referenced within a chapter, where they are relevant to the main topic, for example the relationship between working memory and inhibition, or the role of social cognition in categorization.

As this book is dedicated to viewing language through a cognitive lens, and not vice versa, the chapters are structured accordingly. They focus on how well understood areas of cognition – memory, categorization, attention – shape language, rather than organizing chapters on how linguistic categories – syntax, semantics, and phonology – are affected by cognition. This is because the processes within a cognitive domain have more in common with each other than they do within linguistic ones. For example, the effects of memory cut-across, syntactic, semantic and phonological boundaries, and have more in common with each other than say, the role of attention and categorization in syntax. As Christiansen and Chater note in *Language as Shaped by the Brain* "The real challenge, we suggest, is to delineate the wide range of constraints, from perceptuo-motor to pragmatic . . . that operate on language evolution. Detailing these constraints is likely to be crucial for explanations of complex linguistic regularities, and how they can readily be learned and processed." (Christiansen & Chater, 2008, p. 505). It is indeed a real challenge because of the range of factors at play. The scope therefore is wide-ranging, with the chapters covering areas of cognition that merit book-length treatments on their own and in that respect some depth has been sacrificed for breath. But it was done so for the purpose of laying out the argument and convincing the skeptical; broad coverage is more important in this regard as it emphasizes the interaction between different areas of cognition, each one of which presented in isolation would not provide a convincing explanation for the course of language development. As Goldsmith (2010) notes, if you dig deep enough into any task in acquisition, it quickly becomes clear that in order to model that task effectively, a model of every other task is necessary. Ultimately the diversity of cognition covered here is the very least of what is available to the child and almost certainly represents an underestimate of the domain-general resources that learners draw on when constructing their language.

Chapter 2
Memory

We start with memory first, because, as noted, it is one of the least controversial areas of cognition that has a significant bearing on language and it has the longest history of research that straddles psycholinguistics and developmental psychology. For the purpose of the integrationist account we are pursuing here, we begin by briefly reviewing the typical developmental pathways taken by core processes in memory – encoding, storage and retrieval – so that we can understand the dynamic nature of these resources available for language development.

2.1 The development of memory

In the first few months, the speed and efficiency with which infants encode information, rapidly increases. For example, it typically takes 2-month-olds, four and a half minutes to learn the relationship between the action of kicking and the effect it has on an object. By 4-and-a-half-months old this has typically reduced to two minutes (Davis & Rovee-Collier 1983; Greco et al. 1986; Hill, Borovsky & Rovee-Collier 1988). Relatedly, younger infants also require longer exposure and greater repetition with stimuli to reach the same level of learning as older infants (Barr, Dowden, & Hayne, 1996; Hunter & Ames, 1988; Morgan & Hayne, 2006). Between 2 and 18-months of age, infants' memory storage also rapidly improves, such that older infants show retention over longer intervals than their younger counterparts regardless of the number of opportunities they have to encode the information (Hartshorn et al. 1998; Hsu 2010). The absolute duration of an infant's memory, however, depends on many factors, such as the frequency of stimulus, its spacing over time, and the duration and type of information that is encoded and infants' attention (Rovee-Collier & Cuevas 2009). Eventually, memory retrieval becomes increasingly flexible and independent of context during infancy. Tulving's Encoding Specificity Hypothesis (1983) predicts that memories are more likely to be retrieved when the conditions present at retrieval are most similar with those during encoding. Young infants exhibit a kind of overenthusiastic application of this principle whereby successful recall only occurs in retrieval contexts that minimally depart from those of their encoding. Only later, does this constraint relax to a point where older infants can use a broader range of retrieval cues for recall (including verbal reminders, Imuta, Scarf, & Hayne, 2013) and tolerate much greater mismatch between retrieval and encoding contexts (Hayne et al. 1986; Butler & Rovee-Collier 1989; Hanna & Meltzoff 1993; Hayne, MacDonald & Barr 1997; Hartshorn et al. 1998; Hayne, Boniface & Barr 2000).

From this brief synopsis of memory development it might be tempting conclude that infants are merely forgetful adults that get better with age, but this would be to miss two important points. First, functional approaches to memory emphasize both the strengths and weaknesses of early learning and memory, arguing that for any given stage, memory processes are adapted to an infant's ecological niche (Rovee-Collier 1996). For example, as we will see later, Elman (1993) showed the *benefits* of a limited memory capacity for learning language – indeed the model failed to learn grammatical patterns when memory was a fully formed adultlike resource from the start. This is a specific example of the idea that less can be more in development and, where there is a phased introduction of resource capacity, it leads to critical periods of acquisition such that learning outside these periods risks never acquiring mature proficiency (Newport 1988; Newport 1990).

Second, though the overall picture is of incremental improvement towards adultlike memory, there are important developmental reversals, non-linear trajectories and U-shaped patterns of learning, similar to those seen in language development and, indeed, cognition in general (Van Geert 2011). For example, the perceptual tuning that takes place when older infants can no-longer perceive the same differences in visual and auditory stimuli that were once distinguishable when they were younger (Maurer & Werker, 2014; Scherf & Scott, 2012).

With respect to memory, it has been argued that non-linear changes in development reflect a change in the infants' underlying interest, expertise and attention with similar stimuli (Chi, 1978; Schneider, Gruber, Gold, & Opwis, 1993). That is, what memory can *do* for the infant – what its function is in the infant's wider ecology of the body, environment, relationships, and motivations – changes over time. For example, 6-month-olds find it easier to make simultaneous associations (Cuevas, Giles, & Rovee-Collier, 2009) and remember them longer than older infants (Giles & Rovee-Collier, 2011). At around this time, infants are also beginning to move independently causing them to encounter a greater number and variety of environmental stimuli successively. Because younger and older children occupy different niches, what they perceive, learn, pay attention to and remember about the same event often differs (Rovee-Collier & Cuevas, 2009a; Taylor & Herbert, 2014). Thus the understanding of sequential relationships (i.e., "what comes after what") more closely fits the ecological niche of older infants than simultaneous ones with younger infants (i.e., "what goes with what"; Bhatt & Rovee- Collier, 1994; Rovee-Collier, 1996, 2001). In their review of the topic, Cuevas and Sheya conclude "the same basic learning and memory processes persist throughout infancy, but the temporal constraints on forming associations and the content of what infants learn change with age" (2019, p. 9). Likewise, Turkewitz & Kenny (1982) have argued that infants implicitly solve the problem of perceiving size constancy by initially restricting their depth of field vision to objects which are very close, allowing them to learn about the size of objects unconfounded by the effects of distance. Thus developmental limitations may not only be adaptive in the here-and-now (for example, the immobile, physically immature new-born that does not wander away from its mother), but may also help to shape adaptive pathways of development.

This functional reorganization of the memory system is reflected by the plasticity of the brain architecture that supports it: different networks can underlie the same behavior at different points in development and there is a complex back-and-forth between experience shaping neural connectivity and functional networks guiding behavior (Johnson, 2001). As Johnson puts it "By directing the infant to orient and attend to certain types of external stimulus, some brain systems effectively 'tutor' others with appropriate input for subsequent specialization. In this sense, the human infant has an active role in its own functional brain specialization" (2001, p. 482).

Before we continue, let us pause to consider what we understand thus far about the trajectory of memory developmental and what implications it might have for language learning, Table 1.

Table 1: The potential cognition-language correspondences gives us good reason to suppose that the shape of memory development has something interesting to say about language development.

Memory	Language
The move from simultaneous to sequential memories	Opens up capacity for encoding and storing transitional probabilities and word boundaries; understanding multiword utterances, phrase structure and dialogue
A relaxing of the encoding specificity principle	Allows the use of words and phrases across a greater number of contexts in which they were learned; pragmatic flexibility and generalisation
U-shaped patterns of memory development	U-shaped patterns of grammatical use (e.g., *swam* then *swimmed* then *swam* again)
The importance for learning of the frequency of a stimulus, its spacing over time, the duration/type of information that is encoded and infants' attention	Implications for the trajectory of word, sound and syntax learning; particularly age-of-acquisition and errors (both overgeneralization and omission)

Recall, the argument is to entertain linguistic-internal accounts for language phenomena only after we have exhausted the possibility that they are manifestations of deeper, wider and simpler principles of memory, and as such, general-cognitive explanations represent our default first line of enquiry. In the next section we examine further what developmental psychology has revealed about this relationship and examine the linguistic relevance various subcomponents of memory have.

2.2 Working memory and language development

Language is a performance that needs to be comprehended in the here-and-now before it literally disappears into thin air, unlike written language which can happily sit there until someone decides to read it. For that reason, working memory (WM) plays a crucial role in controlling the online comprehension and production of language. It is responsible for storage and manipulation of information during complex cognitive tasks which often require suspending some information while simultaneously executing a subtask that processes the same or different information (Baddeley 1992). Its resources are of limited capacity though, and can be overwhelmed if the processing demands are too heavy or complex. Thus WM has the potential to play both an enabling and limiting role in defining the scope of words and phrases that are interpretable, learnable and usable.

The incoming speech or signed language creates a stream of information that demands our attention. The systems monitoring this input are a like a worker sitting in front of a conveyer belt with items flowing quickly past them, that, if they are not efficiently packaged right then, will quickly pile up at the end of production line and crash the whole operation. Likewise, if linguistic information is not processed immediately, new words pile up and soon bury old ones, leaving the listener unable to comprehend or produce any language. Cognition has responded to the challenge of a rapid stream of information and a steep signal decay by quickly chunking the stream of information and compressing it into a structured hierarchy (Christiansen & Chater, 2016). Importantly, the same kind of perceptual pressure that creates this "Now-Or-Never" bottleneck is also operative in cognitive domains other than language, such as vision, haptic stimuli, event cognition and non-linguistic auditory stimuli (e.g., Ericcson, Chase, & Faloon, 1980; Gobet et al., 2001; Miller, Galanter, & Pribram, 1960). Furthermore, the kind of forward prediction that this kind of hierarchy buys the user, has been shown to be a common principle of computational design of motor control and wider cognition (Clark, 2013; Pickering & Garrod, 2013; Wolpert,

Ghahramani, & Flanagan, 2001). This has important consequences for what language can be and the kind of representational format it uses or recycles from phylogenetically older capacities. Thus we return to this issue in greater depth when looking at event cognition and grammar in the categorization chapter, as both capacities could be said to use hierarchies as a response to this bottleneck.

Returning to memory, Bever was interested in the extent to which language acquisition was either best interpreted in terms of grammatically defined rules or in terms of the development of the psychological systems underlying perception and memory (1970). He came to the conclusion that "every specific strategy of speech perception is a special case of a general principle of perception, at least in the sense that no general perceptual laws may be violated by a language-specific strategy (1970, p. 53)". For example, consider the sentences (3a) to (3j), representing a continuum of interpretability, with each subsequent sentence containing fewer words between the verb (*call*) and its participle (*up*).

3
- (a) *John called the not very well liked but quite pretty girl on the next block where Jack has lived for years up.
- (b) *John called the not very well liked but quite pretty girl who lives on the next block where Jack lived up.
- (c) ?John called the not very well liked but quite pretty girl who lives on the next block up.
- (d) ?John called the not very well liked but quite pretty girl who lives on the block up.
- (e) John called the not very well liked but quite pretty girl up.
- (f) John called the very well liked and quite pretty girl up.
- (g) John called the well liked and quite pretty girl up.
- (h) John called the pretty girl up.
- (i) John called the girl up.
- (j) John called up the girl.
- (k) John called up the girl who is not very well liked but quite pretty and who lives on the next block where Jack has lived for years.

It is difficult to conceive of a generative grammar in isolation that rules out (3a–g) but that would also permit (3h–k). Rather it seems more straightforward to account for this continuum of acceptability if we appeal to a continuum of cognition, namely, the longer the length of the phrase interrupting the verb and the particle it governs, the greater burden it places on working memory. As Bever points out, the acceptability of (3k) shows that the unacceptability of (3a) is not due to the length of the sentence per se, but to the length of the interrupting phrase between the verb and particle, and thus the burden it places on WM when trying to coordinate these elements. Bever went on to show that other grammatical intuitions could be grounded in domain-general perceptual principles. For example, cases of double embedding (*the dog the cat the fox was chasing was scratching was yelping*), triple negation (*they did not want me not to promise not to help them*), and left-branching (*Coats collars buckles are strong*) are all difficult to process because they violate a perceptual bias, which we can be call superposition: a stimulus may not be perceived as simultaneously having two positions on the same classificatory dimension. Importantly, this principle not only explains the difficulty people have parsing these sentences, but also the difficulty people have in interpreting visual stimuli with the same properties (Figure 2).

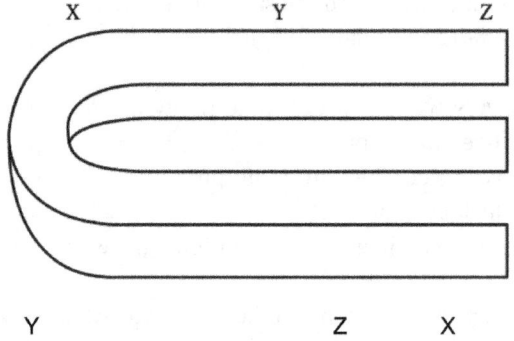

Figure 2: Superposition played out in cognition and language. Example of an impossible non-linguistic figure adapted from Bever (1970) with simultaneous 2- and 3-dimenional interpretations of point Y, and an analogous linguistic example of simultaneous agent and recipient interpretation of word Y.

Centre-embedded relative clauses of the type *the reporter that the senator attacked admitted the error* make a large demand on working memory, causing even adults to misinterpret who-did-what-to-whom 15% of the time (Larkin & Burns 1977). The difficulty arises not only because of the demand the sentence places on working memory – the main clause *the reporter admitted the error* has to be temporarily suspended, stored and then retrieved while the embedded clause *that the senator attacked* is processed. But also because *the reporter* is both the agent of an action in one clause (*admitted*) and the recipient of an action in another (*attacked*); a superposition of roles which seem to pose particular difficulties for human visual and linguistic processing (Bever 1970).

The processing quirks and cognitive biases that Bever described indicates that the developmental trajectory of language acquisition should be in some fundamental sense contingent on the developmental trajectory of memory. This is because of the way memory has the power to shape, control and permit what is linguistically possible. One prediction that follows from the close relationship between working memory and language processing is that individual variation in these abilities should be correlated. The reason being that if two cognitive capacities share similar cognitive routines, skills and resources then being good at one ability should make somebody good at the other. More generally, this focus on individual differences has been argued to offer a crucial source of evidence that speaks directly to the central issues in psycholinguistics, including the extent to which components of the language system interact with one another and cognition in general – a question which is of central concern here (see also Kidd, Donnelly, & Christiansen, 2018).

Many psycholinguistic experiments taking this individual variation approach have demonstrated a deep and enduring relationship between general working memory capacity and various aspects of linguistic ability, including grammatical judgements (Baddeley & Hitch 1974; Ellis 1991; Wulfeck 1993; McDonald 2008a; McDonald 2008b) novel word learning (Atkins & Baddeley 1998), reading comprehension (Baddeley, Logie, Nimmo-Smith, & Brereton, 1985; Daneman & Carpenter, 1980, 1983; Turner & Engle, 1989), understanding complex and ambiguous structures (King & Just 1991; Miyake, Just & Carpenter 1994) and the ability to draw linguistic inferences (Masson & Miller 1983; Cochran & Davis 1987). Furthermore, the correlations between working memory and language have been established for both adults (Daneman, 1987, 1991; Daneman & Green, 1986; Masson & Miller, 1983) and children (Gaulin & Campbell 1994; Swanson 1996).

For example, in a series of experiments King & Just (1991), showed that individual differences in adults' ability to process center embedded sentences (of the type discussed above) are governed by the amount of their working memory capacity available. McDonald, (2008b) found that children's working memory capacity and phonological ability accounted for variance in grammaticality judgments above and beyond that of their age. In particular, working memory capacity was a predictor of comprehension for syntactic structures involving verb morphology and word order. As interesting as these cases are, they provide a rather weak test for the claim that language is built out of domain-general resources, for the following reason. As a test of working memory in this experiment, children were asked to reorder a list of concrete nouns in terms of size of the referent from smallest to largest. Like McDonald, the majority of other studies of this type have also used measures of working memory which have involved some *linguistic* component, such as being asked to read aloud a sentence while simultaneously comprehending another (Atkins & Baddeley, 1998; Daneman & Carpenter, 1980, 1983; Masson & Miller, 1983). Thus they cannot rule out a linguistic-internal explanation for the correlation they establish between memory and language performance. A clearer test of the developmental cognitive linguistics approach would be to measure how non-verbal working memory, such as that used for shapes, constrains and predicts linguistic ability.

Where studies have satisfied this criteria, they have reliably reported correlations between *non-verbal* WM and language in DLD, Autistic Spectrum Disorder (ASD) and bilingual populations (Ebert 2014; Gangopadhyay et al. 2016; Weismer et al. 2017). For example, Ebert (2014) showed variance in non-verbal working memory predicted variance in sentence repetition after accounting for the effect of age *and* phonological short-term memory. Some evidence for the same pattern in typically developing and monolingual populations come from the control arms of the same studies. But the evidence here is more mixed with some failing to find an association in monolinguals (Gangopadhyay et al. 2016) or else find a correlation between non-verbal working memory and some measures of morphosyntactic errors (Weismer et al. 2017) or for some measures of non-verbal working memory and morphosyntactic performance (Adams & Gathercole, 2000). There is evidence from the educational psychology literature that non-verbal working memory predicts reading ability at 9–12 years old (Pham & Hasson 2014) and school achievement at 11 and 14 years old (Jarvis & Gathercole 2003), but here too, it is not a direct test of the cognitive linguistics approach, as language ability in this instance is mediated via reading and more general intellectual abilities. Given that robust associations between non-verbal WM and language have been demonstrated in populations that have a greater language performance variance (ASD, DLD, Bilingual), the mixed picture emerging from non-impaired monolingual data is plausibly a result of this population being at or near-to ceiling performance, leaving little variance for non-verbal memory to correlate with. This quantitative difference between groups would seem a more likely explanation than a qualitative one, given the overlapping nature of function/dysfunction profiles and the fact that non-impaired adults still commit linguistic errors when the WM is placed under enough stress. More individual variation studies assessing the relationship between non-verbal working memory and language in monolingual typically developing populations are needed to confirm this, testing a younger age and/or with greater communicative stress in order to elicit the variance this kind of correlational analysis requires (an in press study that satisfies this criteria will be discussed in Part III).

It remains an open question as to whether increases in short term verbal memory allow for greater vocabulary development (Adams & Gathercole, 1995;

Avons, Wragg, Cupples, & Lovegrove, 1998; Baddeley, Gathercole, & Papagno, 1998; Leclercq & Majerus, 2010) or vocabulary growth expands the boundaries of what short-term memory can do (Fowler 1991; Metsala 1999; Bowey 2006). Leclercq & Majerus, (2010) perhaps get the closest to establishing the directionality of the effect with a longitudinal, follow-up design. Cross-sectional designs show a correlation for one moment in time whereas a longitudinal follow-up of the same population provides something closer to a natural experiment, because levels of initial vocabulary can be treated as if they were pseudo-independent variables. A follow-up of the same cohort of children over a 1-year period enabled them to observe that aspects of WM capacities predict the later vocabulary knowledge, *whatever the initial level of vocabulary knowledge*. This allowed the authors to move beyond acknowledging verbal WM as a critical building block in vocabulary development (Baddeley, Gathercole & Papagno 1998) and suggest causality from WM to language capability. From the point of a developmental cognitive linguistics approach, it is suffice to say the interaction between the two capacities, whatever the directionality, necessitates studying both developmental trajectories if we are to fully understand the growth of either.

Aside from the individual variation approach outlined so far, training studies offer a methodology that moves us even closer towards a casual association than the longitudinal approach. The logic is the familiar from the correlation of individual differences, but in this instance if two cognitive capacities share similar processing routines, skills and resources then *training* on one ability should make someone good at the other. Here the literature appears sparse with respect to kind of studies that would fulfil the developmental cognitive linguistics criteria. In a meta-analysis of 87 WM training studies with 145 experimental comparisons, including nonverbal ability, verbal ability, word decoding, reading comprehension and arithmetic, none of the studies paired a non-verbal working memory training regime that also measured a verbal/language outcome or vice versa – the key comparison for a cognitive linguistics argument (Melby-Lervåg, Redick & Hulme 2016). A more recent meta-analysis of 24 WM training studies reported no transfer between training on verbal short term memory and visual-spatial working memory or vice versa (Gathercole et al. 2019). On the face of it, this seems to provide no evidence for the deep integration account between WM and language, however, in their sample of 24 studies only two of them tested children aged 5 or below with participants typically in mid-adulthood (and as old as 70 years-old in one case). It is not entirely surprising then that WM training failed to transfer to language because the adult linguistic component of the WM system is so well developed, it had effectively nowhere to be trained to. This fits with Gathercole and colleagues' (2019) own theory of cognitive transfer that relies on the creation of novel routines; predicting where transfer should occur between the trained and untrained capacities and how it does so. Essentially the idea is that transfer of WM to other capacities only occurs when both the trained and untrained activities impose the same unfamiliar task demands that are not supported by existing WM subsystems. Key is the creation of new routines or mnemonics that are common across both trained and untrained activities and are functionally required by both tasks in order to succeed. For example, using a strategy for chunking items in WM to link them to multi-chunk items in long-term memory for later retrieval is an acquisition of a skill common to both visual-spatial processing and language (Christiansen & Arnon, 2017; Cowan, Rouder, Blume, & Scott Saults, 2012; Miller, 1956). So the fact that adults do not show memory to language transfer following training is because the cognitive routines to perform these tasks can readily accomplished with existing WM processes and mechanisms – no new routines are needed to functionally succeed at this task and so the cognitive architecture for transfer is not created.

Thus we see a similar pattern in the training studies as the correlational studies. Non-verbal working memory and language correlate in populations with wide variance in their linguistic ability but with mixed findings in monolingual non-impaired population. Likewise, training studies have failed to find robust transfer effects between non-verbal WM and language but these populations have been adults where we expect the linguistic elements of WM to be at or near ceiling, again leaving non-verbal WM little variance to work with. Of the two studies in the Gathercole meta-analysis that used children (2019), one measured only a numeracy outcome (although they did find a domain-general effect of WM; Passolunghi & Costa, 2016). The other study looked at 101 4-year-old children who performed computerized training (15 min / day for 25 days) of either non-verbal reasoning, working memory, a combination of both, or a placebo version of the combined training (Bergman Nutley et al. 2011). Here, they did show a significant effect of non-verbal WM training on a linguistic outcome (Word Span test) when compared with a placebo group. And in a similar training test with 4-year-olds, Thorell and colleagues (2009) report that out of a batch of training tasks and non-trained outcomes, non-verbal working memory training had the largest transfer effect ($d=1.15$) on verbal tests of working memory. In summary when methodology is appropriately configured to test a developmental cognitive linguistics hypothesis, either from populations that have variance in correlational design, or from younger age-groups in the training studies, there is evidence that non-verbal WM significantly interacts with and predicts the development of language abilities.

Eventually, some of working memory's content in transferred to longer-term storage in a process of automatization and skill proceduralization that makes for more efficient memory use and better behavioral decisions based on those memories (Shiffrin & Schneider 1977a; Shiffrin & Schneider 1977b) – a function of memory we turn our attention to next.

2.3 Long-term memory and language development

Long-term memory has traditionally been subdivided into two broad functions. First, a declarative component, wherein information about "what" (e.g., facts, meanings), "where" (e.g., places, landmarks), and "when" (e.g., moments in time) is stored in a network of knowledge and experiences drawn from multiple domains and modalities (Henke 2010; Squire & Wixted 2011). Second, a procedural component that handles the sensorimotor habits and automatic cognitive skills that are difficult, if not impossible to articulate "how" they are accomplished; such as walking, navigation, riding a bike, or more relevantly for language; making predictions or forming rules and categories (Ullman 2004; Eichenbaum & Cohen 2008; Henke 2010; Ullman 2016).

Baars and colleagues underline the difference with the following anecdote (2010). Imagine asking a cyclist how they might avert a crash if their bike started falling to the right. They might say they would try to compensate by leaning in the opposite direction to the fall, which would ultimately make the crash more likely. When physically placed in the same situation the cyclist might contradict their 'declared' response, with an automatic and immediate lean into the direction of the fall, averting the crash. Likewise with language, there are implicit forms of knowledge that are dissociable from, and possibly in conflict with, explicit knowledge, for example, what we might reason about grammatical intuitions and how we use them in naturalistic discourse.

With this broad distinction in place, it is reasonable step to suppose the more idiosyncratic, exceptional and irregular end of the language spectrum is handled by declarative memory and everything that is regular, rule-based and productive by procedural memory. For example, Pinker (1999) argues that the distinction between regular inflection (e.g., *walk-walked*) and irregular (e.g., *come-came*) reflects a fundamental division of labor in the linguistic system; that between a discrete combinatorial system underlying grammar, housed in procedural memory, and arbitrary sound-meaning pairings, housed in declarative memory.

The most direct behavioral evidence that language is organized along these lines comes from the individual variation-type studies, familiar from the WM review. Some investigations with children show that vocabulary and learning abilities correlate with declarative memory but not procedural memory, and some show grammatical ability correlates with procedural memory but not declarative (Kidd, 2012; Lum, Conti-Ramsden, Page, & Ullman, 2012). However, these studies used cross-sectional designs and do not rule out the possibility that different memory systems play different roles in development at different times. There is indirect evidence of such an effect from artificial language learning experiments. For example, syntactic processing at early stages of learning a rule governed artificial language correlated with declarative (but not procedural) memory, whereas the reverse pattern was found at later stages of learning (Morgan-Short et al. 2014). Also, it appears that *which* memory system is more activated by a grammatical task can depend on the demands of input at hand, even at the same point in development. For example, evidence suggests that more complex rule-governed forms can also be learned in declarative memory (Hamrick 2014). And learning a grammar with a heavy reliance on generalization over stored forms correlates with declarative but not procedural memory, whereas learning a more rule-based concatenative grammar showed the opposite pattern (Wong, Ettlinger & Zheng 2013). In his review, Ullman (2016, p. 964) concluded

> evidence from multiple methodologies suggests that declarative and procedural memory may play considerably overlapping roles for grammar, but not for lexical/ semantics, which seems to require a more declarative-type memory . . . rule-governed compositional forms can be not only learned and computed by procedural memory but also stored and processed by declarative memory, via chunking, analogical generalization in associative memory, composition by explicit rules, and other processes.

It seems therefore that there are shared roles for procedural and declarative memory in language processing, especially where the tasks and functions they are used for used require knowledge or skills that are similar. This partial redundancy has its most clear implications for language in the acquisition of sequences, rules, and categories (Poldrack & Packard 2003; Ullman 2004). The fact that both declarative and procedural memory have been associated with syntactic processing is what we would expect if grammar supports a continuum of productivity rather than a strict division of labor between words and rules. The problem with a strict division is, where do the irregular yet productive construction go? (Goldberg, 2019). In most forms of cognitive grammar this problem does not arise because syntactic schemas, idioms, morphology, word classes, and lexical items are all treated as constructions that vary along a continuum of specificity and productivity (Langacker 1987; Fillmore, Kay & O'Connor 1988). If one accepts the premise that language is like this, the developmental implications are that children learn idiosyncratic yet productive constructions (e.g., *Her go to the ballet! My mother-in-law ride a bike! Riddle me this, she explained him the story, he disappeared the rabbit, she considered to say something, the asleep boy*), in the same way as more canonical ones (e.g., *John kissed Mary*). A continuum of productivity would also predict why the level of dependency on declarative memory for lexical items is moderated by many contextual factors including frequency, imageability, mono- versus multilingualism, early versus later stages of learning, gender, handedness and function/dysfunction (Ullman 2016).

The dynamic reorganization of information in memory systems, from working memory to declarative to procedural, may itself represent an adaptive response by language to memory development. Note that it is 'adaptive of language to memory', rather than the other way around, as we assume from the comparative psychology approach, memory has had a longer phylogenetic history than language, and has thus been unfolding in this way in ontogeny before language was present. This is significant as many usage-based theories have emphasized the frequency and importance of lexically-based semi-formulaic patterns in Child Directed Speech and Child Speech, such as the so-called slot and frame patterns like *Where's the* X? *I wanna* X, *More* X, *It's a* X, *I'm X-ing it, Put* X *here, Mommy's X-ing it, Let's* X *it, Throw* X, X *gone, I X-ed it, Sit on the* X, *Open* X, X *here, There's a* X, X *broken* and so on. Decades of research support the general idea that children use these islands of reliability when they are schematizing patterns in their language (Ambridge & Lieven, 2011; Ibbotson, Theakston, Lieven, & Tomasello, 2010; Michael Tomasello, 2003). It may turn out that this linguistic picture of how grammar develops can be grounded in more fundamental properties of how memory itself develops. For example, we know that as the infant moves from preverbal to verbal stages of language development, declarative memory itself is going through simultaneous changes in the way it encodes, stores and consolidates information (Bauer 2006; Rovee-Collier & Cuevas 2009; Mullally & Maguire 2014). More and more memories begin to survive the initially fragile encoding and consolidation stage and transfer to more long-term storage. Not only are more memories stored, but they are of higher quality and more available for retrieval. An increase in the efficiency of memory consolidation means that individual memories can be stored with more features that make them distinctive from one another. This aspect of memory development would seem a prerequisite in supporting a transition from fixed patterns to freeing up schematic patterns, for example, allowing to store what is similar (frame) and what is different (slot). More generally this allows decomposing of phonological and syntactic chunks into separate elements, and the flexibility and productivity of language that this brings.

Previous studies have found that declarative memory performance during the first year of life predicts linguistic performance during the first months of the second year of life (Heimann & Meltzoff 1996; Heimann et al. 2006;

Strid et al. 2006). Furthermore, research has shown that declarative memory measured at 9 months also predicts gestural communication and is positively related to receptive language measured at 14 months and 16 months (Sundqvist et al. 2016). Sundqvist and colleagues stress the domain-general implications of this research (2016, p. 109)

> These findings suggest a connection between the ability to form non-linguistic and linguistic mental representations. These results indicate that the child's Deferred Imitation ability [a measure of declarative memory] when predominantly preverbal might be regarded as an early domain-general declarative memory ability underlying early productive language development.

Finally, there is interesting emerging evidence of the relevant genetic influences on long-term storage and in particular the transfer from declarative to procedural memory (Ullman & Gopnik 1999; Ullman & Pierpont 2005). Intriguingly, the gene that has been implicated in controlling the transfer is FOXP2, originally identified for its role in language, and specifically its significance for grammar function (e.g., Pinker, 2001). Recent findings show that humanized FOXP speeds up learning by promoting the transition from declarative to procedural memory (Schreiweis et al. 2014). Much further investigation is needed here (see Schulze, Vargha-Khadem, & Mishkin, 2018 for the role of Phonological WM and FOXP2), but it raises the possibility that the role of FOXP2 in language function may not lay in controlling language itself but in fundamental processes of memory further upstream in development, manifesting itself only in language because language itself relies on the correct function and development of these more basic systems.

The complexity of these developmental trajectories are perhaps best thought of as a series of interrelated and ongoing cascades of cognitive achievements, of the type investigated by Bornstein and colleagues (2006) for such basic processes as habituation. If an infant sees the same shape, pattern or action, they lose interest or habituate to it quickly. Change a property of the stimulus and they regain interest. Because events and language are experienced sequentially, infants need some memory of the past in order to make a decision about the 'sameness' of the stimulus. Thus a measure of interest can be used to infer something of the infants basic information-processing, categorization and memory ability. Bornstein and colleagues (2006) showed that the more efficient preverbal 4-month-old infants were at habituating, the more likely they were to do better on standardized tests of language comprehension and production when they were 4-years-old. McCall & Mash (1995) suggests the mechanism that mediates this relationship between linguistic performance, general cognition and habituation is inhibition. Infants who efficiently inhibit attending to old or irrelevant stimulus free attentional and cognitive resources to learn something new, whether that be linguistic, spatial, social or something else. More generally, Bornstein and colleagues showed from their large longitudinal sample that perceptual, language, abstract reasoning, and memory tasks unfold in an interrelated cascade of cognitive developmental achievements (Bornstein et al., 2006; also Neisser et al., 1996).

2.4 Computational modelling of memory and language

Further evidence for the role of memory in language learning come from computational approaches. Elman's (1993) starting point was to recognize children are undergoing significant developmental changes at the same time that they are learning language. Like Newport (1988, 1990) he saw that there were some situations in which maturational constraints play a positive role in learning. He gave an artificial neural network the following types of sentences generated by a grammar:

4 (a) boys who chase dogs see girls.
    (b) girl who boys who feed cats walk
    (c) cats chase dogs.
    (d) Mary feeds john.
    (e) Dogs see boys who cats who Mary feeds chase.

The network parsed one word at a time and was scored on how well it predicted what the next word would be. Because the sentences involved the memory-heavy, complex embedded sentences we have encountered before, successful performance needed internal representations that could coordinate elements across the sentence, in short, a grammar. Elman found the network performed best when it was forced to 'start small' with limited access to its internal representations, that is, its memory. But why? Limiting memory reduced the degrees of freedom on prediction by only allowing the model to see a subset of simpler sentences, containing three of the four sources of variance (grammatical category, number, and verb argument type) needed to succeed at this task. Only later, as the model's memory was allowed to undergo a developmental change resembling that found in children, was the final source of variance seen by the model (long distance dependencies). By this time the generalizations that could be made from this final source of information had already been constrained by the first three. Development – the sequence in which information is acquired and organized – mattered.

This is as true for language as it is for any other domain of learning that results in behavior becoming more consistent, flexible and efficient over time, by which we mean skill acquisition in general. For example, the nineteenth-century Russian neurophysiologist, Nikolai Bernstein, pioneered an extremely influential multiple-systems theory of motor development and by doing so overturned the dominate reflex-based explanations of the time (Bernstein 1967). He observed that when infants are planning to execute some movement, there are a vast, perhaps infinite number of options (viz. degrees of freedom) available to perform *the same action*. The solution is for the central nervous system to regulate this redundancy by gradually releasing the available degrees of freedom or the number of independent movements needed at any one time. This isolation of individual degrees of freedom results in lower movement variability to begin with and leads to better task control. For example, Kanemaru and colleagues (2012) found that in three-month-olds there is a dissociation in the movement of the upper and lower limbs, as evidenced by increasing correlations between the velocities of the two arms and between the two legs. Such dissociations have been shown to support intentional action-planning, such a playing with a toy or manipulating an object (Watanabe & Taga 2009). The coordinated symmetry of inter-limb movement patterns provides an example of how the degrees of freedom of the limbs are constrained early on, and as learning continues, they are incrementally liberated as infants' motor actions become more variable, resulting in new task solutions and an internal reorganization of the system (Bernstein 1967; Meulenbroek & van Galen 1988; Bard, Hay & Fleury 1990; Thibaut & Toussaint 2010; Wunsch & Weigelt 2016). In development we should expect similar engineering solutions to similar problems and so we find the benefits of starting small pays off linguistically as it does in biomechanics.

The theoretical concerns of those interested in motor development should also sound familiar to anyone following the debate among language acquisition researchers. For example, "The storage problem is the result of the huge repertoire of human movements. Where are the motor plans for the movements stored? It would seem there would need to be an infinite storage capacity in the nervous system to contain all the plans necessary for the variety of movement available" (Muratori et al. 2013, p. 3) . . . Which for a linguist means a finite grammar creating an infinite number of sentences and the debate over mass storage of forms (e.g., Croft 2001) . . . "The novelty problem, addresses the ability to plan new actions. How is there a program for a movement that has never been performed before?" . . . Which for a linguist means the ability to generalize to novel forms never encountered before, for example *the gazzer mibbed the toma* and . . . "Finally, there is the issue of motor equivalence – the same action can be accomplished using different patterns of coordination. How is this possible if the action is the result of a program?" . . . Which for a linguist means the redundancy in the linguistic system and, for example how to isolate the function of case marking, word-order, animacy when they are all working 'in the same direction'. Because of the interdisciplinary cross-over it also means linguistics can learn from approaches that have worked well in solving some of these issues (Muratori et al. 2013). For example Dynamic Systems Theory proposes that rather than mass storage of motor step sequences, movement is an emergent property (Thelen, Ulrich & Wolff 1991) occurring as the neuromuscular system interacts with the environment as an online adaptation specific to the task at hand (Scholz 1990). Physical movement is constrained by characteristics of the individual (size, cognition, motivation, etc.), environment (light, gravity, etc.), and the task (goals, rules, etc.) (Newell 1986). Notions of emergentism, the importance of social and physical interaction and the role of general cognition in dampening degrees of freedom all play a significant role in the approach advocated here too and are developed further in the final part of the book.

Taking inspiration from Elman's work, and Elissa Newport's more general ideas suggesting learning can be most effective with an incremental roll-out of capacities (Newport 1988; Newport 1990), Ibbotson, López and McKane (2018) went further, implementing not just a limited memory capacity but a memory that actively forgets. Forgetting has traditionally – and understandably – been seen as detrimental to learning, reducing the ability to recall known words and to abstract categories. Recently however, the counter-intuitive notion that forgetting is an aid to word learning and concept generalization has received experimental support in the forgetting-as-abstraction account (Vlach, Sandhofer & Kornell 2008; Delaney, Verkoeijen & Spirgel 2010; Vlach, Ankowski & Sandhofer 2012; Toppino & Gerbier 2014). This work suggests spaced learning – distributing learning events over time rather than massing learning together in close succession – allows time for forgetting to occur between learning events. Vlach (2014, p. 165) hints at *why* this regime might improve learning by suggesting "forgetting promotes abstraction by supporting memory for relevant features of a category and deterring memory for irrelevant features of a category." Using a computational model of word learning, Ibbotson and colleagues found a U-shaped function of errors indicative of a "Goldilocks" zone of forgetting: an optimum store-loss ratio that is neither too aggressive nor too weak, but just the right amount of forgetting to produce better language-learning outcomes. Forgetting essentially acts as a high-pass filter that actively deletes (part of) the referential ambiguity noise and amplifies the signal. The model achieved this performance without incorporating any specific cognitive biases of the type proposed in the constraints and principles account (Golinkoff, Mervis, & Hirsh-Pasek, 1994; Markman, 1992, 1994) and without any prescribed developmental changes in the underlying learning mechanism. Instead, the model's performance is more of a by-product of exposure to input, whereby the associative strengths in the lexicon grow as a function of linguistic experience in combination with memory limitations.

The role of forgetting has been argued to have an important role not just in learning associations but generalizing knowledge to new instances – a fundamental part of the creative aspect of acquiring a language (Vlach, Sandhofer & Kornell 2008; Vlach, Ankowski & Sandhofer 2012; Vlach & Sandhofer 2012; Vlach 2014). Following (Vlach 2014). The "Goldilocks" zone of forgetting adds further support to the idea that a process traditionally thought of as inhibiting learning – forgetting – may actually promote learning words.

Further evidence for the relevance of memory biases in explaining linguistic trajectories comes from so-called optional infinitive errors. Young children have tendency to produce non-finite verb forms in contexts in which an adult would produce a finite verb form. For instance, in these examples from Pine and colleagues (2015, p. 62), English-speaking children produce utterances such as (5a) instead of the correct (5b); Dutch children produce utterances such as (6a) instead of the correct (6b); German children produce utterances such as (7a) instead of the correct (7b); and Spanish children (occasionally) produce utterances such as (8a) instead of the correct (8b):

English
5 (a) That go there
      That go-INF there
  (b) That goes there
      That go-FIN there

Dutch
6 (a) Mama ijs eten
      Mama ice-cream eat-INF
  (b) Mama eet ijs
      Mama eat-FIN ice cream

German
7 (a) Papa Kaffee trinken
      Papa coffee drink-INF
  (b) Papa trinkt Kaffee
      Papa drink-FIN coffee

Spanish
8 (a)   Jugar al fútbol
      (He) play-INF football
  (b)   Juega al fútbol
      (He) play-FIN football

It has been known for some time that the serial order in which information is presented has a strong effect on the ability to recall it, such that recall is boosted for those items that are presented first (primacy) and last (recency) in a string (Murdock 1962). Freudenthal and colleagues integrated this basic bias of memory into a learning model, reflecting the fact that language-learning children too are preferentially sensitive to both the beginning and the end of unfamiliar utterances (Freudenthal et al. 2015). They found that by using this more realistic model of memory, they were able to capture the cross-linguistic patterning of optional infinitive errors in declaratives in English, Dutch, German and Spanish by learning from declarative input, and the cross-linguistic patterning of errors in *Wh-* questions in English, German and Spanish by learning from interrogative input.

2.5 Summary

In this chapter we have considered the role that memory can play in language development, particularly those of working memory, long-term memory and its declarative and procedural components. We also looked at examples of how biases within memory – forgetting, primacy and recency effects – also can play a significant role in learning words and phrases. Our general goal here is to evaluate the extent to which domain-general developmental trajectories, confine, predict and explain the developmental trajectory of the linguistic ones. To that extent, it is clear the unfolding capacity of memory defines a space within which language has to work but also, without it, it could not work at all. This kind of relationship is what we would expect if memory is language's precursor, both ontogenetically and phylogenetically speaking.

We saw that both individual-difference and training studies of memory predict performance on a range of linguistic measures. Furthermore, longitudinal data suggested a strong role for individual differences in memory determining greater language development rather than vice versa. From the early work by Bever, to work on maturational limitations and the complementary evidence of computational models, we saw how memory places various adaptive constraints at various points in development that limit the degrees of freedom on learning. Important in this regard are the downstream consequences of the order in which capacities are introduced upstream. Decision theory provides a general framework to study the impact of these choices and it shows that the sequence in which the same set of decisions are taken can affect the degrees of freedom of subsequent decisions. For example, say I arrive at a restaurant and I have two principal choices: what to eat and what to drink. Say 50 of the 100 meals on offer are best complemented by a red wine and the other 50, by white wine. If I choose what to drink first I have one decision to make (red/white) and then 50 meals to consider whether or not to eat (yes/no), a total of 51 degrees of freedom. If I choose what to eat first, the wine choice is made for me when I select the meal so there are no degrees of freedom left for drink, but now I have 100 meals to consider, and so 100 degrees of freedom: a strategy that is more time-consuming, less efficient and more error-prone than if I had selected my drink first. So the optimal degrees of freedom is obtained by choosing the decision sequence which prunes the most branches off the decision tree to begin with, leaving the largest set of permutations that never need to be entertained. The same kind of decision making heuristics need to employed whenever the combinatorial possibilities rule-out a brute force analysis, for example, the gaming strategies of chess-playing algorithms. Linguists too have often drawn attention to the expressive power and combinatorial possibilities of grammar and asked why certain generalizations (decisions to consider) are possible but not entertained by the child, typically proposing language-internal solutions. Here is where development really matters. What we are beginning to understand is that memory is a powerful non-linguistic force that may have been underestimated in its ability to constrain generalizations. This is because linguistic knowledge has to pass through the bottleneck of what memory can do, and allow, at any stage in development, and that these self-imposed constraints can actually be adaptive.

Of course language is placing the same kinds of maturational constraints on the other cognitive facilities it supports and interacts with so there is nothing special about memory in that regard. It does however underline the importance of studying the interaction between language, memory and cognition as they unfold in an interrelated cascade of development, and it also points to a fertile area of research for years to come for researchers interested in modelling the detailed complexity of this interaction.

Chapter 3
Categorization and analogy

Like memory, the ability to make categories and form analogies, is of such basic importance that it is hard to imagine how language and cognition could function without it. In its absence we would be doomed to treat each new object, action, experience or word as an example of only itself; a class with a membership of one. That would make predicting, navigating and thriving in the physical and social world extremely difficult and it would also rid language of much of its creative power.

In this chapter we study both the development of categorization and analogy as together they seem to rely on a cognitive process that compares two independent elements to a third overarching one, schematically 'x is like y in way z'. For example, a dog encountered for the first time might be categorized as such, using the reasoning that *this dog(x) is like the other dogs I've seen (y) in that it has four legs, barks and has a furry coat(z)*. Likewise with analogies, *the moon(x) is [like] a ball(y) in that they are both round(z)*. This kind of classification structure can of course be applied to the linguistic system too, for example in the caused-motion construction: *Frank sneezed the napkin off the table(x)* is like *Mary sprayed paint onto the wall(y)* in the way *A cause B to move C(z)*. What we want to understand is the contribution cognition and social reasoning makes to the "in way z" comparison, such that generalizations come to satisfy the communicative function the speaker intended and also adhere to the norms of the target language.

Let us start with the observation that people often find analogies made in one direction, $x \rightarrow z$, to be much more acceptable than the other, $z \rightarrow x$ (Tversky 1977). For example, there is a preference for "a scanner is like a copy machine" over "a copy machine is like a scanner". As Tversky points out, this directionality seems odd if one sees similarity as a symmetrical relationship; if x is similar to z then z should be equally similar to x. Viewing categorization and analogy as processes that use the same hierarchical classification structure provides an explanation: scanners are one kind of copy machine and predictive inferences are derived from the more general schema (z) to the more particular instance (x, y), not usually the other way around. And this brings us to the utility of having a categorization-analogy function to begin with. By knowing some properties of a category, other properties can be inferred for free because members of the same class are assumed to share some unobserved properties. If it walks and barks like a dog then it probably smells like one too.

So, categories are essentially prediction engines that pump out best-guesses; and prediction is a general cognitive capacity that appears across domains, organized into a hierarchical cascade of forecasts at different levels of granularity across the brain (Rao & Ballard 1997; Rao & Ballard 1999; Bar 2007; Friston & Kiebel 2009; Lupyan & Clark 2015). With respect to language, error-based models of learning use the notion of prediction to compare expected input with actual input (Elman 1990; Chang, Dell & Bock 2006; Pickering & Garrod 2013). When the prediction matches reality nothing new is learned but the forecast is entrenched; where there is error in the forecast, hearing *mice* instead of *mouses* for the first time, for example, then the category is updated to accommodate the new evidence and alter future predictions (Ramscar, Dye & McCauley 2014). So, our existing memories can help generate analogies and drive predictions, but in addition to interpreting the immediate environment the analogical process also "augments previous representations in a way that fosters increasingly flexible future analogies" (Bar, 2007, p. 282). There is widespread evidence that children generate predictions 'online' during discourse about upcoming phonology (Swingley, Pinto & Fernald 1999), semantics (Fernald, Zangl & Marchman 2008; Fernald, Thorpe & Marchman 2010; Mani & Huettig 2012), morphosyntax (Lew-Williams & Fernald 2007; Borovsky, Elman & Fernald 2012; Lukyanenko & Fisher 2016), and speakers' intentions (Kidd, White, & Aslin, 2011).

Most relevantly for the argument we are pursuing here, is evidence that individual differences in nonverbal prediction correlate with vocabulary size in infancy (Reuter et al. 2018). Reuter and colleagues tested 12- to 24-month-old infants in a visual prediction task and found that the children who were good at the non-linguistic prediction task were also the ones with the highest vocabulary. The predictive payoff of using categories is of course fundamental to a widespread range of linguistic behavior. For example, a number of theorists have proposed that languages have a tendency to align particular semantic roles with different levels of animacy, prototypically animate → agent, inanimate → patient (Dowty 1991; Aissen 1999). The fact that languages with such different lineages as *Hindi, Finnish, Russian, Samoan, Dyirbal, Apachean* and *Papuan* have grammaticalized animacy with syntactic foregrounding structure (e.g., subjecthood) shows that carving the world into animate and inanimate categories is usefully predictive of how things behave and thus buys some information for free (DeLancey & Comrie, 1983; Kibrik, 1985; Mallinson & Blake, 1981; Song, 2001).

The approach of this chapter will hopefully be familiar by now: we consider how the developmental trajectories of non-linguistic categorization and analogizing interact with those of language. For example, to return to the case of animacy, well before children start stringing words together into phrases they have strong expectations about the capacities of animate and inanimate entities, differentiating them on featural, behavioral and intentional properties (Golinkoff et al., 1984; Massey & Gelman, 1988; Rakison & Poulin-Dubois, 2001). Moreover, people the world over converge on a kind of folk-taxonomy of animacy that is remarkably alike (Atran 1998). Because languages generally foreground animacy and agency with syntactic prominence, children learn to expect sentence subjects to be agents of or else govern in some way the other constituents of the phrase. By contrast, children assume that inanimate things, almost by definition, are less likely to be agents (Corrigan, 1988; Poulin-Dubois, Lepage, & Ferland, 1996; Scott & Fisher, 2009; Woodward, Phillips, & Spelke, 1993). So, when inanimate nouns do appear in subject position, they can be a powerful cue of non-prototypical syntax and semantics. Becker has argued that by recruiting non-linguistic understanding of what inanimate agents are capable of, children are guided in their recovery of who-did-what-to-whom in these non-canonical syntax cases (Becker 2005; Becker 2006; Becker 2009; Mitchener & Becker 2011; Becker & Estigarribia 2013; Becker 2014; Becker 2015). That is because they reason inanimates are just not the sort of thing that can be agentive or an experiencer of something, therefore they cannot be the subject argument of the controlling predicate either. The result is that an inanimate subject tends to be interpreted as an argument only of the lower predicate, as is the case in so-called raising (*Bob seems to be lying*) or tough constructions (*Mary is tough to please*). Corroborating this idea is the fact that in languages that allow inanimate subjects in raising and *tough* constructions, they also disallow inanimate noun phrases as subjects of control predicates (various Indo-European languages, plus Tongan, Samoan, Niuean, Chamorro and Maori for raising, and Finnish, Mandarin, Labrador Inukitut, Niuean and Bahasa Indonesian for *tough* constructions). Moreover, inanimate subjects are more generally restricted in their distribution when compared with animate subjects and in some cases they are forbidden entirely in certain contexts (Japanese, Jacaltec, Navajo, Tlapanec, Blackfoot) (Chung 1983; Comrie 1989; Dahl & Fraurud 1996).

Tough constructions have traditionally been difficult to formulate within more formal theoretical frameworks (Chomsky, 1977; Hicks, 2009; Lasnik & Uriagereka, 1988). As was the case for the role of memory in center-embedding, so it seems in this case too: it is more straightforward to account for the graded acceptability of these constructions, the typological pattern and the developmental trajectory of such linguistic phenomena by tracing the developmental trajectory of a graded non-linguistic capacity, namely, animacy. In summary, children's ability to categorize the world into a taxonomic hierarchy of animacy is brought to bear on the categories their languages have grammaticalized

(Golinkoff et al., 2002; Mandler, 2010) and by recruiting this information, it can narrow the degrees of freedom on categorizing the functions of syntactic patterns (Gelman & Koenig 2001; Becker 2014).

3.1 The development of pre-verbal categorization

Infants show basic categorization abilities at birth and within the first year of life they are able to classify visual patterns such as faces and geometric shapes into groups (Bomba & Siqueland, 1983; Slater, 1995; Younger & Gotlieb, 1988). Interestingly, differences in auditory processing and discrimination of non-linguistic sounds in the first year of life significantly predict linguistic comprehension and expression at 36 months-old (Benasich & Tallal 2002). Particularly important in the categorization process is the statistical distribution of items in the learning set, such that increased numbers of exemplars and increased numbers of categories can help infants abstract a generalized category or prototype (Strauss 1979; Bomba & Siqueland 1983; Quinn 1987). Introduced into the categorization literature by Rosch and colleagues, the basic idea of a prototype is that a concept, for example, *bird*, is not defined by a set of necessary and sufficient features – with all members that meet the criteria being equals. Rather, the concept has a graded structure, with fuzzy boundaries, in which some members play a privileged role and thus the prototypical bird is one that shares the most features with other birds and is maximally distinct from non-birds (Rosch 1983; Mervis & Rosch 2003).

By only 3–4 months old children are becoming flexible with how they apply categories and sensitive to subtle changes in the characteristics of the input such that they can make fine-grained *and* broad distinctions of the same stimuli (relevant for the lumper-splitter 'dilemma' discussed later in section 3.4). For example, after viewing exemplars of basic-level animal categories (e.g. cats) and furniture (e.g. chairs) young infants are able to form a category of domestic cats that includes novel cats but excludes birds, dogs, horses and tigers, and a category of chairs that includes novel chairs, but excludes couches, beds and table. They are also able to form a category of mammal that is inclusive of novel mammals but exclusive of birds, fish, and furniture and a category of furniture that inclusive of novel furniture, but exclusive of mammals (Quinn & Eimas 1996). To achieve multiple levels of discrimination at such an early age is impressive and suggests infants already have some appreciation of hierarchical relationships that will later develop into some more sophisticated, for example 'domestic cat' is an instance of the more general category 'cat' which itself is an instance of the more general category 'mammal'.

There is strong evidence infants construct these categories using inductive generalizations grounded in perceptual and attentional mechanisms capable of detecting multiple correspondences or similarities across features (Goldstone 1994; Sloutsky 2003; Murphy 2018). However, which features are the relevant ones? For example, age is more important than height in predicting whether someone is a child but height is a better predictor than age as to whether they are female or not. Moreover the same item can fall into different categories depending on the context; England is simultaneously in the category of The British Isles, United Kingdom, Great Britain, Europe (at the time of writing), planet Earth and so on. This shows us the extent to which categories are not given to us by the structure of the world or objective reality but choices we make to construe the situation from a particular perspective, quite often to adapt to the needs and/or expectations of the audience: I call a dandelion a flower if it's in a bouquet; I call it a weed if it's growing in the wrong place; I call it *Taraxacum officinale* if I'm a botanist; I call it food when feeding it to a pet guinea pig. Asking the question whether a dandelion is a flower or a weed just does not have the same truth-conditional relationship to reality as asking whether 2+2=4. So, our words and constructions are invitations to share our perspective on an object, event or process and not always truth-conditional bearing propositions about the world (Langacker 1987; Langacker 1991). The natural way in which language can subtly bend and insinuate a perspective for listeners will be familiar to any psycholinguistic experimenter who often has to work very hard to *control* these influences across multiple sentences. These linguistic construals, perspective and profile choices can be thought of as manifestations of more basic attention directing strategies and so are dealt with in greater depth in Chapter 4 Attention and inhibition.

The function the category serves is also an important dimension, in addition to similarity. And what is functional or meaningful for the child emerges from physical and social interaction with the world and the subsequent analogies they make to the scripts, events and schemas in long-term memory (Bar, 2007, 2009; Tomasello, 2003). For example, when 14- and 18-month olds were presented with novel hybrid items made from parts of vehicles and animals (e.g., a cow body with wheels and a tractor chassis with cow legs) they resisted creating categories over these dimensions, even though they would have been 'statistically justified' in doing so from their distribution in the input (Rakison & Butterworth, 1998). Instead they generalized over the dimensions they were familiar with because the children had no functional analogue in their experience to date (nor any from the experiment itself) that suggested forming categories of these hybrids had any predictive value about their behavior. The cognitive cost of creating new categories for the hybrids was not offset by the predictive benefit they would bring and so they defaulted to the ones they knew were good predictors of behavior (i.e., things that have legs tend to behave more like other things with legs and things with wheels tended to behave more like other things with wheels). As we will see later, the function of linguistic constructions too – how they behave, what they can do and not just what they look like – deeply canalizes the possibilities over which children generalize categories.

Here we should introduce a note on methodological detail on these studies as it has important implications for establishing the underlying developmental trajectory of categorization. As infants undergo significant cognitive and motor changes in the first year of life, so the measures that assess their categorization skills also need to change. Thus researchers have developed a range of different procedures adapted for different stages of development, including visual preference, object examination, conditioned leg-kicking, sequential touching, and generalized imitation. They all work on the same basic assumption, that categorization abilities are present when an infant responds the same to members of an equivalent class and differently to exemplars from separate groups. In general, studies that have used a familiarization phase (i.e. sequential touching and generalized imitation studies) show infants are able to form categories based on broad, global features whereas those without such a phase (i.e. visual preference, object examination, and conditioned leg-kicking) show infants both form broad categories as well as make finer-grained distinctions, and in some instances are even sensitive to exemplar specific information. Mareschal and Quinn (2001) suggest the difference arises because of the additional learning afforded by the familiarization trials themselves; essentially infants get the extra information they need in the training phase of the study to make finer-grained categorical decisions in the test phase. As we did for memory, we pause to note some immediate correspondences between non-linguistic and linguistic features of categorization in Table 2.

It is clear to see that many non-linguistic categorization processes have linguistic analogues later on in development. Of particular significance to category formation is the statistical distribution of items in the learning set and relatedly, prototypicality effects, which we examine in greater depth below, spelling out the implications for language learning.

3.2 Prototypicality and item weight in categories

Prototypicality effects show in development well before language has been acquired. For example, 3–4-month-old respond as if an unfamiliar shape prototype is more familiar than a previously observed exemplar (Strauss 1979;

Table 2: Categorization phenomena in non-linguistic development and their language counterparts.

Categorization	Language
Prototype and exemplar reasoning about visual and object categories; ability to make broad and fine-grained distinctions	Prototype and exemplar reasoning about linguistic categories; ability to make broad and fine-grained distinctions
Importance of the statistical distribution of items in the class to generalization	Importance of the statistical distribution of items in a novel construction or word
Non-linguistic taxonomic hierarchy including broad and fine-level categorization	Linguistic structural hierarchy including broad and fine-level categorization
Importance of perceptual and functional dimensions of classification and generalization	Linguistic categories based both on similarity of form (e.g., phonological regularities) and of meaning (e.g., the communicative function it serves)

Bomba & Siqueland 1983; Quinn 1987). In adults, the classic study of this effect is by Franks and Bransford (1971), where they argued that in general a prototype comprises a maximal number of features common to the category, often "averaged" across exemplars. They constructed stimuli by combining geometric forms such as circles, stars, and triangles into structured groups of various kinds. Some of these were then shown to participants who were then later asked whether they recognized these and other shapes they had not seen previously. Importantly, one of the exemplars shown at test contained all of the geometric forms together, an exemplar that had actually never been shown previously, but could be considered the prototype if all of the experienced exemplars were averaged. The participants not only thought that they had seen this prototype, but they were actually more confident that they had seen it than the other previously seen exemplars (or distracter items which they had not seen). Note that these effects were established for an ad hoc non-linguistic category. Ibbotson and colleagues (2012) investigated whether the same kind of prototype effects extends to the linguistic domain, namely the transitive argument-structure construction, a fundamental building block present in one form or another in all of the world's languages (Hopper & Thompson, 1980; Naess, 2007).

To transplant the Franks and Bransford methodology from a non-linguistic prototype shape to a chunk of syntax, a working definition of a syntactic prototype was needed. A basic construction in almost all the world's languages is the transitive construction, as in *He kicked the ball*. Building on Hopper and Thompson's (1980) classic investigation of transitivity across the world's languages, Næss (2007) proposes that the prototypical transitive construction is characterized by the maximally distinct argument hypothesis, where the two participants in the transitive clause are maximally semantically distinct from one another. Thus, this 'motion event' (Talmy, 1988) is prototypically realized as an **agent intentionally instigating** an **action** that directly results in the **patient** being **affected**. In line with the gradable nature of concepts advocated by prototype theory, there should be 'better-or-worse' examples of transitivity (Figure 3). For example, the sentence *John cut the bread* semantically overlaps with all the prototypical features, while *the key opened the door*, *John climbed the mountain*, and *John (accidentally) broke the vase*, are all "distortions" from the prototype along the dimensions of agent intentionality, instigation, and affectedness of the patient.

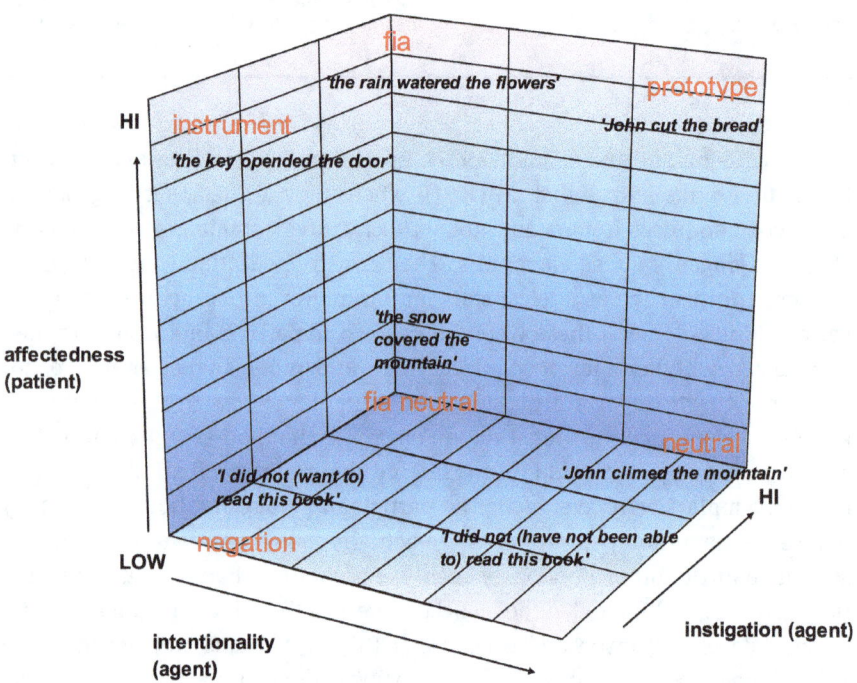

Figure 3: Possible semantic space predicted by Næss' maximally distinct argument hypothesis. These linguistic distortions of the transitive were designed to be the analogue of the geometric distortions of Franks and Bransford's original study.

Ibbotson and colleagues presented many of these distorted prototype sentences to children and adults, followed by a surprise memory recall test which, crucially, did include the prototype. They found, just like Franks and Bransford had for geometric shapes, linguistic constructions with prototypical semantics were the ones most confidently remembered, despite the fact these were the very ones that participants had *not* seen (Ibbotson et al. 2012). Note that this effect of prototypicality was demonstrated, not for some esoteric piece of syntax or idiomatic construction at the 'periphery' of language, but at the heart of a basic canonical grammatical pattern present in many of the world languages. Recall that an encapsulated language module was supposed to have properties unique to language and impermeable to general cognition. The implication of this work suggests that grammar interacts with general cognitive processes at some of the deepest levels we could empirically establish.

Since the introduction of the notion of a prototype into the categorization literature by Rosch and her colleagues (Rosch 1983; Mervis & Rosch 2003), the basic idea has been applied to a wide range of linguistic contexts, including lexical semantics (Lakoff 1987); tense-aspect marking (Andersen & Shirai 1996; Shirai & Andersen 2006); relative clauses (Diessel & Tomasello 2005); questions with long-distance dependencies (Dąbrowska, Rowland & Theakston 2009); subject auxiliary inversion (Goldberg, 2005; Lambrecht, 2012). Lakoff (1987) applied the notion of prototype to both lexical semantics and grammatical constructions. In applying the notion to linguistic constructions, we must attend not only to function – for example, the ditransitive construction prototypically involves transfer of possession – but also to linguistic form – the ditransitive construction prototypically has the form of NP1 +VERB$_{ditrans}$ +NP2 + NP3. In Goldberg's (1995) version of construction grammar there is a focus on the fact that a given form often has a prototypical meaning as well as conventional extensions of that meaning. This is not just confined to metaphorical extensions of prototypical constructions to 'similar' conceptual situations (e.g., the use of the ditransitive construction for acts of information transfer and for benefactives), but also to negation, enablement, future transfer and more esoteric examples *I'm gonna sit right down and write myself a letter.*

In language acquisition, it seems analogy plays a crucial role assimilating new instances to the prototype. For instance, when the learner is trying to comprehend the two sentences *the car is towing the boat* and *the truck is towing the car*, they do not begin by aligning elements on the basis of the literal similarity between the two cars, but match the car and the truck because they are doing the same job from the perspective of the functional inter-relations involved. There is much evidence that people, including young children, focus on certain kinds of relations in making analogies, the most important being spatial and causal relations (Gentner & Markman, 1995; Dedre Gentner & Markman, 1997; Dedre Gentner & Medina, 1998). Thus, crucial for making analogies across linguistic constructions is the meaning of the relational words involved, especially the verbs, and the spatial, temporal, and causal relations they encode (more on this in section 3.3 below).

There are good reasons to suppose the same kinds of category-forming processes are a significant feature cross-linguistically in children's early comprehension and production of basic grammatical constructions (Ibbotson & Tomasello 2009). Evidence from English, German, Cantonese & Polish shows that young children are slow to form abstract constructions because they fail to see the more general applicability of syntactic markers such as word order and case marking. Thus the suggestion is that constructions redundantly marked with multiple cues could have a special status as a nucleus around which the prototype forms – which makes it difficult for them to isolate the functional significance of each cue.

In the non-linguistic domain, sensitivity to the distribution of items in a category has been found to play a significant role in how quickly children form categories across a range of stimuli including shapes (Posner & Keele 1968), spatial relations (Casasola 2005) and social groups (Elio & Anderson 1984). In the early stages of language development, when the type/token ratio is low, the prototype will be closer to the most frequent item. As the type/token ratio increases, with more instances of that category, the average will begin to stabilize, and as the set approaches adulthood levels of exemplars, the prototype of that category will become increasing entrenched and insensitive to new members. If the type/token ratio remains low (as in the ditransitive), the prototype will remain skewed towards the mode (see Figure 4a. below). Another way of putting this is to say the prototype of a particular functional set is weighted towards its most frequent members, so that children are unlikely to understand *read* or *pass* is as good an example of a ditransitive verb as *give*.

The frequency profile for transitives is much flatter (Figure 4b.) but a potential problem this presents for acquisition is that if a construction is often marked redundantly with multiple cues, it may be difficult for children to isolate exactly what job each of these markers is doing – and so to generalize these markers productively. From the perspective of the memory and cognition literature this is analogous to the problem of compound cues for function and category learning. The main point concerning us here is that, when a prototype construction is redundantly marked, children may not be able to isolate the form-function relationship of the syntactic markers involved – what Tomasello (2003) calls the blame-assignment problem – which will limit their productivity with them.

Returning to the non-linguistic developmental trajectories, there is evidence that the weighting of exemplars within a category is important for learning here too. For example, when 10-month-olds were tested to see if they had

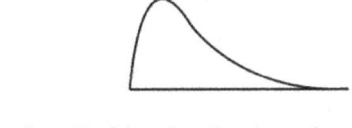

(a)   ditransitive [give, give, give, give, read, pass]

(b)   transitive [get, have, want, take, find, put, do, eat, play, see, like, say...]

Figure 4: Indicative type/token frequency profiles for the ditransive (a) and transitive constructions (b).

acquired a land-animal versus sea-animal category, those who repeatedly experienced a prototypical exemplar of a land animal acquired a category of land animal that excluded sea animals. By contrast, those who repeatedly experienced an atypical exemplar of land animals formed a category of land animal that *failed* to exclude sea animals (Oakes & Spalding, 1997). Relatedly, Elio and Anderson (1984) presented participants with one of two conditions in non-linguistic category learning experiment. In the skewed condition, participants were initially exposed to more frequently represented, more prototypical instances, with the learning set growing gradually to include the full range of members in the category, analogous to the emergent distribution a child would be exposed to in the ditransitive example in Figure 4a above. In the flatter distribution condition, analogous to the transitive example (Figure 4b), participants were trained on a wider sample from the start. Learners were more accurate in the skewed condition, yielding better typicality ratings and accuracy during the test phase on new instances. Clearly, if categories are less distinct, then, the younger children are, the harder these distinctions will be to learn. For example, 10-months-olds, but not 4-months olds, are adept at using co-variation information in the learning set to pull apart two non-linguistic categories that overlap on many features (Younger, 1990; Younger, 1985; Younger & Cohen, 1986; Younger & Fearing, 1999).

In apparent contradiction with this evidence that similarity among exemplars facilitates category learning (Elio & Anderson, 1984; Gentner & Markman, 1994; Sloutsky, 2003) there is also data suggesting increased variation among types facilitates generalization (Bybee 1985; Marchman & Bates 1994; Abbot-Smith & Tomasello 2006). For example, with adults a morpheme is most likely to be generalized across a range of instances when that morpheme is attested

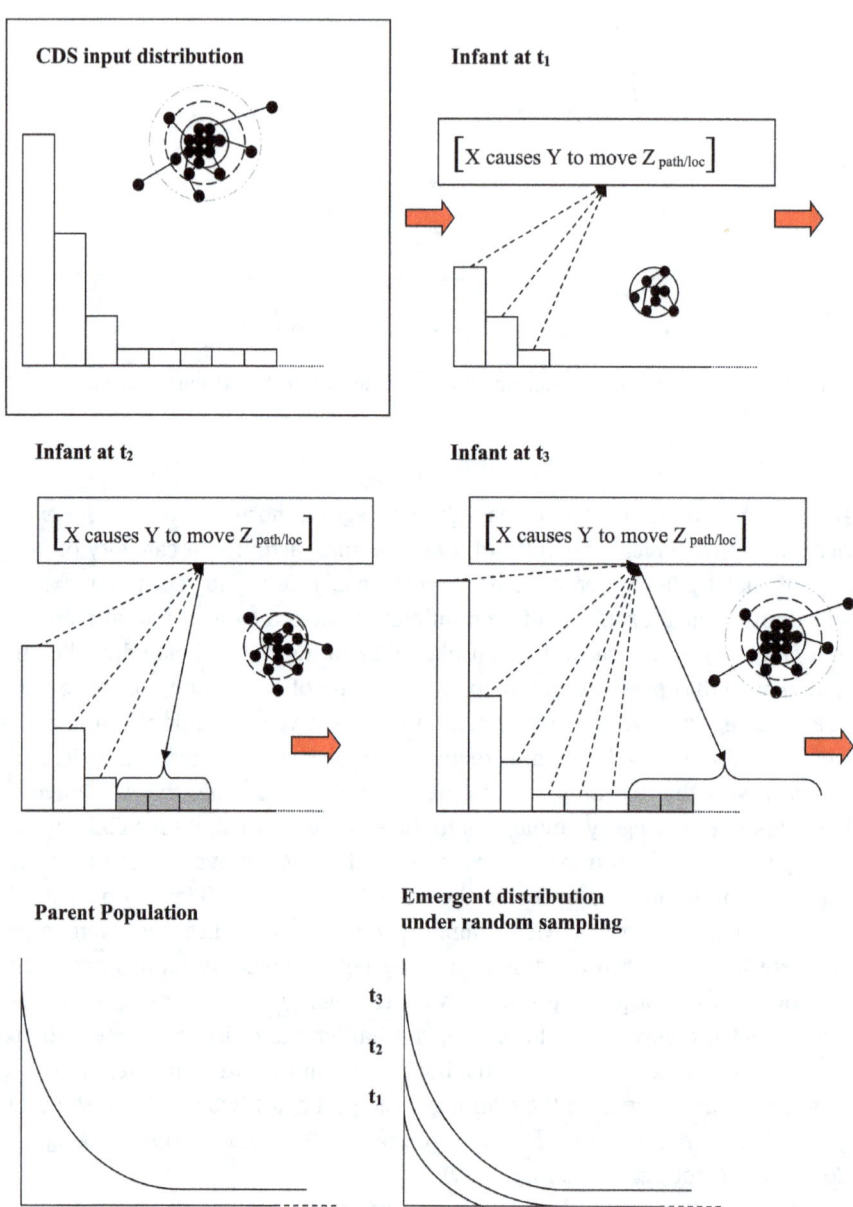

Figure 5: Schematization under skewed conditions. The graph at the top-left represents the verb types and tokens in CDS. To simulate what the child hears, it randomly samples from the CDS input distribution, equivalent statistically-speaking to sampling from a parent population. We then place those samples on the child's own graphs (t_1-t_3) as the child cumulatively builds their own distributions over time. The skewed input of types in CDS makes

with a wide variety of types (Bybee 1985; Bybee 2010a). Matthews and Bannard (2010) found that 2- and 3-year-olds were more likely to reproduce novel phrases when the final position in the phrase was difficult to predict, or in the terms of information theory, had high entropy. The implication being that the high entropy/low predictability slots help to license a wider range of items that could appear there, including ones that had never been heard before.

Boyd and Goldberg (2009) suggest the pattern of results can actually be considered two sides of the categorization coin, playing different roles at different points in development. Similarity across members facilitates category formation to begin with because a cluster features helps the learner identify there is a category to be learnt in the first place, which in turn might be grounded in a basic Hebbian learning advantage where associated concepts in time and space are co-activated (Figure 5). Later on in development, some variability helps to define where the boundaries of that category lie, and what *cannot* be considered a member of that category. This is important as avoiding false positives is as much a part of useful categorization as understanding true positives. For example, a diagnostic test for cancer with a 100% success rate sounds

---

Figure 5 (continued)
it extremely probable that at t_1 the child's first emerging cognitive anchors will be the most frequent types in the CDS. To illustrate, imagine we place all maternal caused-motion utterances in a bag and withdraw verb tokens one at a time. The probability of any verb type being withdrawn is a function of that verb's token frequency in the bag. Say there are ten caused-motion maternal utterances, the probability of extracting the verb 'put' might be 5/10, 'get' 2.5/10, 'take' 1.5/10, 'do/pick' 1/10. This is a kind of Bayesian reasoning of the expected probabilities: given a caused motion event, what are the probabilities that a particular verb will be used in this context. In the model the probabilities are the same for each sample (equivalent to replacing the tokens after each draw) as it makes no sense to say that because a mother has used a verb she can't use it again. The dashed lines in the diagrams represent the semantic contribution of each verb type to the emerging schema. The skewed distribution means the most frequent members of the set have a higher probability of being represented in the early sampling and thus forming the core of the proto-schema. The hypothesis is that the frequency of use reinforces the representation of linguistic expressions in memory, which in turn influences their expectation and interpretation in language use. At t_2 the infant is using this schema to categorize new instances (the shaded bars under the curly brackets) on the basis of the emerging caused-motion schema at that point in time. Those instances that have been categorized at t_2 now contribute to the schema and the categorization of new instances at t_3 but due to the skew of the distribution the semantic weight that these contribute to the overall schema is less than those early exemplars. Thus, the strength of the verb's role in defining the character of schema is proportional to its frequency within that construction. At t_3 instances in the long tail of the distribution are now categorized with respect to cognitive anchor verbs. The graphs at the bottom summarize this sampling process.

impressive until you realize that this could be achieved by just telling everyone they had cancer – not a very useful category. Understanding what is a false positive – not a member of a category – and what is a generalization too far is thus important.

We can add two further points to this picture of similarity and variance from natural language and cognition. First, from the perspective of information theory, if a slot in a string of words or phrase is predictable, it is not informative. For example, actually saying *bucket* in the phrase *He kicked the__* is almost entirely redundant. That is true for a system with a perfect memory, but not for humans who forget in systematic ways. When tokens of experience are repeatedly subtracted out of an emergent category by forgetting (e.g., Ibbotson, López, et al., 2018), repetition of similar items or a prototype helps maintain a pattern in long-term memory long enough for category formation and generalization to establish itself.

Second, and relatedly, in natural language the probability of encountering any given word or any combination of these words is not equal. Specifically, there are a few forms that are encountered relatively frequently whereas most are encountered rarely (Zipf 1935). As Shannon pointed out, this kind of redundancy allows recovery of meaning *xvxn whxn thx sxgnxl xs nxxsy* (Shannon 1951). Interestingly, this is true not only for letter sequences and words but for sequences of words too of the type that form basic formulaic and semi-formulaic patterns. Moreover, there is evidence that exactly this kind of Zipfian distribution helps both children and adults in construction learning by making the meaning and form of a particular construction simpler to identify (Casenhiser & Goldberg, 2005; Goldberg, Casenhiser, & Sethuraman, 2004).

3.3 Event cognition and mapping verbs

This section focuses on learning relational elements of language like verbs, because they seem to be a relatively difficult class of words to acquire, even when between-speaker and inter-language variation are controlled for (Ibbotson, Hartman & Björkenstam 2018). There appears something about the nature of verbs that is a step removed from the perceptual availability of nouns, protracting the trajectory of their acquisition. For example, while *dog* and *cat* may remain stable referents throughout the duration of a scene, who is doing the "chasing" and "fleeing" may alternate. These relational aspects present a wider inferential gap for social and cognitive processes to bridge and thus pose an interesting test-case for the role of domain-general mechanisms in language acquisition.

Like the individual-variation studies introduced in the memory chapter, there is evidence from similar methodologies for the role of non-linguistic categorization in predicting children's linguistic ability. Importantly this effect still persists when linguistic knowledge – lexical and syntactic ability – are held constant. For example, Konishi and colleagues (2016) established that the ability of 14-month-olds to categorize non-linguistic visualizations of an action's path (e.g., around, through, over) and manner (e.g., spin, hop, jog) predicted their verbal comprehension at 30 months, even after controlling for vocabulary levels. This is interesting because we know preverbal infants have the cognitive non-linguistic ability to discriminate both the direction of a figure and the way in which it moves with respect to the ground (Pulverman et al. 2008; Pulverman et al. 2013) and that they use this knowledge for later categorization of path and manner when language is beginning to emerge (Pruden et al. 2012; Pruden et al. 2013). For example, Lakustra and colleagues showed English-speaking infants are able to categorize goal and source paths in dynamic motion events as early as 10 months of age – an age that precedes the acquisition of the relevant linguistic spatial terms *to*, *on*, and *in* (Lakusta, Spinelli & Garcia 2017).

In order to use relational aspects of language like manner, path, and verbs in general, children first have to segment a continuous stream of action into meaningful units, then be able to categorize the same action in different contexts, and ultimately work out how their language expresses these categories (Hirsh-Pasek & Golinkoff 2010). So, while the preverbal action segmentation and recognition may proceed similarly cross-linguistically, by the time the child is learning to speak, this knowledge has to be packaged differently, as different languages have developed different solutions on how to divide the labor between manner and path within their morphosyntactic resources. For example, English packages manner within the main verb and puts path with a prepositional phrase while Spanish glues paths with the verb and outsources manner into optional gerunds (Talmy, 2000). Likewise, different languages have come to different solutions as to how to mark the edge of event boundaries with verbs; with some languages happy with a basic separation between those verbs with built-in endpoints and those without; others like Russian and Bengali go further and make a distinction between changes that occur at the onset or at the end of an event (Malaia 2004; Basu & Wilbur 2010). The burden of communicating events at this level of granularity is either borne by phonology (as with American Sign Language and Japanese; Fujimori, 2012; Wilbur, 2003), morphology (as with Indonesian or Russian; Malaia & Basu, 2013; Son & Cole, 2008) or else by the interaction between the verbs, aspect, determiners and quantifiers (as in many Germanic languages; Ogiela, Schmitt, & Casby, 2014; Van Hout, 2001).

Of course the pragmatic context the child finds itself in when hearing these chunks of language as communicative intentions – a "usage event" – is important in understanding where the meaning of these constructions emerges from. For example, in many of the world's languages grammatical aspect is used to indicate how events unfold over time. In English, activities that are ongoing can be distinguished from those that are completed using the imperfective morphological marker *-ing*. Using video recordings of two children in their third year of life, Ibbotson and colleagues found that the aspectual language that parents used while the child was performing actions – hitting versus hit, for example – respectively mapped onto the functions of the imperfective form which construes events as ongoing and from within, and the perfective, which construes them as completed (Ibbotson, Lieven & Tomasello 2014). This action-perception correspondence provides a strong cue to the child that one of the functions of imperfective morphology is to indicate how ongoing the activity is. More generally, there is mounting evidence from the grounded cognition literature that language develops in a tight association with perception and action (Goodwyn, Acredolo & Brown 2000; Ejiri & Masataka 2001; Childers & Tomasello 2003; Iverson & Fagan 2004; Iverson & Goldin-Meadow 2005; Hahn & Gershkoff-Stowe 2010; Glenberg 2012). When one hears a linguistic symbol, for example *running*, this re-activates stored sensorimotor information associated with running events (Barsalou 1999; Barsalou 2007). This view emphasizes that cognition is a situated activity and as such we should include sensorimotor activities as part of the pragmatic context – a claim that echoes those of early developmental theorists such as Piaget (1952) Werner and Kaplan (1963) and Nelson (1974). With respect to grammatical aspect, the hypothesis is that the embodied event of performing the action facilitates construing the scene from within and blurring the boundaries of the event. This is because, if the verb has imperfective *-ing*, the child is much more likely to be in the midst of action than if the verb is in its perfective form. By building a record of these embodied events in association with the aspectual morphology they do or do not hear, children can begin to form a verb-general notion of what the function of *-ing* is.

Regardless of the way in which a language communicates an event, the first key step on the way to being able to use the discrete, digital elements of language is being able to carve up a continuous, analogue action sequence. The cognitive payoff of doing so is the same reward of categorizing in general: to enable smart behavioral decisions in response to the environment, where future actions are predicted by long-term schematic knowledge of similar actions (Schank & Abelson 1977). For example, observers' eye-gaze predicts which object is the goal of an actor's reach well before the actor's hand arrives at the target object (Eisenberg, Zacks, & Flores, 2018; Flanagan & Johansson, 2003;

Hayhoe & Ballard, 2005). So, by parsing information streams into units of action, these event models can be used to guide comprehension and generate predictions. These become an essential aspect of categorizing the world as scenes of action and interactions constitute much of everyday human experience and naturally enough they come to feature heavily in topics of conversation (Zacks, Speer, Swallow, Braver, & Reynolds, 2007).

Zacks and Swallow (2007) make the following analogy between the temporal segmentation of events and the more well understood problem of spatial segmentation. In Figure 6(a) the scene is carved up into meaningful objects which all perform some relatively independent and coherent function, learned over the course of development by individuals interacting with and using these objects for their own ends. What counts as meaningful will differ among individuals and

Figure 6: Meaningful (a)l and meaningless (b) segmentation of the same scene.

between species. Note that the scene in Figure 6(a) is much easier (for humans) to process and comprehended that its meaningless counterpart (b).

Baldwin and colleagues applied the same meaningful segmentation concept to the temporal domain by inserting pauses into a video that either marked the boundary of an event or else interrupted the middle of one (Baldwin, Baird, Saylor, & Clark, 2001). The infants who watched these videos were more surprised when viewing pauses which disrespected event boundaries, suggesting breaks in the temporal flow of the scene were disruptive in a similar way to the spatial carving of the scene is in Figure 6(b).

By analogy to object boundaries, the definition of what makes a meaningful temporal boundary is experience dependent, grounded in an interaction with and a participation in events themselves. In the Baldwin study, infants were familiarized with one of two movies depicting a woman cleaning a kitchen, involving a salient goal-directed action such as replacing a fallen dishtowel or storing an ice cream container in the freezer. At a fine-grained level of analysis, these types of event boundaries are marked when there is an abrupt or unexpected change in the dynamic perceptual input (e.g., color, sound, movement). Underlining the interconnectedness of systems and the foundational role of memory, there is evidence that being able to segment meaningful chunks, consolidates those events in long-term memory such that individuals who are better able to segment an activity into events are better able to remember it later (Zacks, Speer, Vettel, & Jacoby, 2006). Crucially though, for humans, event cognition means much more than observable perceptual dynamics. At a more coarse-grained analysis, event segmentation also depends on inference of social-cognitive motivations, such as the attribution of goals and intentions to guide comprehension (Richmond, Gold, & Zacks, 2017; Zacks, Speer, & Reynolds, 2009; Zacks & Tversky, 2001). Indeed, infants privilege information about adults' goals at the expense of the specific physical dynamics (Woodward, 2009). Applied to language, Carpenter and colleagues found that at around 24-months-of-age, toddlers can use intentional inference to map novel verbs to discrete actions (Tomasello & Barton 1994; Carpenter, Call & Tomasello 2002) and by 2-years-of-age they are able to use event segmentation skills and intentional inference when mapping verbs to actions embedded in a continuous motion stream (Friend & Pace 2011). This is important as children rarely experience explicit boundaries in ongoing human action so any segmenting ability needs to be powerful enough carve the continuous flow of human action into meaningful units.

Over time, scene segmentation becomes an automatic and rapid skill. Adults can extract the basic whom-did-what-to-whom of a visual scene in a little as 37 milliseconds, as well as encoding other information about the agent's and patient's relationship to the rest of the scene and making behavioral predictions based on that information (Hafri, Papafragou & Trueswell 2013; Cohn, Paczynski & Kutas 2017; Hafri, Trueswell & Strickland 2018). Of particular importance in the scene is the animacy of agents, which is typically the first thing people identify (Webb, Knott & MacAskill 2010). This has implications for the kinds of salience gradient that language has to work with. For example, because preverbal infants privilege animate agents in event cognition it means that language needs a way to overcome this visual default, if the communicate intention is to focus on what happened to the patient. This is most obviously achieved by various passivization syntax that raises the patient to the subject role, and so marks that form for attention. Thus if the function of the linguistic construction is traced to its cognitive precursors, we are better able to define over what dimensions generalizations should be possible. Implementing this idea in a neural network, Takac and colleagues taught a model to represent simple transitive scenes from observing simulated actions. By filling in the slots in a transitive template in the order that mimicked human event cognition – namely agent first, then patient, then action category – the model was able to capture grammatical differences characteristic of event descriptions across languages (Mayberry, Crocker, & Knoeferle, 2009 for integration of vision and language event representations; Takac & Knott, 2016; Takac, Benuskova, & Knott, 2012).

Event structure and linguistic structure also share an important feature in that they are both naturally expressed by a hierarchical construction which can be more or less complex. This has led a number of researchers to claim event cognition operates on a common representational format that integrates information from multiple sources including language and perception (Knoeferle et al. 2008; Altmann & Mirković 2009; Solomon et al. 2015). So, when Pinker and Jakendoff ask "Is all this [syntactic structure] specific to language? It seems likely, given that it is specialized machinery for regulating the relation of sound and meaning. What other human or non-human ability could it serve?" (2005, p.216), the segmentation and coordination of events is one possible reply. For example, both segmenting an activity or a speech stream are not simply a matter of identifying the right event boundaries or the right word boundaries; it also requires tracking how sets of fine-grained events group together into larger meaningful units or stringing words together into syntactically meaningful phrases. The representational similarity with language derives from the fact actions too can be organized into a hierarchy, with overall goals governing a clustering of thematically related sub-goals (Zacks & Tversky, 2001). For example, going to shops might involve leaving the house, driving the car, going in the shops, each one which can be subcategorized; leaving the house might involve putting on shoes, picking up keys, closing door, and driving might involve starting engine, changing gear, parking and so on. Almost all linguistic theories subscribe to some level of hierarchical organization in language, although they may profoundly disagree where this hierarchy comes from and how detached it becomes from meaning. Most theories admit a role for hierarchy to escape the tyranny of form that, for example, prevents an adequate account of long-distance dependencies or the fact the children readily interpret the novel *the gazer mibbed the toma* as a transitive utterance despite sharing few lexical items with that category in their experience.

So, if there is some representational recycling when it comes to event cognition and linguistic hierarchy, then we should expect the behavior of the two systems to be interrelated in complex ways and therefore to have important developmental dependencies between them. When people are asked to describe scenes in terms of their major and minor events, coarse-grained events tend to focus on describing objects, using more precise nouns and less precise verbs, whereas fine-grained events focus on actions on those objects, using more precise verbs but specifying the objects less precisely (Zacks, Tversky, & Iyer, 2001). This general picture outlined here is not to imply any one-to-one mapping between the hierarchical structure of events and the language, rather the claim is that they can access to the same representational structure.

As we noted in the Introduction to the book, it seems reasonable to suppose from the comparative psychology literature that our ancestors were segmenting and organizing motion-perception long before they were using linguistic information structure – given how wide-spread motion-perception is in our phylogenetic neighborhood. So it also seems reasonable to suggest some of those segmenting and hierarchical cognitive processes employed for motion-perception would have been available to systems performing similar functions and executing similar goals. Event cognition is also prior to language in ontogeny as well as phylogeny and this has important implications for the claim that language uses forms specifically for its own purpose. Clearly, different languages construe the same scene in different ways, and the morphosyntactic resources a language has available to it can predict where people look in a scene (Flecken, Von Stutterheim, & Carroll, 2014 for German and Arabic; see also Gennari, Sloman, Malt, & Fitch, 2002; Papafragou, 2010; Papafragou, Hulbert, & Trueswell, 2008 for Greek) even in the absence of using spoken language at the time of the event (Flecken et al. 2015). Note though that the feedback from language to event segmentation can only play a significant role when language comprehension or production is "up and running". So, like memory, because event segmentation is acquired before language, it is a representational format available to language by the time it needs it, Figure 7.

If hierarchy is the solution what is the problem? Recall the from the Now-Or-Never bottleneck of memory, this hierarchical chunking strategy is a general

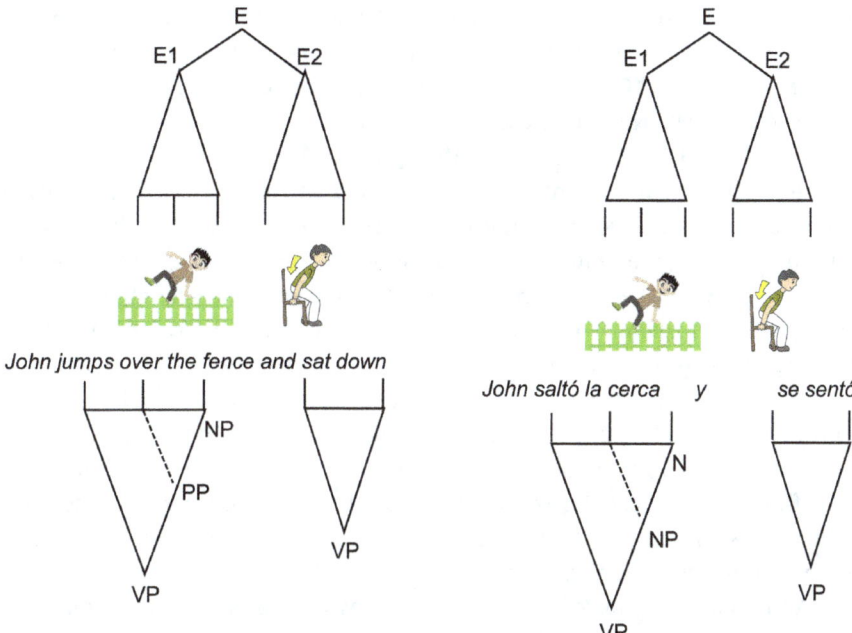

Figure 7: Event structure (E), perceptual events, utterances, and a partial syntactic constituent analysis (NP, VP, PP) for English and Spanish. Note the structure above is not tied to an particular theory – almost all linguistic approaches commit to some representational hierarchy but disagree as to how it originated and functions. Whether instantiated in phrase structure or functional schematization, in essence they are both merely asserting that linguistic categories exist and specifies differences are overlooked for the sake of generalities.

cognitive solution to the deluge of incoming perceptual sensory information and its rapid signal decay (Christiansen & Chater, 2016). While all linguistic structure might be processing history, not all processing history is linguistic. So, importantly, the same kind of hierarchical organizational principles have been demonstrated for memory, action and problem solving (Ericcson, Chase, & Faloon, 1980; Gobet et al., 2001; Miller, Galanter, & Pribram, 1960). In each case, detail-rich bottom-up information is recoded, compressed and passed up to the next level as a more abstracted and chunked representation. Language has evolved to fit this cognitive niche allowing linguistic chunks to exist at the same time across acoustic, phonological, word, and discourse levels (Christiansen & Arnon, 2017). This chunk-and-pass solution allows cognition to capture the inbound information in a maximally distinct and efficient way, and reduces the chance of interference between overlapping representations. Because this hierarchical structure is a domain-general format, language use shows the same practice effects as other domains, namely, repeated use of a chunk in the hierarchy leads to greater degrees of automaticity in a drive for cognitive efficiency (Bybee & McClelland, 2005; Heathcote, Brown, & Mewhort, 2000; Logan, 1988; Newell & Rosenbloom, 1981).

Mandler (1992, 2007) suggests that prior to language, infants construct image schemas that store fundamental components of an event. These image schemas are a kind of perceptual re-description of an event that is analyzed within the infant's attention. Some of the most common image schemas are constructed around relational components of dynamic events: containment-support (putting things in a container vs. putting things on a surface), path-manner (the trajectory of the action with respect to the ground vs. how the action is performed), source-goal (beginning point of an event vs. its ending point), and figure-ground (the moving or conceptually movable point vs. the reference entity or stationary setting; (Choi & Bowerman, 1991; Jackendoff, 1983; Lakoff, 1987; Langacker, 1987; Talmy, 2000). According to Mandler these common image schemas are later combined to derive basic conceptual categories such as animacy, causality, and agency.

Although these concepts are universally expressed, as we know, different languages encode them in different ways. Gökson, Hirsh-Pasek, and Golinkoff (2010) showed that for some basic image schemas, infants start with language-general concepts that are gradually construed in language specific ways. Infants parse events and generalize components of these events in ways that lay the groundwork for the learning of relational terms such as verbs and prepositions (McDonough, Choi & Mandler 2003; Pulverman et al. 2008; Lakusta et al. 2011). Gokson and colleagues (2010) argued that sensitivity to these basic constructs (such as figure vs. ground, source vs. goal), is universal in two senses: (a) irrespective of the language environment in which infants are raised, they detect these non-linguistic components of events, and (b) infants attend to fine-grained distinctions in events even when these are not codified in their native language (Göksun, Hirsh-Pasek, & Golinkoff, 2008; Hespos & Spelke, 2004). This is in the spirit of Kemmer's (2003) cognitive typology approach where the basic idea is that recurrent typological patterns reveal the distinctness of a number of basic contrasting types of event to which human beings are sensitive. These conceptual categories are used in the chunking and organization of conceptual information for the purposes of formulating, manipulating, and communicating thought. So, early on in development how events are construed in mental space (the conceptualization, Figure 8) bears some relation to how they are construed in perceptual space.

In the example of the caused-motion construction, there is evidence that people represent causation as patterns of force paying particular attention to

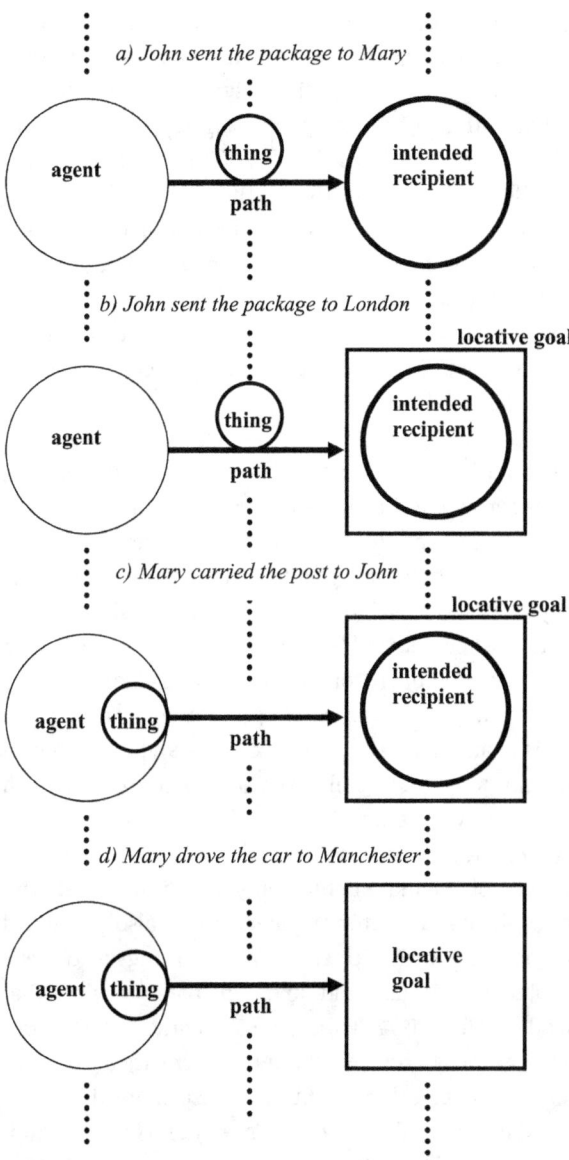

Figure 8: The functional alignment of constructions based on their event construal; a relevant domain of analogy for argument-structure constructions like the caused-motion construction, elaborated from Lakoff and Johnson's (1999, p.32) source-path-goal schema (see also Kodama, 2004). There is good evidence that the alignment of relational structure and mapping between representations is a fundamental psychological process underlying analogy and similarity across a range of domains (Gentner & Markman, 1994, 1995, 1993; Goldstone, 1994; Goldstone & Medin, 1994; Goldstone, Medin, & Gentner, 1991).

the dynamics of the event (Gennari et al., 2002; Talmy, 1988). Because dynamic properties can be sensed, a physicalist approach to causation not only grounds causation in the world, it also explains how causation might be experienced in our own bodies, and why such notions of causal power, energy, and force are not just side effects of statistical dependencies (Wolff 2007). Argument structures are differentiated into different families of use on the basis of these properties, such as "X cause Y to move to Z." At some point children begin to make categorization decisions based on the relationship between participants in an event – for the caused-motion construction this means they realize this particular type of utterance is an example of a convention that is put to use where the intention is to communicate "X causes Y to move to Z," this is pattern finding based on "things are what they do" (Nelson, 1985, 1996).

One manifestation of this domain-general process allows inter-construction mappings and is shown by the vertical dotted lines shown in Figure 8. They are analogies/categorizations in the sense that X is like Y in way Z: Utterance a) is like utterance b) in that they construe the agent, thing, and path in similar ways; utterance b) is like c) in that they construe path and goal in a similar way; and utterance c) is like d) in that they construe agent, thing, and path in a similar way. They are placed in this order as a) is more like b) than it is like c) or d) with respect to the relationship between participants; b) is more like c) than it is like d) and so on. The model framework is also tagged with psychological descriptions such as agent, goal, and intention. This is an important point: the goals and intentions of people do not present an infinite range of equally relevant generalizations with respect to the common (communicative) ground established between communicator and recipient. The ability to represent such psychological states is predicated by a fundamental social ability of shared intentionality and intersubjectivity (Tomasello, 2003). In Figure 8, the social-cognitive framework is also populated with a basic conceptual repertoire that is able to represent such things as objects, forces, goals, causes, paths, substances, space, and time – the types of things that language after language encodes (Allan, 1977; Bybee, 1985; Denny, 1976; Pinker, 1989; Talmy, 1988). Therefore, learning grammar is thought of here as categorizing over these types of concepts and image schemas, but it is also more than that. Because psychological states are also tagged onto this framework it is pattern finding through a unique social-cognitive lens, allowing us to see patterns that no other species can while making other possible patterns deeply unintuitive or not entertained at all. Abstract grammatical patterns are conventionalized patterns of shared experience; patterns of experiences that can be organized on the basis of behavior, for example whether their actions are intended to accomplish something similar. Thus right from the start, wider knowledge of how people work is brought to bear on finding patterns in grammar.

Emphasizing the role that event cognition can play, is not to diminish the contribution of syntax and semantics in narrowing the degrees of freedom on what words and phrases can mean, *once* some syntax or semantics has been acquired (Fisher, 2002; Gleitman, 1990; Maguire & Dove, 2008; Maguire, Hirsh-Pasek, & Golinkoff, 2010; Naigles, 1990; Yuan & Fisher, 2009). For example, different sentential contexts make some word classes much more likely interpretations than others, as these examples (9a-f) show (MacWhinney 2005):

9   (a) Here is a pum   (count noun).
    (b) Here is Pum   (proper noun).
    (c) I am pumming   (intransitive verb).
    (d) I pummed the duck   (transitive (causative) verb).
    (e) I need some pum   (mass noun).
    (f) This is the pum one   (adjective).

Likewise, by knowing something of what words mean, one can infer the syntactic word order if there is some stable correspondence between the two, for example, agents of actions tend to be subjects of a sentence, patients and themes tend to objects and goals, locations and instruments tend to appear as oblique or indirect objects (Pinker, 1984). As important as these processes are, they play a less significant role in the story of developmental cognitive linguistics because their focus is on how linguistic information (grammar or semantics) can guide linguistic generalizations, either of a known syntactic slot to a novel word or a known word to a inferred syntactic slot. That is, explaining a linguistic pattern with respect to a linguistic process, but not grounding it in an independent cognitive motivation that might support the emergence of language in the first place. What is of more interest here is how the non-linguistic categorization of events might share the hierarchical structure on which later syntactic and semantic bootstrapping can work. Furthermore, because event-segmentation is independent of language it can provide an escape to the circularity of linguistic-internal reasoning. For example, Frank and colleagues give the following example of a 'chicken and egg' problem with respect to word learning (2009, p.1).

Linguistic-internal chicken and egg problem

"If a child can understand what the sentential context is, it would be easy to learn the meanings of individual words, and once a child knows what many words mean, it is easy to infer the sentential context."

If we replace one element of the way the problem is stated above with a independently motivated domain-general element, we can escape its circularity:

Domain-general and linguistic statement

"If a child can understand a speaker's communicative intentions, it would be easy to learn the meanings of individual words, and once a child knows what many words mean, it is easy to infer the sentential context."

The escape route appears not just because we have reference to a system independent of language but because intention-reading, like memory and event categorization, emerges in development before infants begin building their language and thus the knowledge and representational structure that they offer is available to them.

3.4 Lumping and splitting

A supposed tension in the analysis of categorization is how to account for the lumping behavior of those that see generalizations, the connections and the commonalities between items and the splitters of this world who see the differences, carving the semantic space into ever smaller distinctions and sub-sub categories. Recall that by only 3–4 months old, children are becoming flexible with how they apply categories and sensitive to subtle changes in the characteristics of the input such that they can make fine-grained *and* broad distinctions of the same stimuli (Quinn & Eimas 1996). Here we apply this non-linguistic capacity to make broad and fine-grained distinctions, to the linguistic domain of the caused-motion construction and its more general form, the X cause Y schema, suggesting how item-based knowledge *and* generalizations can emerge from the same representational hierarchy.

In Figure 9, as the schematicity has increased from level to level the semantic content has decreased. This obviously represents a problem for a model of schematization if it cashes-out meaning as the output of the most abstract node: At the most general level it is schematic of everything and predictive of nothing. However, this symbolic assembly is a composite of all the levels it dominates; a form-function pairing. This is consistent with the evidence for graded representations of linguistic knowledge (Goldberg 1995), and in fact, one instantiation of this view – radial prototype conceptual structure – is produced as a by-product of "seeing" through the cumulative layers of abstraction, shown in Figure 9 as an arrow running from one end of the symbolic assembly

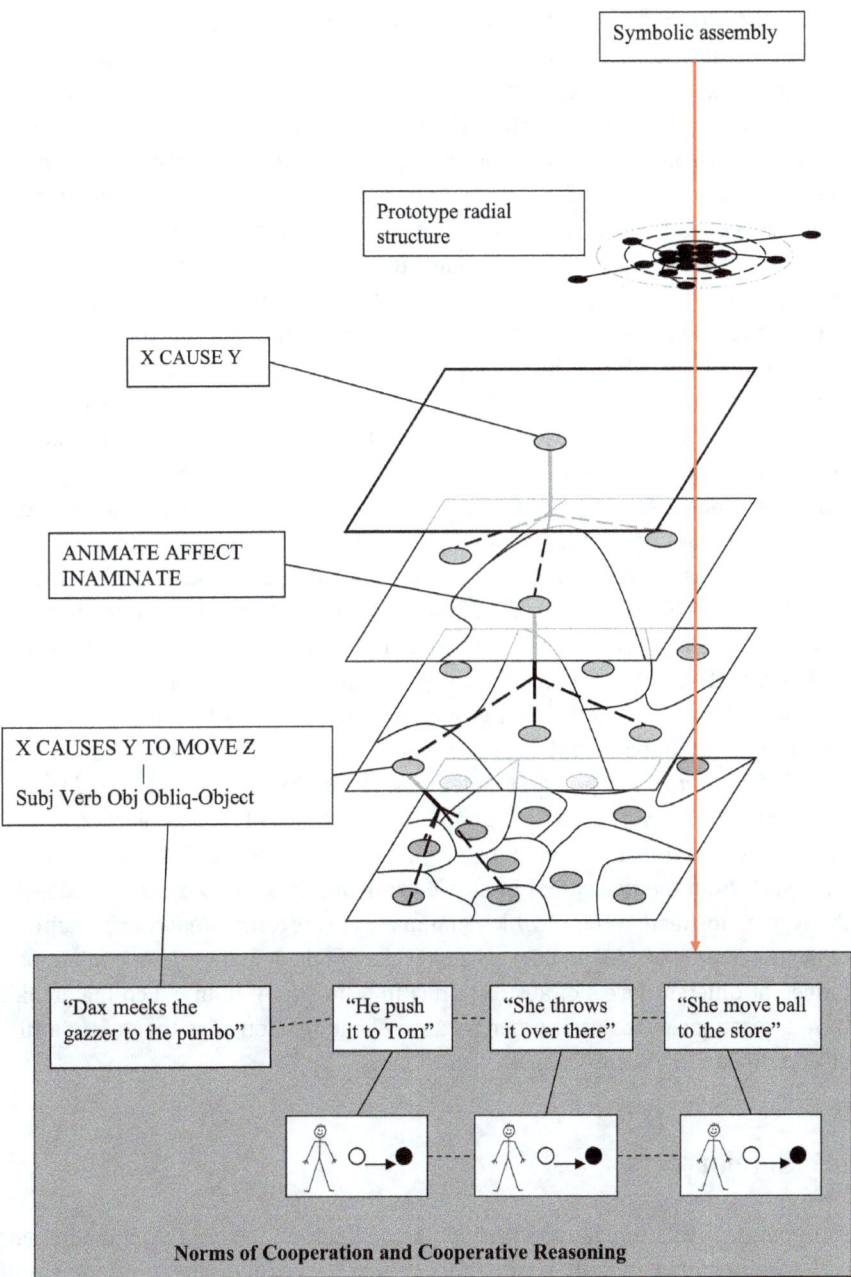

Figure 9: A schematization of the X cause Y event, the caused motion event forms part of this abstraction; the symbolic assembly is viewed through the four planes and incorporates the activated schemas it dominates.

to the other. Thus this is not a situation where we need to choose between supposedly dichotomous views of representations: we retain item-specific knowledge (e.g., exemplars) and we can abstract over them (e.g., prototypes or some other kind of schematized form). More important, after a period of development, the formal pole (toward the perceptual end) of this symbolic assembly may stop short of phonological content, that is, after sufficient evidence on which to generalize the construction can detach from the perceptual input. Thus, the caused motion schema comes to represent a grammaticalized event, free of phonological content in the sense that whether the noun phrase can enter the argument slots is not determined by its phonological properties.

The flexibility of analogy making that this kind of hierarchy buys, is impressive for many reasons, two of which are (i) it takes place at multiple levels of representation – from surface generalizations to functional generalizations and everything in between, and as a result of this (ii) the things being compared need not share any functional characteristics (a blue dog and a blue pencil are both blue) nor any perceptual characteristics (a blue taxi and a red boat are both means of transport), thus analogies made on the basis of how things behave can be made over vastly different degrees of specificity and domains (Holyoak & Koh 1987; Gentner, Rattermann & Forbus 1993). This includes the social–cognitive ability to understand you by analogy to myself, as well as the type of functional similarity that group constructions into families, such as ditransitives, resulatives, and caused motion or *the goat ate the woman* with *a woman tickled a goat*. The adult state for such a network in usage-based theory is basically the memory traces of hundreds of thousands of usage events organized into families of form and function pairings. Because, at some point in development we detach from the perceptual input we can make concept-to-concept analogies, the type of abstraction out of which grammatical categories are formed. Figure 10 represents the process of analogy as a type of mental cut-and-paste operation, performed at different levels of abstraction (1 to 4 in Figure 9), in which hierarchies have a resonance with each other because of the relationships they encode (the objects, forces, goals, causes, paths, substances).

3.5 Summary

Our goal here was to evaluate the extent to which understanding domain-general development can help to constrain, predict and explain the development of linguistic trajectories – categorization in this case. Many aspects of infants preverbal categorization, prediction and analogy-making skills correlate with their later linguistic ability. The behavior of infants and pre-verbal young children

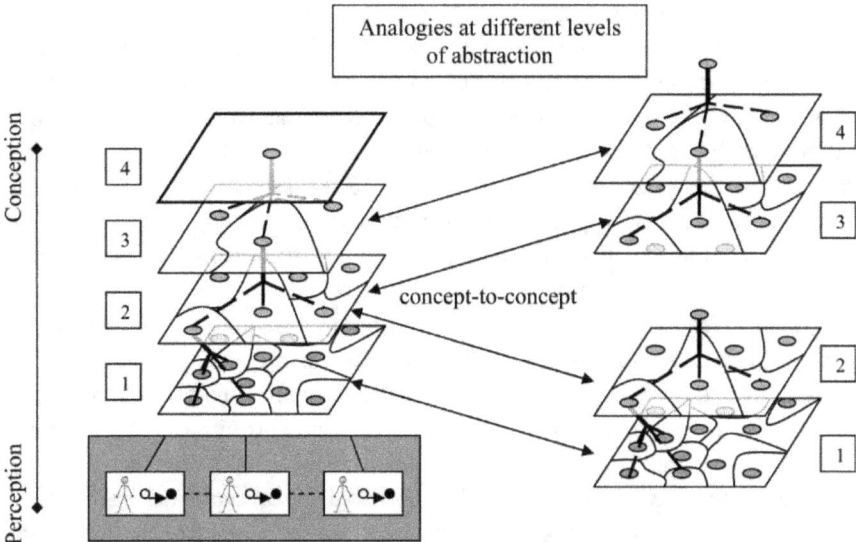

Figure 10: "Hierarchical resonance". Analogies are formed at various places on the perceptual conceptual continuum.

show they process non-linguistic input in a hierarchical way; from the taxonomic classification of broad and fine grained categories to the broad and fine grained categories of event structure. We saw how similarity across members facilitates category formation early on because a cluster of features help the learner identify there is a category, and later on, some variability helps to define where the boundaries of that category lie, and what *cannot* be considered a member. The distribution of natural language helps both children and adults in construction learning by making the meaning and form of a particular construction simpler to identify (Casenhiser & Goldberg, 2005; Goldberg et al., 2004). In summary it is worth clarifying what the implications for learning are of this. Skewed input is not a necessary condition for learning constructions, as we saw in the flat distribution of the transitive, although it may help compared to a flat one. Furthermore, skewed distributions cannot be sufficient either, because any randomly generated slice through a large enough corpus will be Ziphian in nature – whether that maps on to a meaningful category or not. So, the point we make here is twofold. From the perspective of developmental cognitive linguistics it is important enough to show the same kinds of within-category-item-weight considerations have a significant role in determining non-linguistic generalizations as well as linguistic ones as it speaks to a common process. Second, the fact that Ziphian distributions cut across meaningful categories shows how important function is in defining the scope of category formation – a message that repeatedly comes through from the categorization and event cognition literature synthesized here. It should also be noted that this skewed distribution in language seems conveniently suited to category learning. There is good reason to suppose both categorization and the memory systems it relies on emerge before language both in phylogeny and ontogeny. Thus rather than it being a fortunate fact that natural language has this distribution, it is more likely that language adapted to fit the cognitive niche of human cognitive processing if it was to remain intergenerationally transmittable.

Children show prototypicality effects before they acquire language and after they acquire language too. Recall that this effect of prototypicality was demonstrated, in one instance, not for some esoteric piece of syntax or idiomatic construction at the 'periphery' of language, but at the heart of basic core grammar present in many of the world languages (Ibbotson et al. 2012). More generally, the same processes have been shown to be at work in lexical semantics, tense-aspect marking, relative clauses, questions with long-distance dependencies, and subject auxiliary inversion to name a few. The implication being that grammar interacts with general cognitive processes at some of the deepest levels we could experimentally establish. We have seen that in many instances it seems more straightforward to account for the graded acceptability of constructions, the typological pattern and the developmental trajectory of such linguistic phenomena by tracing the developmental trajectory of a graded non-linguistic capacities.

Important in this story too has been the role of embodied cognition, which simply stated emphasizes that cognition is a situated activity. Abstract symbols acquire real-world meaning by ultimately being grounded in terms of the agent's experience of the physical world. Of most importance to language seem to be categories constructed around relational components of dynamic events, such as containment-support, path-manner, source-goal, and figure-ground, forming the most basic conceptual categories such as animacy, causality, and agency. We focused on learning relational elements of language like verbs, because they seem to present a wider inferential gap for social and cognitive processes to bridge and thus present a high bar for domain-general acquisition mechanisms to clear. Developmental psychologists and linguistics have asked "given an infinite number of generalizations a child could make, why do they make the ones they do?" The embodied view of cognition combined with a domain-general understanding of categorization and a social-cooperative model of communication shows why an infinite number of generalizations are not available to the learner to begin with. "Fifty years ago, it was widely held by the most prominent philosophers and psychologists that language is just a matter of conditioning and some obscure general notion of "induction" or "analogy." (Chomsky, 2011, p.264). While this book as a whole hopefully makes it clear that language is certainly not just a matter of analogy, this chapter aimed to make it a less obscure notion and therefore its relevance and significance in predicting the developmental trajectory of language acquisition clearer. The predictive payoff of categorization is of fundamental importance for language. Linguistics has learned a lot from what we know about forming categories and constraining generalizations from the non-linguistic literature and hopefully will continue to benefit from what psychology has to offer in this regard.

Chapter 4
Attention and inhibition

As we have seen, memory, categorization and analogy all play a key role in shaping the course of language development. However, in order for something to be memorized efficiently or categorized it first needs to fall within the spotlight of attention. When perception delivers more data to cognition than would be processable or relevant to the goals of the system, there needs to be criteria that privileges some sources of information over others. That gating and ranking of the information helps us to move from a reflexive and automatic set of behavioral responses to those that are more adaptive, flexible and creative. All of that requires effortful control and that takes time to develop. So what to attend to, what not to attend to and what to inhibit become important cognitive bottlenecks on the kinds of information available for language development and can further dampen the degrees of freedom available for linguistic generalizations.

4.1 The development of attention and inhibition

New-borns primarily allocate their attention in a reflexive way to marked perceptual contrasts in the environment, focusing on objects, patterns and actions that change size, intensity, shape, color or else are a departure from the familiar in some way (Fantz 1963; Fantz 1964; Colombo 2002). The ability to detect such differences is supported by a visual system able to coordinate saccadic and smooth-pursuit movements of the eye from birth. At the this early stage however, the general immaturity of the visuomotor system prevents infants scanning the scene extensively and constrains attention of stimuli to within 30 degrees of the visual field (Aslin, 1987; Lewis & Maurer, 1992). Once infants' attention does land on an aspect of the scene, they often have difficulty disengaging from it, displaying so-called sticky fixation (Colombo, 2002; Haith, 1980; Hood, 1995). Within a couple of months though, the expansion of the visual field, physiological changes in the retina and cortical visual pathways, and moderation of inhibitory mechanisms that caused sticky fixation, all allow infants more voluntary control over their attentional resources. Infants become increasingly able to intentionally direct their attention to aspects of their environment that interest them most and resist distractors that do not, as they come to recognize, categorize and sort their experience of objects, actions, patterns and people.

Their new found volition is expressed with less interest for static and simple objects and greater attention given to more complex and dynamic stimuli (Courage, Reynolds, & Richards, 2006; Ruff & Saltarelli, 1993) as well as more social-referencing from and joint-attention with their caregivers (Bakeman & Adamson 1984; Bertenthal & Campos 1990). Their greater voluntary control of inhibitory mechanisms also allows them to achieve important cognitive milestones such as the A-not-B task (Diamond, 1985), deferred imitation (Barr & Hayne, 2000; Barr et al., 1996) and means-end problem solving (Willatts & Rosie 1989). Thus there appears to be a two-part 'orientate and investigate' nature to early attention; a spatial network directs where attention should be deployed in the environment, then a recognition network investigates properties of what it is looking at (Ruff & Rothbart, 1996).

By the time language is starting to emerge, young children show an ever greater ability and willingness to engage in longer sustained or focused periods of attention, moving from 5- to 10-seconds at 3-months-of age to several minutes or more over the first two years (Reynolds & Richards, 2007; Ruff & Capozzoli, 2003). In these episodes, the infants' social and cognitive activities are processed with greater depth and more efficiently, as well inducing a state of arousal – decreased heart rate, activation of the noradrenergic and cholinergic neurochemical systems – that is optimal for learning and performance (Oakes & Tellinghuisen, 1994; Reynolds & Richards, 2007; Richards, 2003; Ruff & Rothbart, 1996). In sustained attention infants are also less distractible by the periphery and slower to orientate to it (Hicks & Richards, 1998; Hunter & Richards, 2003; Richards, 1997; Ruff & Capozzoli, 2003).

Individual variation in attention performance predicts differences in later infant cognitive function and childhood intellectual performance (Bornstein & Sigman, 1986; Fagan, 1984; Rose & Feldman, 1995). It has been proposed that this relationship is mediated by speed of processing, processing strategy, and the ability to disengage attention (Colombo, 1993; Colombo, Freeseman, Coldren, & Frick, 1995; Colombo, Richman, Shaddy, Greenhoot, & Maikranz, 2001). For example, Colombo and colleagues (2001) found that infants who spent a relatively long time fixated on a stimulus were more likely to continue looking even after they had lost interest, whereas short-lookers, could shift attention by disengaging more easily once interest had faded. In general, those short-lookers went on to have higher measures of IQ and vocabulary in later childhood (Bornstein & Sigman, 1986; Colombo, 1993; Colombo, Shaddy, Richman, Maikranz, & Blaga, 2004; Rose & Feldman, 1997). The mediating role of processing efficiency has developmental implications because attention is a zero-sum game – the decision to attend to one stimuli is a decision not to attend to another, and the more time spent inattentively looking at something is time not spent processing, and thus learning about something else.

So, there is a shift typically occurring around 9 months of age, in all aspects of attentional responding – orienting towards, selection of, and maintenance on a stimuli – from a reflexive responses to those that come under greater intentional control. This voluntary control is exercised in increasingly focused and longer episodes of sustained attention – frequently shared as joint attention. This lays the foundation for important components of executive function, critical for the development of higher order cognitive skills and behaviour such as self-regulation, social-reasoning and language (Reynolds, Courage & Richards 2011).

The other face of attention, in a sense, is inhibitory control, because of its capacity to defocus a stimuli or block a response, filtering what can or should fall within the spotlight of attention. This capacity has the ability to withhold or delay a response in the face of other conflicting responses and we see it all the time in the everyday lives of children, such as when they resist eating a treat they would like but have been told they cannot have or in the simple game Simon Says. Inhibitory control develops as part of an infants' wider physiological, attentional, cognitive, emotional, and behavioral regulatory processes which support behavior that is increasingly less impulsive, more planned and goal-directed (Berger, 2011; Calkins & Fox, 2002). As such, inhibitory control is an important predictor of all kinds of developmental outcomes that are associated with the function or dysfunction of these capacities, such school readiness (Blair 2002), health (Moffitt et al. 2011), and psychopathology (Dale & Baumeister 1999).

Inhibitory control was once thought to emerge only in middle to late childhood, as the demand to perform more complex, higher-order integrative tasks becomes more frequent and more intense (Welsh, Friedman & Spieker 2006). However, recent research suggests inhibitory control emerges in a stable form as early as 6-months of age (Holmboe et al. 2018), and is visible in the inhibition of neonatal reflexes and reaching responses throughout the first year of life (Diamond, 1990). The development of such behavior is associated with the increased activation in the second-half of the first year of life in the prefrontal cortex; an area of the brain whose function is thought to support a range of self-regulating behaviors including inhibitory control (Diamond, 2002; Friedman & Miyake, 2017). Interestingly, infants with a genetic variation associated with more efficient processing in the prefrontal cortex have higher level of inhibitory control (Holmboe et al. 2010) and, in a study of over 300 twin-pairs assessed longitudinally, genetic influences accounted for approximately 60% of the variance in parent-rated inhibitory control at 2 and 3 years (Gagne & Saudino 2016).

Between the period of 6–12 months, infants' capacity for inhibitory control is expanding (Bell & Fox, 1992; Diamond, 1985). For example, in the A-not-B task, a toy is repeatedly hidden in location A and the infant repeatedly reaches out to retrieve it. After several examples of this, the location is switched to a new location B, where again, the child must reach out if they want to retrieve it. To successfully reach out to location B on the switch trial, it is argued, involves resisting the established pattern or inhibiting the response of reaching for location A – and success on this task has been correlated with the integrity and functioning of the prefrontal cortex (Baird et al., 2002; Kimberly Cuevas, Swingler, Bell, Marcovitch, & Calkins, 2012; Diamond & Goldman-Rakic, 1989; Diamond, Zola-Morgan, & Squire, 1989). However, because there is typically a delay between the last location A trial and the switch Location B trial, it also is a measure of working memory – without some memory of the Trial As there is no dominant response to inhibit. A purer test of inhibitory control therefore is the Freeze-Frame task, where success is dependent on infants' ability in the here-and-now (thus minimal demands on working memory) and involves inhibiting gaze to peripheral distractors in order to focus attention on a centrally presented stimulus (Holmboe et al. 2008). Performance on both tasks is correlated at 9 months suggestive that they both recruit common cognitive resources associated with inhibitory control (Holmboe et al. 2008).

Other researchers have decomposed the notion of inhibition further into its "cool" and "hot" components (Martin-Rhee & Bialystok 2008; Zelazo & Carlson 2012); with externally generated conflict engaging a type of cool perceptual inhibition (e.g., in the Stroop tests that require a response of *Moon* to a picture of a Sun and vice versa) which develops earlier, and inhibition that is engaged by motivational hot conflict (e.g., in the Less is More game where correct choices yield more winnings or the Tower game where children tend to prefer to take more turns), which tends to develop later on. This view of inhibition shows different facets of inhibitory control possibly coming online at different points in development, in a process that has been described as heterotypic continuity (Kopp 1982; Raffaelli, Crockett & Shen 2005).

In conclusion, both attention and inhibitory control change over the course of development from early reliance on external sources for control or attention that is reactive and impulsive to environmental stimuli, to later internal, self-initiated forms of inhibition and attentional deployment (Berger, 2011; Calkins & Howse, 2004; Kopp, 1982). This is supported by underlying improvements in infants' ability to engage, disengage, shift, and inhibit attention as well as more time spent practicing these skills as they spend more time alert and awake. Beyond these significant changes in the early years, effortful control continues to develop into mid-childhood, developing ever more sophisticated strategies to negotiate conflict/inhibition, detect and repair error and in general, slow down behavioral responses (Rothbart & Bates 2006).

As before, if the developmental trajectory of language is dependent on domain-general capacities such as attention and inhibition (Table 3), we should expect to see one predicting the other. Kannass and Oakes found that attentional abilities at 9-months old predicted language abilities at 31-months-old (2008). Interestingly though, the relationship of this prediction was significant in opposite directions dependent on the task used. In the single-object task, a toy was presented to the child in isolation, thus engaging exogenous aspects thought to be most relevant in controlling attention at an early age – things like familiarity which are less under the control of the infant. The multiple-object task presented stimuli that were in competition for attentional resources – designed to be a measure that taps volitional control over attention as the child decides whether to maintain attention on one target toy, resist distractor toys, or distribute attention among all the toys. As they predicted, shorter attention time was negatively correlated with vocabulary in the single-object task and positively correlated with vocabulary in the multiple-object task. Why? The authors conclude the same measures in different tasks or the same measures at different ages reflect different underlying processes. Essentially there is no competition for attentional resources in the single-object task so a short looking time is employed by children who have learnt to recognize, disengage and move their attention away. In the multiple-object task there is competition for

Table 3: Attention and Inhibition processes and their relevance for language acquisition.

Attention and Inhibition	Language
Attentional system allows for some sources of information to be privileged over others	Supports topicalization, stress distinctions, figure/ground comparisons and generally allows information to be structured on a continuum of communicative focus
Increases in selection, resistance to distractors, and narrowing of attentional focus.	Allows sustained periods of attention and joint-attention with other language users, longer chunks and dialogue to be processed.
A shift from attention and inhibition as driven by external perceptual features to those internally generated motivations and conflicts	Relevant for the complex feedback loops between language comprehension and production
Increasing control of competing stimuli, error detection and greater ability to inhibit	Greater ability to weigh and resolve cue competition, resolving syntactic ambiguity; resisting tempting, but wrong overgeneralizations

resources, so it taps inhibitory control – here longer looking time shows children who can effectively ignore the distractors and focus on what they need to for longer. In both cases they represent efficient processing strategies and it seems that being efficient at these tasks means the child is also efficient at acquiring language, as the longitudinal data suggest.

4.2 What attention can do for language and language acquisition

Understanding the interface between attention and language – and attention and grammar in particular – has been a central concern in many functional linguistic theories (e.g., Langacker, 1991; Talmy, 2012) and an important topic in psycholinguistic research (Ferreira & Henderson, 2004; Trueswell & Tanenhaus, 2005). Directing attention via referential and perceptual priming causes people to construe a scene in a particular way and typically this is reflected in the linguistic structures people use (Turner & Rommetveit, 1968; Myachykov, Thompson, Scheepers, & Garrod, 2011; Posner, 1980; Prentice, 1967; Tomlin, 1995, 1997). For example, the same state of affairs in the world can be encoded by the use of different linguistic devices to communicate a nuanced range of perspectives:

10 (a) the roof slopes gently downwards
   (b) the roof slopes gently upwards

The two scenes referring to the same roof can be mentally viewed or 'construed' from either above (10a) or below (10b) (Langacker 1987). Languages have of course evolved many different ways to alter how a particular concept is construed in the mind including different structural frames:

11 (a) the dog chased the cat
   (b) the cat was chased by the dog

Note that the scenes in (10a–b) and (11a–b) are truth-conditionally equivalent in the sense that the state of affairs in the world which requires the statements to be true is the same for both. For example, in (10a) and (10b) there is a roof that exists such that it is angled at x degrees. The different expressions are therefore not describing different facts about the world rather they are conventionalized and prefabricated ways of expressing different perspectives. Some of the most extensively investigated attention-directing devices are those components of dynamic events, including those that highlight the conceptual distinctions of containment/support, path/manner, source/goal and figure/ ground discussed in the Categorization and analogy chapter (Choi & Bowerman, 1991; Givon, 1995; Jackendoff, 1983; Lakoff, 1987; Talmy, 1988, 2000). The notion of figure/ground – whereby some information is highlighted with respect to relatively stable background – has been particularly well studied in relation to the English subject. For a similar conceptual division see "frame/highlighting" (Fillmore 1976) and "base/ pro ling" (Langacker 1987).

The subject of an English clause is a 'mosaic' of prototypical coding and behavioral features (Keenan 1976). For example, the subject typically comes before the verb and triggers agreement with it (e.g., *She smiles*, not *She smile*), has a special pronominal form (e.g., *She smiles*, not *Her smiles*) and entails certain structural properties (e.g., only the subject can leave in *She smiled at him and left*). Cross-linguistically speaking, there have been about 30 different grammatical features that have been variously attributed to the concept of "subject" (for example controlling verb agreement, determining the actor in a subjectless second coordinate clause and so on) and any one language 'subject' is only a subset of these features which do not necessarily overlap.

The overall developmental picture is that children acquire the different features of the English subject gradually and at different times in a 'mosaic' fashion (Rispoli 1991). Young children identify 'subject' as the most animate participant, or the first-mentioned participant, or the agent, which suggests something less abstract than an adult-like notion of subject (Corrigan 1988). Experimentally, Braine and colleagues (1993) have shown that mastery over the notion of English subject appears at around 5–6 years of age. Consistent with this, typically children do not produce full passives in spontaneous speech until about 4–5 years-of-age however performance can be significantly boosted when the passive form is supported with case marked pronouns (Ibbotson et al. 2010) with training (Brooks & Tomasello, 1999; Pinker, Lebeaux, & Frost, 1987) and when the passive form is more frequent in the ambient language relative to Indo-European languages (Allen & Crago, 2008 for Inuktitut; Pye & Poz, 1988 for K'iche' Mayan; Suzman, 1985 for Zulu). Following Croft (2001) one explanation for this relatively late and piecemeal acquisition pattern is that in reality, abstract constructions such as intransitive, transitive, passive and there-constructions actually have their own subject. They may only be united by analogy later on in development under something like a highly schematic subject-predicate construction (Tomasello, 2003).

The subject position is also associated with certain discourse properties – for example, given information, whereas the object position is associated with new information (e.g., Halliday, 1985) and the foregrounding of items that appear in that position and, by definition, backgrounding other items in the clause. Depending on the choice of linguistic terminology this function is also been variously referred to as figure-ground, perspective, theme, aboutness and prominence (Langacker, 1991; MacWhinney, 1977; Talmy, 1988). Tomlin has shown that the foregrounding function of subject can essentially be re-described in terms of the cognitive concept of attention (1995, 1997). The key idea here is that attentional mechanisms privilege some forms of information over others by 'gating' perceptual input, sustaining focus on what is foregrounded. What is foregrounded then becomes the subject of the sentence. This is most clearly exemplified by the active passive alternation in English, the function of which allows speakers to focus attention on what the agent did (active) in contrast to what happened to the patient (passive). The utility of defocusing the agent's role in an action or state of affairs has not escaped many politicians, most famously realized in the non-apology apology . . . *mistakes were made* . . .

To test the hypothesis that subject-is-theme-is-attention Tomlin (1995) asked participants to watch prototypical transitive scenes of two fish approaching each other until one swallowed the other and swam away. Tomlin manipulated the attention of participants by placing a flashing red arrow above one or other of the fishes 75ms before the eating action was completed. Participants were asked to keep their eyes on the character the arrow pointed at and describe what they saw. The majority of adult speakers performed as the subject-is-theme-is-attention hypothesis predicted: on the cued agent animations (the arrow was above the fish that was doing the eating) the agent was assigned the subject position, and the clause was active. On the cued patient animations (the arrow was above the fish being eaten) the patient was assigned subject position and the overall clause was passive. Gleitman and colleagues (2007) obtained similar results even when the cue was implicit (participants were largely unaware of the cue because it appeared so briefly), although with a decreased effect size of passivisation.

Items that appear at the start of an utterance occupy a salient slot and thus could trigger structural organization somewhat independently of grammatical status (MacWhinney 1977). Because the sentence initial position is confounded with Subject role in English transitive sentences, it is difficult to differentiate between a linear-ordering versus a grammatical-role account of the priming effects. To do so we must turn to languages that permit, under certain pragmatic contexts, more flexible word orders. Three studies analyzed perceptually primed structural choice in Russian (Myachykov & Tomlin, 2008), Finnish (Myachykov, Garrod, & Scheepers, 2010), and Korean (Hwang & Kaiser 2009). Overall the studies suggested that in flexible word-order languages the extent of perceptual priming is consistently weaker than in the fixed word-order languages. Myachykov and colleagues (2010) propose that speakers universally attempt to employ the grammatical-role assignment mechanism in order to represent the perceptually salient referent but this interacts in complex ways with the availability and reliability of the linguistic resources of the particular language. In languages like Russian and Finnish, for example, passives are rare or largely dispreferred and as a result, a linear-ordering mechanism is used to accommodate referential salience in terms of word order.

The exact nature of the attention-grammar interface is still uncertain and of course, subject position is one attentional cue among many others. For example, in unmarked cases, English tends to correlate theme with given information and subject position, and focus with new information and object position (and usually also prosodic stress). The famous Moses illusion takes advantage of this pattern: when asked *How many animals of each kind did Moses take on the Ark*, most people respond *two*, even though it can be independently established that they know that it was Noah, not Moses, who took the animals on the Ark (Erickson & Mattson 1981). The fundamental role of attention in this process is underlined by the fact the illusion can be ameliorated when attention is focused on the incongruent item using structures such as clefts (12a) and there-insertions (12b) (Traxler 2012).

12 (a) It was Moses who took two of each kind of animal on the Ark.
    (b) There was a guy called Moses who took two of each kind of animal on the Ark.

So, while Tomlin and others have demonstrated the importance of attention for the creativity and productivity of linguistic patterns for adults their role in language acquisition has been much less researched. For example children do not experience little arrows hanging over the subject in the way they did over the fish in the Tomlin experiment – what is of more relevance to the cognitive and social world of the infant is how they can manipulate the attention of others and have their attention manipulated with social cues, such as eye-gaze.

Humans show a strong sensitivity to eye-gaze from birth (Farroni, Csibra, Simion, & Johnson, 2002). We know infants as young as 3-months-old can perceive the gaze direction of adults and that this perception triggers corresponding shifts of their own attention – so even very young infants can use eye-gaze as a cue to engage in joint attention (Hood, Willen, & Driver, 1998). Neonates can follow gaze if the pupils are seen to move (Farroni, Massaccesi, Menon, & Johnson, 2007) and at around 5-months-of-age they can discriminate between very small horizontal deviations (5 degrees) of eye gaze (Symons 1998). Like adults, infants process facial features in a deeper way when gaze is directed towards them as compared with averted gaze (Farroni et al., 2002; 2007; Farroni,

Massaccesi, Pividori, & Johnson, 2004; Hood, Macrae, Cole-Davies, & Dias, 2003). Clearly, the capacity to use another person's eye gaze as a cue to attention develops very early in life; however, to begin with this might be achieved with rather low-level, low-mentalizing mechanisms, for example, the perceptual geometry and luminance of the eye (Ando 2002). Compared with other primates, humans have a relatively large white sclera surrounding a small dark pupil and iris making eye-gaze discrimination relatively easier in humans than in other animals (Kobayashi & Kohshima 1997). Supporting the low-mentalizing interpretation of eye-gaze sensitivity, a wide range of species have a very accurate ability to determine whether they are being looked at (Burghardt & Greene 1988; Perrett & Mistlin 1990; Burger, Gochfeld & Murray 1992) and nonhuman primates such as adult rhesus monkeys can discriminate between photographs depicting direct gaze and gaze averted by 5 degrees, the same ability that has been reported in human infants (Campbell et al. 1990; Symons 1998).

Although infants' eye-gaze sensitivities may be based on relatively simple mechanisms (gaze perception), young children soon begin to integrate eye-gaze information into a more sophisticated picture of how other people work including their future intentions and mental states (Baron-Cohen, 1994; Striano & Reid, 2006). Joint attention performance at 20 months predicts theory of mind abilities at 44 months (Charman et al. 2000) underlining eye-gaze as a key component in the development of social cognition in early life. Baron-Cohen and colleagues (1995) found that children aged 3 and 4 years old deduce the direction of gaze of a schematic face and they can ascribe mental states such as desires on the basis of the direction of gaze (see also Lee, Eskritt, Symons, & Muir, 1998). Thus, understanding that direction of gaze can indicate which objects a person knows exists, is currently attending to, and holds a mental state about can help a child infer much about the current visual world, although this understanding may not be as flexible as adults when cues conflict (Pellicano & Rhodes 2003; Freire, Eskritt & Lee 2004).

Eye-gaze following at 6 months has been shown to correlate with vocabulary size at 18 months (Morales, Mundy & Rojas 1998; Morales et al. 2000) and in noun learning, children can use eye-gaze, head posture and gesture to infer speakers' referential intention (Baldwin, 1991; Carpenter, Akhtar, & Tomasello, 1998; Gergely, Bekkering, Király, & Kiraldy, 2002; Woodward & Sommerville, 2000). Nappa and colleagues (2009) showed that 3-, 4- and 5-year-olds used the eye-gaze of the speaker to infer the meaning of novel relational verbs (of the type chase vs. flee) in linguistically uninformative contexts (e.g., *He's mooping him*). Thus children who saw a speaker looking at the chaser when they uttered the novel verb were more likely to attribute 'chase-like' semantics to the novel verb. The opposite effect was found when a speaker looked at the flee-er.

Change in gaze direction is one of several behavioral cues that individuals use in combination with changes in facial and vocal displays and body posture to mark the intention to act on an object (Mumme et al. 2007). Crucially, just prior to speaking, adults are more likely to look at the subject of their sentence than any other character (Gleitman et al., 2007; Griffin & Bock, 2000). This raises the possibility that children could use this cue in the input, probabilistically at least, to build a correspondence between the perspective of an event and how that perspective is expressed in their language (Nappa et al. 2009). Just as verbs such as chase and flee can lead to different construals of the same (perceptual) scene so can argument-structure constructions like the active-passive alternation, which are basically perspective-taking devices.

As the evidence we have reviewed suggests, and in line with the general cognitive linguistic framework, there is a close relationship between attention and linguistic performance (Givón, 1992; Landau & Jackendoff, 1993; MacWhinney, 1977; Osgood & Bock, 1977; Talmy, 2007). Specifically, it raises the possibility that young children could use the social cognitive cue of eye-gaze – which directs attention – to infer the function of grammatical subject – which is grounded in attention. Ibbotson and colleagues investigated this hypothesis by exploring if even young children could use the active passive alternation (essentially a choice of subject) in a way that is consistent with the eye-gaze of the speaker. The idea is that if the function of subject position is grounded in attentional mechanisms (Tomlin, 1995, 1997), then we would expect that developing attentional abilities should interact with developing linguistic ability to assign a subject. Thus we would expect different age groups to perform differently.

Testing that idea Ibbotson and colleagues found that 3- and 4-Year-Olds and adults were able to use speaker-gaze to choose a felicitous subject when describing a scene (Ibbotson, Lieven & Tomasello 2013).

In this study the experimenter looked at the participant, engaged eye contact, looked at the target animal (either the agent or patient of the impending action) looked back at the participant and then finally looked back to the target animal again (Figure 11). Thus the idea was to establish triadic joint-attention between speaker, addressee and referent. The experimenter then performed the action while continuing to look at the target referent. Shortly after the action had begun the experimenter asked, *what's happening*? The response to that question was then recorded, specifically whether the subject of the sentence (either agent or patient) was congruent or incongruent with the eye-gaze of the speaker/experimenter. For example, if the speaker was looking at the agent of the action and the participant responded with the agent in subject position (i.e., active: *agent-V-patient*) it was coded as congruent. If the participant

Figure 11: In this example, *the cat is taming the dog* or depending on your perspective *the dog is getting tammed*. The eye-gaze of the experimenter cues attention towards either the agent of the action (far left), neither agent nor patient (control condition in center) or the patient of the action (far right).

responded with the patient in subject position (i.e., passive: *patient-Aux-V-(agent)* it was coded as incongruent.

We found that older children and adults were able to use speaker-gaze to choose a felicitous subject when describing a scene with both agent-focused and patient focused cues. Integrating attentional and grammatical information in this way allows children to limit the degrees of freedom on what the function of the Subject might be. To succeed at this task is not trivial. We do not know for sure all the steps needed to produce the appropriate response but at the very least, the following processes are all credibly involved. First, both children and adults need to understand that following gaze establishes reference. Subcomponents of this ability are recognizing that looking is intentional behavior directed to external objects and events; that looking results in the mental experience of seeing an object or event; and that others share in the capacity to see things (D'Entremont et al. 2007). Second, participants need to coordinate where their attention has been focused with a linguistic representation. This involves selecting the construction that best serves the function of foregrounding a participant, which in this case is the subject position. Part of this ability requires suppressing the preferred information structure and most heavily entrenched form (the active) when one needs to describe a scene from the perspective of the patient. There is evidence that this maybe more of a challenge for the 3-year-olds because they have the strongest preference for describing the scene with an active in the absence of social cues. In addition, success on the experiment not only requires attention for a given trial but the ability to switch attention between trials. Thus inhibitory control, attentional flexibility, and working memory are all implicated in giving the correct response. As reviewed earlier, all these capacities are in the middle of significant periods of reorganization and development around the time the children were tested in this study (Hughes 1998). Finally, participants need to produce a string of nouns, verbs and auxiliaries that not only satisfy the grammatical requirements of who did what to whom but also conform to the social-pragmatic demands of the context.

Salomo (2010) note that children have more difficulty giving pragmatically appropriate responses to sentence-focus questions of the type *what's happening?* than either argument-focus questions *who is VERB-ing?* or predicate-focus questions *what is AGENT doing?* This pattern corresponds with sentence-focus questions being relatively less frequent to the other types in child directed speech. In this experiment, the eliciting questions were deliberately chosen to assess the role of social cueing in isolation (i.e., *what's happening?*). To the extent that sentence-focus questions are more pragmatically difficult, this seems to affect the youngest age group in this study the most. Again, one possible explanation for this is in terms of the development of underlying domain-general capabilities – the idea is that argument-focus questions and predicate-focus questions help to anchor the relevant piece of information (either verb or agent) in short term-memory, from which the appropriate response to the question is constructed (an advantage which is not present in sentence-focus questions). Although more infrequent in child directed speech, sentence-focus questions may benefit the most from the support of social cues precisely because they are linguistically uninformative. Indeed, Nappa and colleagues (2009) found the strongest effect of social cues on verb learning in the linguistically uninformative condition. Using the design in this study, one might predict an even stronger effect of subject choice alternations (and perhaps at younger age) where linguistic anchoring (e.g., *what's happening to the cat?*) acts in coalition with social cues (e.g., speaker looks at cat).

It is also worth noting that the experiments that have focused on the relationship between attentional states of speakers and communicative intentions have mainly focused of word learning (e.g., Baldwin, 1991; Tomasello & Farrar, 1986). The adult-like function of subjecthood makes it a much more abstract and less concrete learning challenge than learning words, which, in the usage-based framework at least, means that mastery of subjecthood requires more evidence and more experience with using it. While the 3-year-olds in this study probably possess many of the social-cognitive foundations that the 4-year-olds do, success on the task needs competence in linguistic and executive control domains as well as effective connections between these domains.

The performance of the 3-, 4-year-olds and the adults in this study provides further support for the subject-is-theme-is-attention attention hypothesis (Tomlin, 1995, 1997). More generally, the methodology used a more ecologically valid cue (eye-gaze) than the red arrow hovering above a participant, but one which plays a similar role: it is an attention-directing cue that foregrounds one character and, by definition, backgrounds the other. Importantly, we know adults are more likely to look at the subject of their sentence than any other character (Gleitman et al., 2007; Griffin & Bock, 2000). This raises the possibility that young children could be using the social cue of eye-gaze in situ (which directs attention) to infer the function of grammatical subject (which is grounded in attention). Previous work suggests the function of the subject position can be grounded in terms of attention and information structure. One powerful source of directing attention that we know young children are sensitive to is eye-gaze. It has been shown before that social-cognitive cues help children learn words but this is the first demonstration that eye-gaze could be important in learning something as abstract as subject role.

In conclusion, the methodology advocates exploring linguistic cues in combination with the social-pragmatic context. By using eye-gaze we have been able to consider a broader range of cues than a traditional corpus-based approach to the development of language. By doing so, we have been able to get closer to reconstructing the rich social-pragmatic-linguistic world in which the child actually grows up. The ongoing challenge is to explore ways in which social-pragmatic skills interact with prodigious pattern-finding abilities in a way that which explains the emergence of other aspects of linguistic knowledge.

4.3 What inhibition can do for language and language acquisition

When sentences are syntactically complex, unusual, or ambiguous they place a particular demand on the executive function to select one among different (competing) sentence representations (Novick, Trueswell & Thompson-Schill 2005; Choi & Trueswell 2010). And of course to begin with, for young children most sentences are unusual, most of the time – just when their immature inhibitory control is in development. Thus compared to adults and older children, 4- to 6-year-old children show substantially greater difficulty in inhibiting and revising their initial misinterpretation of noncanonical or temporarily ambiguous sentences (Trueswell et al. 1999; Novick, Trueswell & Thompson-Schill 2005; Choi & Trueswell 2010; Woodard, Pozzan & Trueswell 2016).

Ibbotson and colleagues explored a specific hypothesis about the relationship between inhibition and language development (Ibbotson & Kearvell-White 2015). The basic idea was that the grammatical ability to produce an irregular past tense form, for example, *fly* → *flew*, depends on the ability to inhibit a temping but incorrect response, *flyed*. Specifically, the correct form *flew* is facing unwanted competition from analogous patterns such as *tie* → *tied*, *die* → *died* and *lie* → *lied*. So, to put it very simply, if children are to learn language they must learn patterns and they must learn exceptions to those patterns. Giving the correct linguistic response involves suppressing this competition by using a cognitive faculty that is independent of language – inhibition.

The prediction is that those participants who are good at avoiding the overgeneralization error on a linguistic task (e.g., *flyed*) should also be good at inhibition on a non-linguistic task, The Stroop. The implications of this are first, it provides evidence that performance on a linguistic and non-linguistic test are recruiting the common cognitive faculty of inhibition, strengthening the case that language is deeply integrated with the rest of cognition, Second, it provides new insights into the process of language acquisition as these overgeneralization errors have traditionally received a very linguistic, domain-internal analysis (Ambridge, Pine, & Rowland, 2011, 2012; Ambridge, Pine, Rowland, & Chang, 2012; Marchman, 1997; Plunkett & Marchman, 1993). A positive result would open the door to more cognitive-based explanations of the phenomena, for example, the retreat from overgeneralization errors witnessed in child development could be the result of maturing inhibitory control. Third, it identifies a source of individual variation in language ability which may in turn have implications for linguistic interventions, particularly for those at the far end of the spectrum of language ability like those with Developmental Language Disorder.

As a test of grammatical ability Ibbotson and colleagues used a past tense elicitation task where participants heard a standard frame . . . *every day I fly, yesterday I . . . .* and had to complete the sentence. As a test of domain-general inhibition they used the Sun-Moon Stroop task which involves participants responding *sun* to a picture of a moon and vice versa. There is evidence to suggest bilinguals are better than monolinguals at Stroop tests as they are well practiced in the skills of cognitive control and conflict resolution which switching between languages requires (Bialystok et al., 2005; cf. de Bruin, Treccani, & Della Sala, 2015; van Heuven, Conklin, Coderre, Guo, & Dijkstra, 2011). Here we test whether the variation within monolinguals is also related to their ability to inhibit. To test this we use 5-year-old participants because adult monolinguals are at ceiling performance on the past tense elicitation task, meaning that there would be no between-participant variation to investigate. It is worth noting however, that these errors are not entirely absent from adult speakers, especially when the speaker is tired or under some communicative stress suggesting these too could be elicited under different experimental conditions than the ones we used here.

It could be that those children who are good at the Stroop test simply know more words or are a little older and this makes them better at the grammatical task. For this reason we also recorded each participant's vocabulary ability and age in months. All three variables were assessed to see what extent they predict grammatical ability. The main hypothesis is schematically summarized in Figure 12 below.

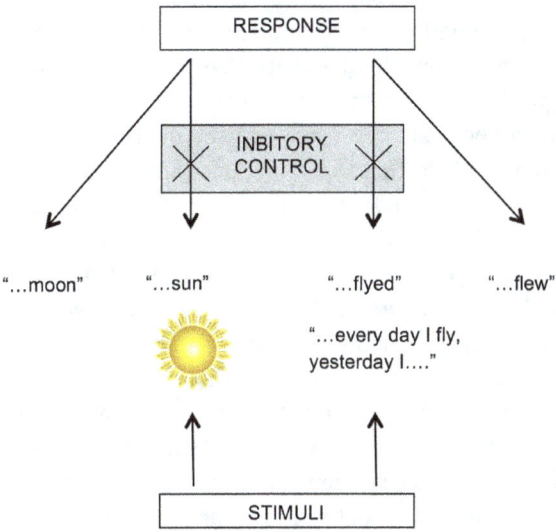

Figure 12: The linguistic and non-linguistic stimuli of Ibbotson and Kearvell-White (2015), recruiting a common cognitive resource in order to succeed at the task.

Ibbotson and Kearvell-White found evidence that individual variation in grammatical ability can be predicted by individual variation in inhibitory control (Ibbotson & Kearvell-White 2015). Testing 81 5-year-olds using two classic tests from linguistics and psychology (Past Tense and the Stroop), they showed that inhibitory control was a better predicator of grammatical ability than either vocabulary or age. The explanation given is that giving the correct response in both tests requires using a common cognitive capacity to inhibit unwanted competition. From other work we have already reviewed in the categorization and analogy chapter we know grammatical constructions such as the transitive can behave in similar ways to non-linguistic categories (Ibbotson et al. 2012), and from the present chapter we also know speakers can use the eye-gaze of the speaker to work out the meaning of novel verbs and grammatical constructions (Nappa et al. 2009; Ibbotson, Lieven & Tomasello 2013). We perhaps can add past tense formation to that list of core linguistic abilities that are integrated at deep level with the rest of cognition. If the developmental trajectory of grammatical ability is in some sense dependent on the developmental trajectory of inhibition then the question is whether it makes sense to study these topics independently.

Overgeneralization errors have received a lot of attention from developmental psycholinguists as they are thought to be a window in the processes that underlie linguistic creativity: Adults do not say *flyed* so children must have created that form for themselves. One particular concern is how children 'retreat' from these errors if they never receive explicit feedback that they are incorrect. Currently, the three main solutions to this problem – pre-emption, entrenchment and semantic class – are all born out of a very linguistic-internal analysis. Our result does not negate the need for these explanations (which offer more fine grained predictions than inhibition could) but it does suggest they should be considered alongside more cognitive based explanations. We know inhibitory control is maturing throughout the years that children's overgeneralization errors are reducing (Leon-Carrion, García-Orza & Pérez-Santamaría 2004). It is possible therefore that inhibitory control accounts for some of the individual variation in past tense performance that linguistic accounts do not (and vice versa).

In summary, grammatical errors involving past tense formation and errors of performance on the Stroop test are significantly related. What appears to be the most parsimonious explanation for this relationship is that giving the correct response in both tests requires using a common cognitive capacity to inhibit unwanted competition. That performance on a linguistic and non-linguistic test are recruiting a common cognitive faculty of inhibition, strengthens the case that the complexity of language emerges through the interaction of cognition and language use over time. The implications are that understanding the developmental trajectory of language acquisition can benefit from integrating the developmental trajectory of non-linguistic faculties, such as inhibitory control.

The main pattern of these findings has been recently replicated by Yuile and Sabbagh (in press) with a stricter test of the developmental cognitive linguistics approach; they required children point to a white square when the experimenter said "grass" without requiring a verbal response from the child (cf. sun/moon) and still found their level of inhibitory control was associated with their production of irregular forms. Building on this, recent work by Gandolfi and Viterbori (2020) suggests that it was not inhibitory control per se that was responsible for this effect, but a more finer-grained distinction of the executive function called interference suppression that is specifically associated with grammatical complexity. In their study, they looked at 62 typically developing children aged 24–44 months and investigated whether early inhibitory control skills are longitudinally associated with language outcome. They gave children a batch of five inhibitory control tasks and a language test at Time 1 and receptive and morphosyntactic tests a year later at Time 2. Hierarchical multiple linear regression analysis showed that all language production measures at Time 1, as well as later receptive morphosyntactic ability at Time 2, were significantly associated with the interference suppression score, even when early lexical and grammatical measures, age, and mother's education were included in the analysis. Furthermore, using Principle Components Analysis they identified two significant components of inhibitory control that predicted language outcomes. The first was Response Inhibition – the early ability to inhibit prepotent but inappropriate motor or cognitive responses – and the second was Interference Suppression – the more advanced ability to manage cognitive conflict and filter out irrelevant information from complex stimuli involving a substantial role for working memory.

4.4 Summary

This chapter has hopefully shown that attention and inhibition can do a lot for the language learner; gating information that becomes the subject of categorization and longer-term memory processes, mediating the relationship between social-cognitive cues and recovering constructional meaning from the environment, and inhibiting pattern overgeneralization responses that would fall outside the norms of the language. These self-regulation processes emerge around the second-half of the first year of life and help us from being controlled by our immediate environment, the foundation for more adaptive, flexible and creative behavior to come. More than that, they are available to language when infants are starting to put words together into larger meaningful strings and phrases. Our understanding of children's cognition and social reasoning has progressed significantly; however, there is still so much work to be done to work through in detail how this knowledge interacts with emerging syntactic representations. The work presented here is a step in that direction and investigated whether eye-gaze influences the choice of grammatical subject for young children and adults (which it did) and whether performance on a grammatical test that recruits inhibition was related to a visual test that recruits inhibition (which it was). The linguistic notions of subjecthood or verb-tense marking are in principle abstract ones. Integrating attentional, inhibitory and grammatical information in this way allows children to limit the degrees of freedom on what the function of certain linguistic constructions might be and allows linguistic theory to ground abstract functions in deeper cognitive and communicative principles (Goldberg, 2007; Langacker, 1991; Tomlin, 1995, 1997).

Chapter 5
Social cognition

Social cognition is the final chapter of Part II for two reasons. First, as we have seen, intention-reading, shared attention and other forms of intersubjectivity have emerged as important factors that cut-across all the other cognitive domains we has explored thus far. For example, intention-reading in some way or another plays an important part in how events are segmented; the way categories are formed and generalized along functional dimensions; the mapping between attentional stimuli in the environment and argument-structure constructions; and what falls within the scope of attention, what gets inhibited and thus what gets passed on to long-term memory for consolidation and later use. Second, as mentioned in the Introduction, the cognitive domains examined in previous chapters may be considered the minimal and necessary requirements that support language acquisition and use. But without the additional restriction placed on the degrees of freedom by cooperative action, they may not be sufficient to get human language acquisition "over the line".

And the reason for thinking so is simple: many other species have the ability to memorize, categorize, show inhibitory control and selective attention but they do not use symbolic communication in anything like the way we do – even when born and raised in a rich communicative and cultural environment (Beran, 2015; Emery & Clayton, 2004; Fujita & Matsuzawa, 1990; Herrmann & Tomasello, 2015; Kuhl & Miller, 1975; Menzel, 1973; Spinozzi, 1996). Christiansen and Chater state "*language acquisition is nothing more than learning to process*: to turn meanings into streams of sound or sign (when generating language), and to turn streams of sound or sign back into meanings (when understanding language)" (original emphasis, Christiansen & Chater, 2016, p. 10). It is not that anyone is suggesting (to my knowledge) that giving chimpanzees improved "Chunk-and-Pass" or "Right-First-Time" processing strategies would turn them into talkers and to be fair to Christiansen & Chater, human uniqueness is not the target of their argument in this context. But it underlines how the general-processing argument can only go so far, especially as in this example, when the same perceptual bottlenecks ("Now-or-Never") are both domain general and species-general too.

Before we examine the developmental picture of how social cognition interacts with language, it is worth considering why it could help further dampen the degrees of freedom on linguistic generalizations. The default psychological status of a communicator's utterances is one of referential intention, that is, a communicator wants the recipient to attend to something; an action, an object, some aspect of the scene, the speaker's attitude toward a scene, or a proposition. The communicator is also likely to have a social motive for doing so; I want you to do something, to feel something, to know something, or to share something that I think you will find useful or interesting, and this assumption of helpfulness guides the search for communicative relevance (Sperber & Wilson, 1986; Tomasello, 2008). The motivations, beliefs and knowledge of others are not represented as an infinite landscape of possibilities, so if language significantly interacts with social cognition, linguistic generalizations are not equipotent in every direction either. For example, in ongoing discourse communicative acts are modified by what the speaker and recipient know together, the common ground and joint attention that they have established over the course of their communicative history, which narrows the linguistic options on how utterances are interpreted. So, before we consider the developmental picture, there are reasons to suppose that a understanding of social cognition – in addition to the non-social aspects of cognition we have considered thus far – has an important function in constraining what language can mean. What this chapter aims to do is lay out some of the mechanisms of how that works.

At a very broad level, social cognition describes those intuitions engaged when trying to understand the intentions of others. The foundation of this reasoning enables infants to categorize people versus objects, use social cues such as eye contact, body movements, tone of voice and facial expressions to understand, predict and control behavior. Ultimately this matures into an understanding that intentional beings are capable of desires, knowledge and beliefs that might be different from our own and, crucially, a motivation to coordinate these intentions to accomplish ever more complex forms of cooperative acts: giving and taking objects, rolling a ball back and forth, building a block tower together, putting away toys together, pretend games of eating and drinking, pointing-and-naming games, going for a walk together, taking a piano upstairs, playing a symphony (Hay 1979; Hay & Murray 1982). Of particular interest for us is the development of a subtype of social cognitive behavior that may underpin the fabric of symbolic communication, and is thus the most likely candidate for the species-unique contribution to the language acquisition process. As before, we summarize the non-linguistic trajectory of social-cognitive development and map the ways in which these processes can plausibly constrain and predict the trajectory of language development.

5.1 The development of social cognition

When neonates are just hours old, they prefer to look at faces that show a direct gaze rather than an averted one, and soon thereafter focus in on the eyes and mouths of other people (Farroni et al., 2002; Jaffe et al., 2001; Johnson & Morton, 1991; Cassia et al., 2001). From just about as early as it is possible to measure, infants orientate themselves and attune their perception towards voices, faces and eye-contact in a way that suggests they are born to seek out socially relevant stimuli in the environment (Rochat & Striano, 1999; Striano & Reid, 2006). As they are scanning their world for social cues, infants shift their gaze approximately 50,000 times a day so that by 3.5 months old they have made something in the order of 3–6 million eye movements (Bronson, 1994; Haith, Hazan, & Goodman, 1988). It is also worth noting the raw amount of experience this generates, for example, by 2 months old infants will have amassed 200 hours of visual experience (Johnson, Amso, & Slemmer, 2003). Presumably, this includes many instances of how objects behave in space and time – a source of experience that must be controlled for before concluding the innate origins of infants' intuition of physical motion. Their early social exchanges are characterized by a back-and-forth of emotionally contingent smiles, touches and vocalizations, such that by 2- to 3- months old they show surprise or distress when their experience deviates from this (e.g., an unresponsive face), and try to repair the breakdown by reengaging their partner (Keller et al. 1999; Adamson & Frick 2003; Striano & Bertin 2005a; Striano, Henning & Stahl 2005).

As their sensorimotor abilities become more coordinated infants are able to sit independently and soon gain enough stability to correct for the destabilizing forces caused by turning the head, twisting the torso, and moving the arms (De Onis 2006). This is not just an isolated fact about their motor development – becoming increasingly mobile and dexterous presents new opportunities for acquiring knowledge about the world that has knock-on effects across a range of perceptual, cognitive, and social domains – including language, as we shall see (Adolph & Franchak 2017).

With independent sitting, infants' hands become free from their supporting role and are available for more sophisticated bimanual object exploration such as fingering, transferring, and rotating. This in turn facilitates learning more about the three-dimensionality of objects (Soska, Adolph & Johnson 2010) and more generally, infants' burgeoning manual skills allow for more direct learning about object appearance (Baumgartner & Oakes 2013), object size (Libertus et al. 2013), and multimodal information about objects (Eppler 1995). With infants' greater experience of the way the physical world works, comes greater experience of how to get what they want. To be become good at that, entails understanding there are multiple ways to achieve the same goal and several goals compatible with one means. For example, the exact same configuration of physical movements (means) involved in putting a cup on a piece of paper could be the goal of finishing a drink, using the glass as a paperweight, putting a tired arm down, giving the glass away, signaling for another drink and so on. They can only be thought of *as* different if they are categorized with respect to their goals – the same kind of reasoning employed when deciding if someone is waving or drowning, for instance. Locomotion gives infants new ways to reach their goals because, if what they want isn't where they are, they need to move. Infants find different ways to meet this challenge by log-rolling from place to place or pivoting in circles using auditory information to calculate the shortest rotational distance to their caregivers (van der Meer, Ramstad & van der Weel 2008). When confronted with obstacles such as steep slopes, cliffs, and stairs, infants search for alternative means of descent – scooting, crawling, sliding, and backing strategies that suggests they are employing means-ends problem solving ability in combination with the ability to represent goals, spatial locations and use tools (Gibson et al. 2006; Kretch & Adolph 2013; Karasik, Tamis-LeMonda & Adolph 2016). Around 6-months-of-age, infants start to realize that an object can be used as a means to get another object: 31% of 6-month-olds intentionally pull a support to retrieve a toy in comparison with 19% of infants who showed no such desire. By 8-months, 69% of infants intentionally pull the support with only 6% showing no interest (Munakata et al. 1997; Willatts 1999; Menard 2005).

There is a large amount of evidence suggesting infants' action production and action perception develop in very close relation (Bell & Adams, 1999; Falck-Ytter, Gredebäck, & Von Hofsten, 2006; Hespos & Baillargeon, 2006; Matthews, Ellis, & Nelson, 1996; Pelphrey et al., 2004). For example, Daum and colleagues (2009) found that 6-month-old infants' ability to perceive the goal of a grasping action from the aperture size of an actor's hand during a grasp was related to their own grasping competence. Specifically, *only* those infants who were already able to perform a grasping action were able to encode the goal of another person's grasping action. The common coding principle provides a theoretical framework for understanding such correspondences, whereby the perception of an action and the control of an action share a common representational format (Prinz, 1990, 1997). A large amount of evidence converges on the idea that perceived events can have an impact on planned actions and vice versa (Brass et al. 2000; Stürmer, Aschersleben & Prinz 2000; Brass, Bekkering & Prinz 2001; Schubö, Aschersleben & Prinz 2001; Wühr & Müsseler 2001; Hamilton, Wolpert & Frith 2004; Miall et al. 2006; Repp & Knoblich 2007). With respect to the developmental sequence, there is evidence that infants' causal actions develop before their causal perceptions (Schlesinger & Langer 1999; Loucks & Sommerville 2018); that infants' causal perceptions develop before their causal actions (Daum, Prinz & Aschersleben 2009) and that they more-or-less develop simultaneously (Sommerville & Woodward 2005). Whatever the direction – whether infants reason "others are like me" because they recognize their means and ends in others (Moore & Corkum 1994; Meltzoff 2005) or infants reason "I'm like others" based on an inference of other people's actions (e.g., in imitation Tomasello, Kruger, & Ratner, 1993) – the key idea is that some point means-end reasoning comes to have a interpersonal currency – they are the kind of things that can be shared, they have intersubjectivity.

So, now we are at a point where we can begin to retrace our steps from motor-acquisition to its relevance for language acquisition via social cognition. An intention is a means-ends bundle that says: I want to achieve *x* in way *y*. Inherent in that idea is an understanding that things could have been otherwise. Without such a concept it is difficult to see how to differentiate between successful and unsuccessful action or furthermore how actions that are unsuccessful could be the result of an accident versus trying but failing. This distinction between unwilling versus unable relies on an intentional interpretation of behavior and begins to emerge at around 9-months of age (Behne et al. 2005). By around this time, infants are both sensitive and able to initiate social exchanges that are dyadic in nature – person to person – and also triadic – usually, person to object to person (Carpenter et al. 1998; Striano & Bertin 2005b). Triadic attention is developmentally important because it is not just about the capacity to represent objects of mutual interest, as if perceived in parallel. Rather, it defines a situation where individuals *share each other's* perceptions and intentions so that they can be coordinated on a common goal, and whereby this cooperation is kept on track by monitoring the goal-directed behavior and perceptions of the partner. For example, cues such as eye-contact and tone of voice help infants establish when information is intended for them and when it is not (Farroni, Johnson & Csibra 2004; Grossmann, Striano & Friederic 2006). The shared attentional space that this defines, sets the stage on which much of early language is played out, and where the majority of the referential action takes place (Baldwin & Moses, 2001; Brooks & Meltzoff, 2005). By selectively attending to goal-relevant aspects of the situation, infants' "doing together" becomes truly triadic. Now the infant has the mental representational ability and motivation in place to make the transition from *a toy* being the object of triadic shared-attention to *language* itself being the object of triadic shared-attention.

Much of this book treats language as 'dynamic system' (more on this in the final chapter) and the cascading sequence of events just described is a prime example of this in action: Sitting upright frees the hands for more time spent manually exploring the world. More time exploring the world is more time spent learning how to obtain goals in the face of obstacles given the way the world works. More experience with means-ends manipulation and more experience of others' means-ends behavior helps the infant analogize their own intentions to others and recognize the intentions of others in themselves. This experience with representing means-ends of the self and the intentions of others sets the stage for ever greater communicative acts, as well as the motivation to convert cooperative ways of thinking (e.g., shared-intentionality) into cooperative action (e.g., symbolic communication). It also emphasizes the continuous dialogue between brain, body and behavior, in co-constructing developmental pathways. This embodied cognitive dynamics approach aims to understand and model such complex dependencies, for example, beginning to use facial gestures, talk and the acquisition of other social skill milestones, sets off a new cascade of developmental implications: the body presents opportunities to implement behavior and behavior presents new challenges for the brain to solve (Spencer & Perone 2008; Schöner 2009).

After the first year of life, where so many of these social cognitive abilities emerge, the developmental picture thereafter is one of infants refining ever more sophisticated social-inference perception with more planned and elaborate cooperative behavior; they move from being able to represent other people's perceptions, to their intentions, to what they know, and finally what others believe – including an appreciation of how those beliefs might be different from the ones they hold.

5.2 Social cognition, cooperative action and language

In comparison with the rest of the natural world, humans are not particularly fast, strong or ferocious. Individually, we are a pretty unremarkable-looking sociable ape sitting at the end of the mammal branch on the evolutionary tree. Together, of course we have the ability to put our minds together to bring down a mastodon, build a cathedral and share a language. The latest comparative psychology research on social cognition suggests than chimpanzees (and even to some extent other non-human primates and birds) have the ability to represent others' goals, intentions, perception, knowledge and even beliefs (Call & Tomasello, 2008a; Dally, Emery, & Clayton, 2006; Emery & Clayton, 2001; Flombaum & Santos, 2005; Krupenye, Kano, Hirata, Call, & Tomasello, 2016; Santos, Nissen, & Ferrugia, 2006). Beliefs are a particularly interesting case because of the space they occupy between the self, others and the world. Beliefs can be wrong, of course, as the subjective inner experience of the world is riddled with biases and paradoxes that the world itself is not, hence "you are entitled to your own opinions but not your own facts". So, to predict someone's behavior based on their beliefs requires coordinating someone's attitude to the facts and the facts themselves. The question for us is what it takes, cognitively-speaking, to reason about beliefs and its relevance to language acquisition.

Tomasello argues that young children and chimpanzees can predict the behavior of others, based on a system that tracks the epistemic states of others (what they know) without those states being subject to a direct comparison or embedded in anyway within their own beliefs (Tomasello, 2018). Essentially, chimpanzees never progress beyond this stage of reasoning (Figure 13) and they never have the motivation to, either, if sharing intentions are tied to cooperative acts rather than competitive ones. Children however, eventually do develop a shared-intentionality that begins to emerge at 5 years-of-age, only after a period where performance dips at around 3-years of-age. One possible explanation is that, en route to representing more complex relationships between others' belief and self-belief, self-belief provides unhelpful interference with

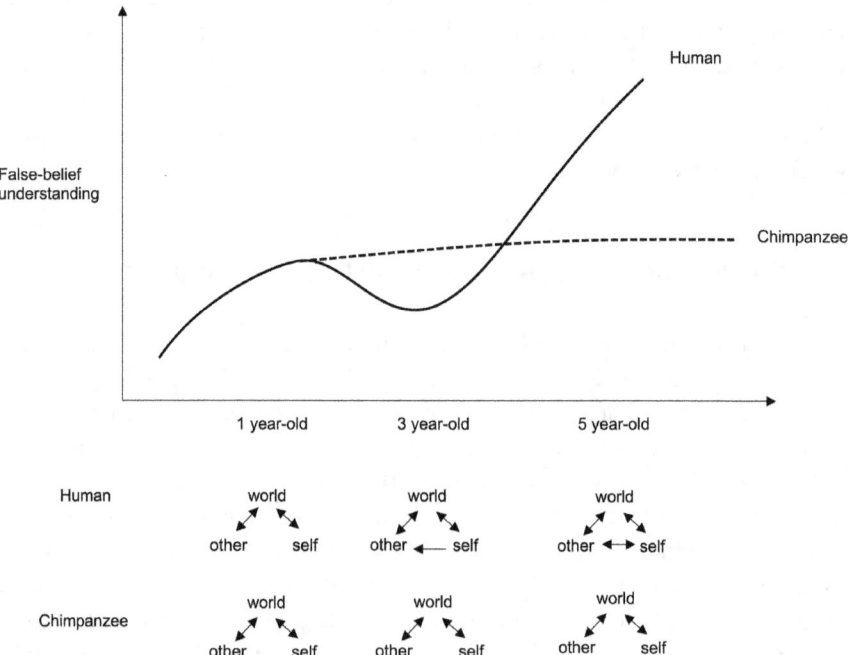

Figure 13: The U-shaped developmental trajectory of false-belief understanding in humans, its relationship to chimpanzee development and the kind of mental coordination needed to predict belief-based behavior.

reasoning about others, and it does so usually in one direction. Thus the "pull of the real" at this age means it is difficult override or inhibit the 1st person perspective being confused with or projected onto that of others. The ability to flexibly manipulate representations in a way that can represent a conflict of interpretations (false belief in others) emerges later, perhaps a result of a more general improvement in executive function skills that are also going through major development around this time (See Chapter 4).

Compared to humans, what other species seem to lack is the motivation to convert these basics of cooperative thinking into widespread cooperative behavior. Thus while the story from decades of comparative psychology research has been one of acknowledging an ever-expanding repertoire of social cognitive *perception* for non-human apes; the picture from naturalistic observations of non-human ape *behavior* has remained relatively static. For example, to see two chimpanzees spontaneously cooperate by carrying a log or working together to fashion a tool, remains an unlikely event. Which begs the question of why non-human apes would have the cognitive capacity for cooperative action if it does not serve cooperative behavior, at least not to the extent that it does in humans? It may be that the same or similar perceptual abilities in this regard generate behavior at different points on the competitive-cooperative continuum, dependent on the different ecological demands of the species' history (Tomasello, Melis, Tennie, Wyman, & Source, 2012). The behavioral effect of this is that, in chimpanzees at least, it is more likely that cooperative perception serves more self-regarding preferences, and apparent prosocial behavior arises as a by-product of these motivations. For example, in primates, grooming can be reciprocated and has the benefits for the groomer of reduced stress and a host for parasites (Zamma 2002; Shutt et al. 2007; Gomes, Mundry & Boesch 2009; Aureli & Yates 2010), consolers of others are likely to receive less aggression themselves (Koski & Sterck 2007; Koski & Sterck 2009), and where non-human apes do share food it tends to be, although not always, that they are harassed into doing so or else begged for it by others (Mitani & Watts 2001; Stevens 2004; Gilby 2006). Chimpanzees will help other chimpanzees access food by performing an action as long as it is of low-cost to themselves. However, they are just as likely to prevent another chimpanzee from getting food with the same action, thus they are no more prosocial in this regard than they are spiteful (Tennie, Jensen & Call 2016).

The relevance to language is this. More than anything else, language is not just a cooperative way of thinking, it is cooperative behavior. It needs to be cooperative behavior – and not just cooperative cognition – because that is the medium in which informing, sharing and requesting works. From this perspective, language is intention made public. Why would anyone want to make their intentions public? Because then, you know what I want and I know what you want, and when we know together it is just a lot easier to coordinate these perspectives towards a common goal than if I were keep this information private. And if I were to keep it private it would put an upper limit on the efficiency and scale of the cooperative acts we could achieve together (Duguid et al. 2014). One case where we might want to keep reasoning about intentions private is if these intentions were not in the best interest of all parties, that is, if I wanted to put my reasoning-ability to more competitive ends, then publicizing them risks others taking counter-action against me to protect *their* interests.

However, humans have both the motivation to see collaborative opportunities where others (e.g., chimpanzees) might see only competitive ones, and we also have the cognitive ability that allows us to put those motivations into practice. When the outcomes of both parties are perceived as a non-zero sum calculation, then going public with intentions makes sense, especially because talking is of such low cost to the individual. The process requires online coordination such that it is not just about representing the intentions and beliefs of others but the back- and forth of cooperative action, and perceptually monitoring each other's' behavior to keeps the goals on track. This distinguishes it from social interaction in general because communicative acts are characterized by their coordinated, mutual responsiveness (e.g., turn-taking in conversation) with a shared goal participants hold together. In language the cooperative goal is not to build a tower together or get a toy (which can be achieved non-linguistically) but typically to share, inform and request information. Interestingly, this transaction can often be a non-zero calculation for both parties because if I share some information it doesn't mean I have any less of it, making it more a mutualistic act than a prosocial one.

Tomasello (2008) has advanced the theory that these key cooperative motives of sharing, informing and requesting have created stable functional pressures that have acted on language for long enough to shape the course of grammaticalization. For example, requesting help in the immediate you-and-me here-and-now requires little in the way of grammar (e.g., "that, here, now"), but, nevertheless, requires common ground such that that reference of those deictic expressions ("linguistic pointing") can be recovered from the context. This is language as tool-use for getting things done in the world, where it can be used can advance a common goal. As anyone who spends time around children knows, language's imperative function to express desire, emerges robustly with the word *want*. Associated with a requesting motivation, children produce these forms a year or more earlier than the corresponding belief verbs and comprehend them earlier also (Bartsch & Wellman 1995; Perner et al. 2003). Sharing – wanting to share emotions and attitudes with others, and informing – wanting to help others by informing them of useful or interesting things – require more sophisticated linguistic strategies that can package these cooperative motives. Where there are multiple relevant objects and actions there is pressure to combine phrases (e.g., connectives) in a way that disambiguates between objects (e.g., nouns, prepositions, quantifiers), identify items or events displaced from the here-and-now (e.g., tense), how they unfold over time (e.g., aspect, adverbs) and how elements in the scene relate to each other (e.g., verbs and argument structure constructions). Finally, the motive of expressing and sharing emotions and attitudes, particularly through narrative, requires a way to express a speaker's relationship to an assertion (e.g., modals, evidentials) discourse-coordination devices (topic-elaboration-termination) and structure (onset-unfolding-elaboration) that enable relations to be tracked across multiple events and participants.

A summary of the relevance of social cognition for language is given in Table 4.

Table 4: Some elements of social cognition that impinge on and underpin the language acquisition process.

Social Cognition	Language
Means-ends differentiation	That others, like me, can differentiate means-ends, have intentions and can read others' communicative intentions
Motivation to turn cooperative perception into cooperative behavior	That symbolic communication is designed to achieve the cooperative goals of requesting, informing and sharing; keep conversation on track
Ability to construct, maintain and terminate shared attention, common ground	Triadic attention, referential language in the here-and-now you-and-me, the use of deictic language; track and coordinate supra-sentence coordination like topic, new/old information.
An understanding that others have different knowledge, beliefs and understanding	Supports a host of so-called metalinguistic abilities including, irony, hyperbole, understatement, humor and metaphor.
Normative reasoning (more on this below)	We say things this way

5.3 Social cognition and language development

Carpenter and colleagues followed 24 infants between 9- and 15-months of age, measuring them every 2-months on their level of attentional engagement, eye-gaze and point following, imitations of two different kinds of actions on objects, imperative (*give me that*) and declarative (*look at that*) gestures and comprehension and production of language (Carpenter et al. 1998). First, they found that the age at which the social cognitive skills emerged were significantly correlated with each other. This might be because, as argued by others elsewhere, joint attention, play, imitation, language and theory of mind, all form part of a shared social-communicative representational system in infancy that only becomes increasingly specialized and differentiated as development progresses (Charman et al. 2000). Second, Carpenter and colleagues found that two of these social-cognitive measures – the amount of time infants spent in joint engagement with their mothers and the degree to which mothers used language that was attuned to their infant's focus of attention – predicted infants' earliest linguistic communication. Subsequently, Brooks and Meltzoff (2005) found a strong positive correlation between gaze-following behavior at 10–11 months and subsequent language scores at 18 months and Charman and colleagues have found imitation ability at 20 months was associated with language production ability at 44 months (Charman et al. 2000).

The mechanisms by which such associations are mediated are fairly well understood in the case of intentions, namely, that triadic shared-attentional space made possible by intention-reading narrows the degrees of freedom on referential language (Baldwin, 1995; Baldwin, 1993; Tomasello & Farrar, 1986). At a basic level this requires understanding what we see together is shared and also the capacity to track that information over space and time. For example, when adults say to 12- and 18-month-old infants *Oh, wow! That's so cool! Can you give it to me?* while gesturing ambiguously in the direction of three objects, infants hand over the object that is new to adult even though it was not new for the infants (Tomasello & Haberl, 2003). Responding appropriately under these conditions needs the common ground we have established together; the kind of common ground that becomes necessary to interpret a whole range of linguistic constructs. For example, it has been extensively demonstrated that infants use this type of intentional inference to constrain interpretations of conventionalized verb meanings and novel verbs (Poulin-Dubois & Forbes, 2006; Poulin-Dubois & Forbes, 2002; Tomasello, 1995). Furthermore, children rely on intentional inference to map verbs to discrete actions (Tomasello & Barton, 1994), map novel verbs to both concurrent and impending actions (Tomasello & Kruger, 1992) and to actions that have occurred in the past (Akhtar, Carpenter & Tomasello 1996). As well as infants internal perception and understanding of intentionality, the use of intentional-type language by others can provide a strong cue to meaning. For example, Carpenter, Akhtar, and Tomasello (1998) had an experimenter say *There!* or *Whoops!* after completing an action. Children were much more likely to imitate the action associated with intentional linguistic description than the accidental one. Likewise, words such as *Uh-oh*, or *Oops* reveal a speaker has not achieved their goal, and are used by two-year-olds to abandon a possible association between a new noun and an object or a new verb and an action (Tomasello, 1995). In general, toddlers' action re-enactments and verb-to-action mapping conform to the perceived intention of the agent executing the action (Carpenter, Call, & Tomasello, 2005; Tomasello & Barton, 1994).

For children to productively and normatively use this kind language depends on their acquisition of non-linguistic conceptual distinctions, namely, the types of things people are capable of believing, knowing, seeing and so on. As we saw in the case of explaining patterns of tough or raising constructions where non-linguistic knowledge was brought to bear on what animate entities were capable of, for example, so too here in the case of novel verb and noun acquisition. Again, this is not to deny the syntactic and semantic contribution of words and phrases to this process once some language has been acquired (e.g., Papafragou, Cassidy, & Gleitman, 2007). Neither does it diminish the complex feedback relationship between cognition making language possible and language highlighting, reinforcing and pushing the boundaries of what cognition can do (to be explored further in the final section). But this intersubjective cooperative behavior is evident in humans before they develop language, so the enabling role of social cognition that allows these patterns to happen – allows language to happen – is logically antecedent to language itself.

5.4 Normative reasoning – we say things this way

People see themselves as belonging to families, cliques, nations, clans, religions – and of course languages. In conversation, listeners are quick to identify how their interlocuter compares with their own group on a whole range of membership criteria, for example adults can detect a foreign accent within 30ms of speech – basically enough time to say hello – and reliably infer others' gender based on only a single vowel utterance (Lass et al. 1976; Flege 1984; Klatt 1989). For those conversational partners who are judged to be part of the native-accent in-crowd, they are rated more positively in terms of their social status, education, professional success, and credibility than those with a foreign accent (Fuertes, Gottdiener, Martin, Gilbert, & Giles, 2012; Giles & Billings, 2004; Lev-Ari & Keysar, 2010; Pantos & Perkins, 2013; Ryan, 1983). The in-group bias begins early in life with children (both monolinguals and bilinguals) more likely to befriend native-accented peers over foreign accented ones – and accent is a more important factor in this regard than is race (Kinzler et al. 2009; Souza, Byers-Heinlein & Poulin-Dubois 2013).

Being part of a group also comes with expectations about how one ought to act and think – norms. For example, I tacitly expect other English speakers to put adjectives before the noun they modify. Cross-culturally, people seem particularly adept at reasoning about normative matters compared to non-normative matters (Cosmides & Tooby 2008). By 3-years-of-age children are better at reasoning about violations in deontic conditionals, e.g., if x then y must/should do z, than they are with indicative conditions, e.g., if x then y does z (Cummins, 1996b, 1996a; Harris & Núñez, 1996). We also know young children from diverse cultural backgrounds "overimitate" adults' behavior, for instance copying nonfunctional means to a goal-directed action (Lyons, Young & Keil 2007; Nielsen & Tomaselli 2010). By comparison, Chimpanzees in same situation drop the unnecessary steps and focus in on the goal (Tennie, Call & Tomasello 2009; Whiten et al. 2009). This is important as the ability to produce high fidelity copies of cultural tools is a necessary precursor for cumulative cultural evolution to work: if you can't copy a wheel then you will have to wait for someone to reinvent it. Moreover, the advantage of a general adaptation to imitate is that it doesn't need to specify "copy what works" because the fact that enough adults are doing it shows at the very least it works well enough for them to still be alive (on average). Chimpanzees seem to exhibit some evolutionary precursors of normative cognition (tolerant societies, well-developed social-cognitive skills, empathetic competence) but appear to lack the cooperative behavior motivation that would convert quasi-social norms into human-like collectivized norms (Tomasello & Rakoczy, 2003; von Rohr, Burkart, & van Schaik, 2011). Thus it seems natural selection has favored some important elements of the architecture of normative cognition – a disposition to learn prevalent norms (imitation) to comply with norms and enforce them (Boyd, Gintis, Bowles, & Richerson, 2003; Robert Boyd & Richerson, 1992; Chudek & Henrich, 2011; Henrich & Boyd, 2001).

Of course we see the human proclivity for groupishness and normativity in many aspects of language use but so-called over-generalization errors provide a particularly interesting case because they break with the group convention, hence the 'error'. Below are the three main suggestions in the linguistics literature that would help children rule out some overgeneralizations or retreat from them once they have occurred and, in one way or another, are all based on patterns of use (Ambridge, Pine, Rowland, Chang, & Bidgood, 2013).

1. Entrenchment (Braine & Brooks, 1995): the more often a child hears a verb in a particular syntactic context (e.g., *I suggested the idea to him*) the less likely they are to use it in a new context they haven't heard it in (e.g., **I*

suggested him the idea; (Ambridge, Pine, Rowland, et al., 2012; Perfors, Tenenbaum, & Wonnacott, 2010).
2. Pre-emption (Goldberg, 2007): if a child repeatedly hears a verb in a construction (e.g., *I filled the cup with water*) that serves the same communicative function as a possible unattested generalization (e.g., **I filled water into the cup*), then the child infers that the generalization is not available (Ambridge, Pine, & Rowland, 2012).
3. Construction semantics (Pinker, 1989): constructions are associated with particular meanings (e.g., the transitive causative with direct external causation). As children refine this knowledge, they will cease to insert verbs that do not bear these meaning elements into the construction (e.g., **The joke giggled him*; (Ambridge et al., 2011)).

Ibbotson used the *Google Ngram* database, a corpus of 5,195,769 digitized books containing ~4% of all books ever published, to test the role that verbal semantics, pre-emption and skew play in generalizations (Ibbotson 2013a). Using 828,813 tokens of un-forms as a test case for these mechanisms, we found verbal semantics was a good predictor of the frequency of un-forms in the English language over the past 200 years – both in terms of how the frequency changed over time and their frequency rank. There was not strong evidence for the direct competition of un-forms and their top pre-emptors, however the skew of the un-construction competitors was inversely correlated with the acceptability of the un-form (cf. Categorization chapter). We suggest a cognitive explanation for this, namely, that the more the set of relevant pre-emptors is skewed then the more easily it is retrieved from memory. This suggests that it is not just the frequency of pre-emptive forms that must be taken into account when trying to explain usage patterns but their skew distribution as well.

In practice, in can be difficult to tease apart the role that entrenchment and pre-emption play, and it seems possible to have entrenchment without pre-emption but not vice versa. They can be visualized as two sides to the same coin, Figure 14. If the semantic niche is already full, then the creative use of that item is blocked or pre-empted for that niche (but without sufficient entrenchment there is nothing to do the blocking). The number of balls in Figure 14 is supposed to indicate the role of frequency in this process. The incoming words (or phrases) need to find their niche and if it is already full then the word cannot occupy that niche. The more a word appears in that niche the more it is associated with it. Entrenchment is like preferential attachment in network behavior in this sense – the "go to" way for expressing that niche.

As ever, with developmental cognitive linguistics approach, it is instructive to see what the value-added is of differentiating between pre-emption and

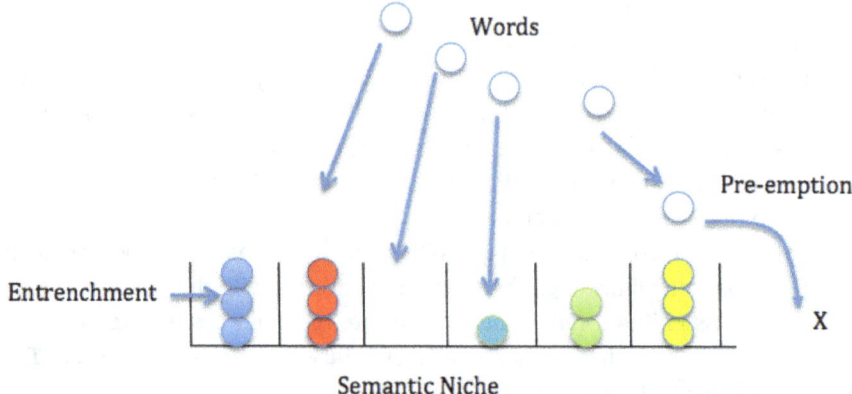

Figure 14: Entrenchment and pre-emption as two sides of the same linguistic process. Note how the same argument applies to incoming argument-structure constructions as it does to words.

entrenchment if we translate the linguistic examples into non-linguistic ones. For example, it has been claimed that once a word becomes highly entrenched, it should not be available for any different uses. Let's see what that argument might look like for a non-linguistic example. The more I see a potato peeler being used in the context of peeling potatoes the more I associate it with that frame, performing that function, in that context. That doesn't prevent me using the item in a novel context such as using it to lift the lid off a hot saucepan or use it as doorstop. However, if I have a doorstop already, then that functional niche is filled by the doorstop itself and I'm probably less likely (pre-empted) from generalizing its function in that direction (if I own a doorstop). Everyone agrees the more the potato-peeler is used in the context of peeling potatoes the more it will be the "go to" tool for that function. However, when the function demands improvisation (e.g., a lid-lifter upper or an extension of the double-object construction *I'm gonna write myself a letter*) then there is nothing to stop that item being exported out of its regular context, particularly if there isn't an off-the-peg tool already doing the job.

Despite being normative by nature, clearly children do not imitate all they hear because (a) sharing, informing and requesting works when it is part of a dialogue of old and new information, not just repeated information (b) languages would show no signs of change (c) linguistic innovations (and more general cultural ones) would not be possible and (d) no adult says *we go-ed to the shops* or *the joke giggled him* – and that fact is at the heart of the productivity we are trying to explain. But it also the case that language acquisition has to be a massively conforming, conservative and reproducible process for languages to survive from one generation to the next and for its users to share a common symbolic repertoire. To the extent that the linguistic solutions for overgeneralizations work at all, they are underwritten by a normative social-cognitive force that essentially stipulates, we, the people, say things in this way, as arbitrarily as we choose to do so – and what is interesting is that children feel compelled to behave in line with that force.

There is a huge amount of evidence from social psychology that people conform, obey and act the way they do because they are quite simply not willing to behave differently from others in their group (Williams & Nida, 2011 for a review). Behaving differently from your peers, linguistically or otherwise, risks being kicked out of the group and that comes with some heavy social, physical and emotional consequences, so much so that it has been referred to as social death. Being ostracized is felt as a threat to a sense belonging (Baumeister & Leary 1995), self-esteem (Steele 1988), sense of control (Seligman 1975), and of meaningful existence (Greenberg, Solomon & Pyszczynski 1997). The affective response is one of sadness and anger and – speaking to its universality – is experienced similarly irrespective of personality type (Williams 2009). The emotional pain caused by ostracism has been shown to be experienced like that of physical pain (Eisenberger, Lieberman & Williams 2003) and analgesics designed to target physical pain have had success in ameliorating the pang of social exclusion better than placebos (DeWall et al. 2010). Longer-term exclusion leads to feelings of insignificance, alienation, worthless, high levels of depression, suicidal ideation and other psychological difficulties (Williams & Nida 2011). For most social creatures, ostracism simply means death so early detection and sensitivity to behaving at the edges of the normative distribution can maximize an individuals' chance that they adaptively avoid this fate (Gruter & Masters 1986). Not surprisingly then, adults and children (Over 2018) either directly or indirectly go to great lengths to stay part of the in-group and avoid being ostracized.

No-one is going to kick a child out on the street because they overregularized a verb, or I hope they would not. But what this shows is how sensitive children become to the social distance between where *they* are at in relation to the norms of their group. And the use and acquisition of language is played out against that background of this wider matrix of emotional, social and biological motivations as much as any other group-level behavior. Being part of a group can deliver a sense of belonging, self-worth, control, and meaning. But this can be taken away if one deviates too far from the norms and the dark side of this groupishness can motivate us-them intolerance, radicalism, hostility and violence. To stay in the group, then, comes with expectations about how one ought to act, think and behave – and that includes linguistic norms. Interestingly, people take steps to reduce the social distance in conversation, for example by imitating one another's intonation, clarity, posture, speech rate, regional accent and speech style intonation (Delvaux & Soquet, 2007; Giles, Coupland, & Coupland, 1991; Goldinger, 1998; Kappes, Baumgaertner, Peschke, & Ziegler, 2009; Lakin & Chartrand, 2003). This process of phonetic, structural and stylistic convergence has the effect of increasing affiliation and the extent to which conversational partners like each other (LaFrance & Broadbent 1976; Chartrand & Bargh 1999; Dijksterhuis & Bargh 2004; Stel & Vonk 2010). When the social distance is reduced though imitation, interactions flow more easily, there is more perceived positive sociability towards the speaker, and interlocuters are more likely to act prosocially towards each other by being more helpful or generous, for instance (Van Baaren et al. 2004; Pardo, Jay & Krauss 2010; Pardo et al. 2012).

The balance of creativity and conformity will not always be the same throughout development but in the end, overgeneralizations get crushed under the normative weight of examples that essentially just mandate: we say it this way. For instance, based on a sample of child-directed speech Cameron-Faulkner and colleagues (2003) estimate – and broadly corroborated by similar analysis of a more diversely collected sample (Wells 1981) – English-speaking children hear, every day, something in the order of 7,000 utterances – including about 2,000 questions, about 1,500 fragments, about 1,000 copulas, and about 400 complex utterances. To pick an example of one grammatical construction; this means an average infant born into an English-speaking environment will have heard 766,500 examples of a Subject-Verb-Object construction by the time they are two-years-old. Note that even though overgeneralization errors have attracted a lot of theoretical interest (for the reason that they are the 'windows on productivity' mentioned earlier) errors themselves represent a relatively small proportion of largely error-free (normative) language. For example, by 3-years-of-age 71% of utterances are free of all grammatical errors, not just errors that over-regularize (Eisenberg, Guo, & Germezia, 2012). So while the production of overgeneralization errors may offer interesting insight into what is linguistically possible, the motivations for their retreat and broader developmental trajectory may be better explained by motivations that lay outside the linguistic system itself (see also the role of inhibitory control in their developmental trajectory, Chapter 4). In summary, overgeneralizations errors temporarily occupy a small space left over by a domain-general categorization system (a kind of linguistic spandrel), but it is space that eventually becomes a normative no-go area due to in-group motivations.

More broadly, there are many cross-linguistic examples of where cultural normative cognition interacts with language in a way that constrains grammatical interpretations (Everett 2012). For example, Kulick (1992, p. 2) describes New Guinean communities that have

> purposely fostered linguistic diversity because they have seen language as a highly salient marker of group identity . . . [they] have cultivated linguistic differences as a way of "exaggerating" themselves in relation to their neighbors . . . One community [of Buian language speakers], for instance, switched all its masculine and feminine gender agreements, so that its language's gender markings were the exact opposite of those of the dialects of the same language spoken in neighboring villages; other communities replaced old words with new ones in order to "be different" from their neighbors' dialects.

Thus the function of gender agreement here is grounded, acquired and understood in terms of its normative role to the in-group and by implication, the out-group. Kulick also gives examples from the Selepet speakers of a New Guinean village who, overnight, decided to change their word for *no* from *bia* to *bune* explaining that they wanted to be distinct from other Selepet speakers in a neighboring village. Swopping gender agreement to be different from your neighbors is probably not motivated by a drive for communicative efficiency (indeed, in the short term it probably reduces efficiency) or by any other the more cognitive aspects of language we have examined thus far – memory, categorization, attention and inhibition. Thus the need to consider social cognitive factors here, particularly the role of normative reasoning and infants' proclivity to reason normatively about language. This means infants' search for communicative relevance is guided by a set of motivations, beliefs and knowledge that is not represented as an infinite landscape of possibilities, because people's normative motivations, beliefs and knowledge are not represented that way either. For example, Everett discusses three example where systematic linguistic behavior is played out over a normative landscape (2012, p. 194):

1. When a concept is sufficiently prominent in a culture, that is part of the shared values, it can predict what is left unsaid, as in the case of Amele, a language spoken in New Guinea. It is an SOV language but when the meaning of "giving" is expressed the verb is omitted. Roberts (1998) argues that there is no verb "to give" because giving is so basic to Amele culture that this can be left backgrounded. For example

13 Jo   eu   ihaciadigen
    House   that   Show
    'I will show that house to you'

The verb ihac means "to show" but in the example below the verb is omitted

14 Naus   Dege   Houten
    Name   name   Pig
    'Naus [gave] a pig to Dege'

2. Speakers of Wari', an Amazonian Indian language, report on others' thoughts, character, reactions, and other intentional states by means of a quotative structure. Regardless of whether people say something or not they are quoted as saying so in order to communicate what the speaker believes they were thinking. Everett (2012) argues this structure can be traced back to, and explained by, the way Amazonian Indians use a metaphor of "motives" and "will," as in *the sky says it is going to rain, the Tapir says it will run from me,* and *John said he was tired of talking with us,* even when John did not say this, but he behaved as though he did. Because of this the verb *to say* is omitted and the quotation structure (capitalized below) in Wari' acts as the verb:

15 MA' CO MAO NAIN GUJARÁ nanam 'oro narima, taramaxicon
    'Who went to the city of Guajará?' [said] the chief to the women.'

    (Everett, 2012, p. 196)

In Wari a high cultural value is placed on evidence for beliefs and since intentions require first-hand evidence this created a linguistic niche filled by the quotative structure which does not commit the speaker to first-hand knowledge.

3. Relatedly, Pirahã, another Amazonian language, requires evidence for assertions – a declarative has to be witnessed, heard from a third party or reasoned from the facts. Pirahã marks this with a suffix, for example – hiai (hearsay), sibiga (deduced or inferred), and xáágahá (observed). The verb and the objects implicated by the verb are obliged to be licensed by the verb's evidential suffix. The culture places high value on evidence for declarations, which in turn is realized on the evidential suffix, which in turn controls the verbal frame. Because in most languages evidentials are limited to main clauses, the claim is that embedding clauses (recursion) is not possible in Pirahã on a clausal level – as a subordinate clause would not be licensed by the evidential, violating the cultural/grammatical constraints.

The main point is that the linguistic behavior in these instances are best described as a reaction to the normative niche it satisfies, and because children are in good place to reason normatively, they are in a good place to make generalizations that make normative sense.

5.5 Discourse and narrative

By the time children are talking *about* things, one of the challenges is to make the content of what they are saying relevant to the conversation. That necessities a level of social cognitive ability to coordinate knowledge between speakers over time, for example by initiating a topic, mutual elaboration and development of a theme, and eventually its termination. To begin with, children are quite poor at this and child–adult conversations rely heavily on scaffolding from adults to maintain a topic. For instance, adults typically respond to the child's initial response with a follow-up question, prompting them to continue the thread of the conversation (Kaye & Charney 1980). The following conversation involves a 2-year-old recorded by Peterson (1990, p. 438)

> Child: He bite my leg.
> Adult: What?
> Child: Duck bite my leg.
> Adult: The dog bit your leg. Oh, oh, the duck. Oh boy!
> Child: Me go in the water.
> Adult: You went in the water?
> Child: Yeah. My leg.

Notice the topic of the conversation comes out of nowhere and the pronoun 'He' is used before the child has established the common ground as to who 'he' is. This phenomena is of great importance because reference and perspective is of such fundamental importance to language. Herb Clark has emphasized the notion of reference as a dynamic, interactive process grounded in discourse, so instead of saying *He was drunk* it is more likely for speakers to say *you know that guy we saw yesterday . . . the one with the beard . . . and the parrot on his shoulder . . . no, not that guy but his brother . . . yeah, well he was drunk* (Clark, 1982; Clark, 1985). Hopefully, by this stage of the book, the author and reader have constructed a large enough landscape of common ground together such that by now we are able to reference ever more abstract and complex ideas. Interestingly, for any writer, in can take time to re-establish common ground with *their self* if they have been away from this landscape for a long period. Speakers opt for references in the "middle" of this common ground to begin with – the ones most likely to be shared by both parties – and thereafter spend time in conversation pushing the boundaries of this ground, stretching and pinning down new areas of references while checking they are taking their listeners with them by monitoring for signs of comprehension or confusion. As an aside, this monitoring is thought to be the reason why talking on a cell phone is more dangerous than talking with your in-car passengers. Your fellow adult passengers can observe your attention because they share it with you and they cooperatively withdraw conversation at hazardous times, freeing your attentional resources to make better driving decisions. Those on the other end of the phone cannot do this so they can overwhelm attentional resources at critical times.

Children are starting to get the topic-comment function of discourse around 2.5 years of age as they add to, elaborate and strengthen common ground in discourse. But they still have difficulty keeping track of specific referents ('he', 'she', 'it') as they participate in different events over time and ordering events in time in the same sequence they actually occurred. In contrast, older children are better at laying common ground, avoiding ambiguity and correcting themselves (Karmiloff-Smith 1986). For example, in a longitudinal study of conversations between two young girls between the ages of 4 and 6, McTear (1985) noted the emergence of greater topic continuity in their conversation as utterances came to serve the dual role of responding to a preceding utterance as well as providing the starting point for further talk. Dorval and colleagues (1984) showed that even 8-year-olds were nearly as likely to have unconnected sentences in their conversations as connected ones, with significant improvement not seen until age 11 or so. Clearly, coordinating a topic between speakers is a skill that takes time to master.

Being good at conversation also requires that you keep track of whether your partner understands what you are saying. When a partner clearly does not understand, young children tend to just repeat the failed message verbatim, while older children are more likely to revise their messages, presumably understanding that saying things differently might help (Tomasello, Farrar, & Dines, 1984). As children get older they become increasingly adept at repairing conversation if it breaks down, appropriately responding to requests for clarification, confirming what was heard or refining meaning in response to questions (Garvey 1984).

As children develop, the content of their conversation gradually moves from observations and comments about the here-and-now to a more 'decontextualised' discussion about absent people and things involved in past or future events. Conversation begins to provide the platform, and the motivation, to take longer and longer solo turns in conversation; these eventually develop into narratives of connected passages relating a sequence of events, real or imaginary – in other words, telling a story (Labov & Waletsky 1967). Storytelling is a complex skill, requiring the narrator to keep track of what is being said from word to word (so that the sentences make sense) as well as paragraph to paragraph (so that the plot makes sense). Typically, stories start with a brief statement of what the story is about, providing the 'who, where and when' of the action to follow. Then the 'unfolding' is the center of the story and consists of one or a series of complicating actions that lead to a high point, and then finally to some to resolution or result. Children develop towards mastering this structure over time: Children aged 3–4 display very primitive narrative structure; sometimes providing two or three dynamic events related in time but, more typically, storytelling consists of lists of unrelated referents and events (Applebee 1978). At around this time children are more likely to focus on the most salient aspects of a scene, rather than the events that advance the story. By 5 years old, half of children give adverbial sequencers like 'then', 'and then' or 'next' and by approximately 8 years of age, more children begin to use adverbial time clauses and create complex relationships between events (Pearson and Ciolli, 2004). A causal structure starts to emerge with relationships that are at first local and only later become more global (Trabasso and Rodkin, 1994). At an intermediate level, children may manage one or two well-formed episodes, but are not able to sustain the organization throughout. Among the many stories analyzed by McCabe and Peterson (1991), one frequently seen category includes those that end at the high point (i.e. do not manage to bring the story to a resolution). At the most mature stage, children ensure that the causal sequence of the whole story makes sense at a global level, and that events relate to an initial goal and an attempt to reach the goal. The outcome is reached with respect to the goal and includes evaluative commentary (Berman and Slobin, 1994). With these multiple components to introduce and co-ordinate it is not surprising that many of the elements of successful storytelling and narration are still developing as children move into adolescence (Hickmann 2002).

Mature narratives present not only 'what happened' but further engage the listener in giving a perspective on the emotional motivations and consequences of the events. Over the period between 5 and 9 years of age, children begin to incorporate more and more of this emotional coloring into their stories, and offer more insight into the characters' cognitive states, such as surprise, guilt or jealousy, in relation to the story (Berman and Slobin, 1994; Pearson and Ciolli, 2004).

5.6 Summary

Our examination of how social cognition allows language to happen concludes the middle section of this book and our tour of the contribution that psychology has made in understanding the mechanisms driving language development. In this chapter we were especially concerned with the development of a subtype of social cognitive behavior that underpins the fabric of symbolic communication, and thus the most likely candidate for the species-unique contribution to the language acquisition process. To do so, it was necessary to take a sideways glance at what we share, cognitively and behaviorally with our closest evolutionary relatives, and where we differ. Compared to humans, what other species seem to lack is the motivation to convert the basics of cooperative thinking (e.g., shared-intentionality) into widespread cooperative behavior (e.g., symbolic communication). It may be that the same or similar cooperative thinking generates behavior at different points on the competitive-cooperative continuum, dependent on the different ecological demands of the species' history. The behavioral effect of this is that, for our closest relatives at least, it is more likely that cooperative perception serves more self-regarding preferences, and apparent prosocial behavior arises as a by-product of these motivations. This matters because, more than anything else, language is not just a cooperative way of thinking it is cooperative behavior. It needs to be cooperative behavior because that is the medium in which informing, sharing and requesting work. And there is evidence that these motivations have been in place for long enough to act as historically significant attractor spaces for languages to evolve into – thus languages have arrived at similar design solutions (parts of speech, narrative structure) to similar problems of packaging sharing, informing and requesting.

We examined the wider matrix of emotional, social and biological motivations that are aligned to keep behavior normative and how the use and acquisition of language is played out against that background. To stay in the group, comes with expectations about how one ought to act, think and behave – and that includes linguistic norms. Infants' search for communicative relevance and linguistic generalizations are guided by a set of motivations, beliefs and knowledge that is not represented as an infinite landscape of possibilities, because people's normative motivations, beliefs and knowledge are not represented that way either. The importance of social cognition in narrowing linguistic generalizations evident from the developmental data converges with evidence we reviewed in Part I from modelling work. Computational approaches to language acquisition have had more success understanding utterances when the linguistic cues combine with social cues such as face recognition (Asoh et al. 2001; Ido et al. 2006) pointing and eye-gaze direction (Hanafiah et al. 2004; Stiefelhagen et al. 2004; Toptsis et al. 2005). Computational word learning models also perform better when they integrate the speakers' intentions and pragmatic context into their learning algorithms than when they use distributed statistical information alone (Frank, Goodman & Tenenbaum 2009; Smith, Goodman & Frank 2013).

The cognitive domains examined in the previous chapters may be considered the minimal and necessary requirements that support language acquisition and use. But without the additional restriction placed on the degrees of freedom by intersubjective behavior, they may not be sufficient to get human language acquisition "over the line". That is because many other species have the ability to memorize, categorize, show inhibitory control and selective attention but they do not use symbolic communication in anything like the way we do. The intersubjective cooperative behavior that language is an example of, is not evident in other non-human apes but it is evident in humans and emerges before they develop language. So, the enabling role of this social cognitive ability that allows language to happen, is logically antecedent to language itself and thus a plausible candidate for the species-unique contribution to the language acquisition process.

Part III

Chapter 6
Developmental cognitive linguistics

This final section of the book begins by compiling a summary of the language-cognition interactions explored throughout Part II and contrasts this evidence with the modularity of language claim. It then goes on to explore a possible analytic framework in which to study Developmental Cognitive Linguistics and tackles some outstanding questions raised by the approach itself: what is the role of language in reorganizing cognition; how does one think about language differences and language similarities; some of the challenges of 'doing' developmental cognitive linguistics; an example of complex dynamic properties in action with a dynamic network analysis of emergent grammar; a test of the directionality of cognitive transfer; and finally some concluding remarks.

Below is a collection of all the summary boxes for each of the domain-general areas we have considered – memory, categorization, analogy, attention, inhibition, social cognition – and their relationship to significant areas of language development.

Let us briefly remind ourselves of where we started.

> It would surprising indeed if we were to find that the principles governing [linguistic] phenomena are operative in other cognitive systems, although there might be certain loose analogies, perhaps in terms of figure and ground, or properties of memory, as we see when the relevant principles are made explicit. Such examples illustrate . . . that there is good reason to suppose that the functioning of the language faculty is guided by special principles specific to this domain . . . (Chomsky, 1980, p.44)

So, an important point is that, historically-speaking, this modular view is not some straw-man idea that represents an isolated point of view – it is a way of thinking that has deeply permeated the language acquisition field, both theoretically and methodologically. Some of the greatest supporters of the encapsulated view are simply incredulous that things could be otherwise: "doubting that there are language specific, innate computational capacities today is a bit like being still dubious about the very existence of molecules, in spite of the awesome progress of molecular biology" (Piattelli-Palmarini, 1994, p.335). That is why the developmental cognitive approach is an important enough project to pursue even if it turns out to be wrong. I hope the contrast between the opening quote and the summary Table 5 (and all the in-chapter references on which it is based) makes the point self-evident: we have moved beyond "loose analogies" thanks to the detailed and persistent work of thousands of psychologists, psycholinguists and linguists over many decades who have detailed the relationship between language

Table 5: A summary of the ways in which domain-general processes support, shape and constrain the development of language.

Domain-general cognition	Language
The move from simultaneous to sequential memories	Opens up capacity for encoding and storing transitional probabilities and word boundaries; understanding multiword utterances, phrase structure and dialogue
A relaxing of the encoding specificity principle	Allows the use of words and phrases across a greater number of contexts in which they were learned; pragmatic flexibility and generalization
U-shaped patterns of memory development	U-shaped patterns of grammatical use (e.g., *swam* then *swimmed* then *swam* again)
The importance for learning of the frequency of a stimulus, its spacing over time, the duration/type of information that is encoded and infants' attention	Implications for the trajectory of word, sound and syntax learning; particularly age-of-acquisition and errors (both overgeneralization and omission)
Prototype and exemplar reasoning about visual and object categories; ability to make broad and fine-grained distinctions	Prototype and exemplar reasoning about linguistic categories; ability to make broad and fine-grained distinctions
Importance of the statistical distribution of items in the class to generalization	Importance of the statistical distribution of items in a novel construction or word
Non-linguistic taxonomic hierarchy including broad and fine-level categorization	Linguistic structural hierarchy including broad and fine-level categorization
Importance of perceptual and functional dimensions of classification and generalization	Linguistic categories based both on similarity of form (e.g., phonological regularities) and of meaning (e.g., the communicative function it serves)
Attentional system allows for some sources of information to be privileged over others	Supports topicalization, stress distinctions, figure/ground comparisons and generally allows information to be structured on a continuum of communicative focus
Increases in selection, resistance to distractors, and narrowing of attentional focus.	Allows sustained periods of attention and joint-attention with other language users, longer chunks and dialogue to be processed.
A shift from attention and inhibition as driven by external perceptual features to those internally generated motivations and conflicts	Relevant for the complex feedback loops between language comprehension and production

Table 5 (continued)

Domain-general cognition	Language
Increasing control of competing stimuli, error detection and greater ability to inhibit	Greater ability to weigh and resolve cue competition, resolving syntactic ambiguity; resisting tempting, but wrong overgeneralizations
Means-ends differentiation	That others, like me, can differentiate means-ends, have intentions and can read others' communicative intentions
Motivation to turn cooperative perception into cooperative behavior	That symbolic communication is designed to achieve the cooperative goals of requesting, informing and sharing; keep conversation on track
Ability to construct, maintain and terminate shared attention, common ground	Triadic attention, referential language in the here-and-now you-and-me, the use of deictic language; track and coordinate supra-sentence coordination like topic, new/old information.
An understanding that others have different knowledge, beliefs and understanding	Supports a host of so-called metalinguistic abilities including, irony, hyperbole, understatement, humor and metaphor.
Normative reasoning	We say things this way

and cognition. Their work has led us to a position where we can now state with some precision the many nuanced, complex and powerful ways in cognition enables, predicts and confines the acquisition of language – in other words, answer Chomsky's call to make "the relevant principles . . . explicit". I hope it is also evident by now that the evidence casts serious doubt on the claim that language use or any encapsulated language faculty "is guided by special principles specific to this domain". The developmental trajectory of language is contingent on those domain-general trajectories because there is representational recycling and information exchange across cognitive borders and this is how cognition generates abstractions and constrain generalizations. In combination with the converging lines of evidence from neuroscience, cross-species comparisons and artificial intelligence, the developmental cognitive linguistics approach has made significant contributions to answering the long-standing questions of language acquisition research and offers much more potential to do so in the future.

6.1 Dynamic systems theory and developmental cognitive linguistics

How can we start to organize, make sense of and analyze what is by definition a complex emergent process? One framework that seems particularly well-suited to the task is dynamic systems theory (DST) (Smith & Thelen, 2003; Thelen & Smith, 1994). It seeks to examine complex questions about the interrelatedness of the whole and its parts, particularly those relationships that are nested in some way into complex hierarchical feedback loops – in other words exactly the kinds of relationships between language and cognition we have been attempting to understand throughout the book (Bogartz, 1994; Smith, 2005). *Developmental* systems theory is a similar approach to DST, and it also captures the incremental progress and multilevel interactions that shape development, but has tended to focus on how development unfolds through a transactional model of gene-epigenetic-environment interactions (Johnston & Edwards 2002), whereas DST developed from a more formal background of the mathematical analysis of complex physical systems (Gleick, 1998; Smith & Thelen, 2003). Regardless of these differences in emphasis, as Spencer, Perone, and Buss summarize (2011, p.261)

> A key characteristic of systems metatheory that both approaches [developmental systems theory and dynamics systems theory] share is the rejection of classical dichotomies that have pervaded psychology for centuries: nature versus nurture, stability versus change, and so on (for discussion, see Spencer et al., 2009). In their place, systems metatheory takes the "organism in context" as its central unit of study, an inseparable unit in which it is impossible to isolate the behavioral and developmental states of the organism from external influences. Furthermore, behavior and development are emergent properties of system-wide interactions that can create something new from the many interacting components in the system   (Munakata & McClelland, 2003; Spencer & Perone, 2008; Thelen, 1992)

That "something new" in the case of developmental cognitive linguistics would be language itself and the "system wide" interactions are those relationships that we have been studying between language, memory, categorization, attention, inhibition, social cognition, body and culture. The DST framework is less interested in the what, the when, and the outcome of development and more interested in the how, the why and the process (Elman et al., 1996; Plumert & Spencer, 2007; Thelen & Smith, 1994). As an example of this way of thinking in action, consider the classic set of studies conducted by Esther Thelen on motor-development, specifically the developmental trajectory of kicking and stepping reflexes. If you hold a new-born upright and let the soles of their feet touch a flat surface, they reflexively try to take steps by placing one foot in front of another. The motor coordination required to accomplish this is very similar to that required to kick, yet the stepping reflex, present at birth, disappears within the first three months of life and kicking steadily increases in frequency throughout development with no interruption. In a longitudinal design, Thelen and colleagues noted that it was the heavier babies and those who gained weight the fastest that were the ones to stop stepping first (Thelen, Fisher, & Ridley-Johnson, 1984). This fact led to the idea that it required more strength for infants to lift their legs upright in a stepping position than when they were lying down in a kicking position – hence why the chubbier infants were the ones to give up stepping first. To test this conjecture they strapped weights to the legs of 2-month-olds, equivalent to that which they would gain in the next month of development, and this had the effect of reducing stepping. With older infants whose stepping had begun to disappear, they immersed them in water up the waist so that their legs weighed less, whereupon the stepping behavior reappeared. The dynamics of weight gain in combination with the physical properties of body orientation, they revealed, could explain the different developmental trajectories of stepping and kicking.

There are two relevant lessons from this. First, at the time Thelen was trying to explain this pattern, the leading explanations were that either (1) the disappearance of stepping was a result of the maturation of certain cortical centers thought to inhibit the behavior (2) that stepping was innately programmed to disappear (e.g., Andre-Thomas & Autgaerden, 1966). Neither of these arguments could explain how Thelen had demonstrated that both stepping can be reduced in infants that could already step and be made to reappear in those that could no longer do so. Thelen concluded multiple factors cohere in a moment in time to create or hinder these reflexes. DST had a revolutionary impact in how developmental researchers thought about motor development and it has the same potential to change the way people think about cognitive development too. For example, multiple factors cohere in a moment in time to create language: the split-second processes of producing and comprehending speech; the years an individual takes to construct their language; the centuries over which languages evolve. The second lesson from Thelen's work is that, the kind of individual-differences approach needed to uncover the relationship between elements in the motor-system (e.g., chubby babies stopped stepping first) is the same approach we have been taking in the developmental cognitive linguistic approach too (e.g., those children who are good at grammatical inhibition are those that are good at non-verbal inhibition too (Ibbotson & Kearvell-White 2015)).

Figure 15 is an attempt to visualize what developmental cognitive linguistics would look like from a DST perspective – the similarities with Waddington's epigenetic landscape are not accidental (Waddington 1957). Time is represented as moving forward from X to Y. The grey horizontal plane represents an infinite landscape of possible developmental trajectories for language (the ball) to develop into and thus an infinite range of possible languages – similar to the

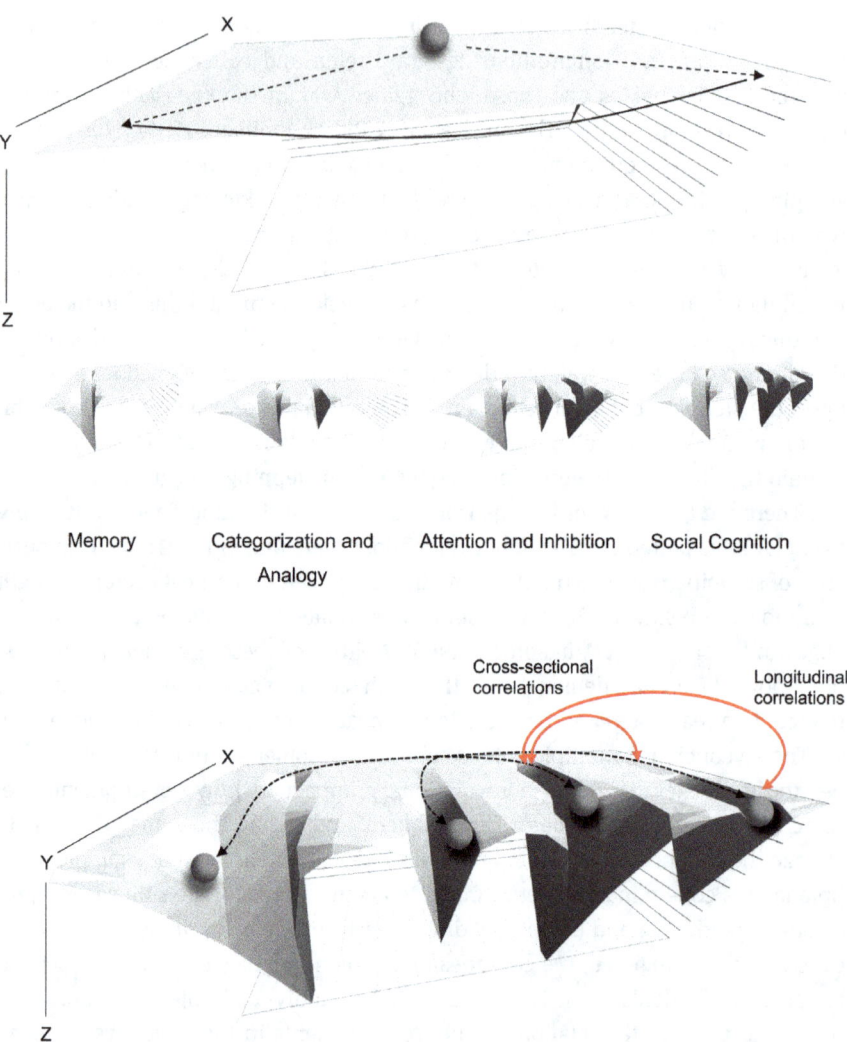

Figure 15: A Dynamic systems approach to visualizing developmental cognitive linguistics.

pluripotent cell prior to differentiation (Waddington 1957). This brings us back to the two fundamental problems that language acquisition research has concerned itself with: (1) children have syntax but they don't hear it, what they hear are utterances, so the question it begs is one of process; how to do children get the former from the latter? (2) whatever process governs this transition, in theory it is also possible for it to generate a grammar that sprawls beyond what it should. So, in theory, in a plane decoupled from the influence of cognition, there are infinite degrees of freedom consistent with a finite sample of grammar that a learner is exposed to.

What we have tried to show is that, in practice, the integration of cognition into the learning process can massively reduce the combinatorial possibilities on what words and phrases can mean. As different cognitive capacities emerge and develop they come to channel the course of language development (axis Y-Z), or in the terminology of DST they may be mathematically characterized by considering behavioral patterns as the attractor states of a dynamical system. So, qualitative change occurs in the system when there is a change in the layout of the attractors or when a new attractor appears. For example, recall that the dynamic reorganization of information in memory systems, from working memory to declarative to procedural, may itself represent an adaptive response by language to memory development. This is significant as many usage-based theories have emphasized the frequency and importance of lexically-based semi-formulaic patterns in Child Directed Speech and Child Speech (Ambridge & Lieven, 2011; Ibbotson, Theakston, Lieven, & Tomasello, 2010; Tomasello, 2003). It may turn out that this linguistic picture of how grammar develops can be grounded in more fundamental properties of how memory itself develops. For example, we know as the infant moves from preverbal to verbal stages of language development, declarative memory itself is going through simultaneous changes in the way it encodes, stores and consolidates information (Bauer 2006; Rovee-Collier & Cuevas 2009; Mullally & Maguire 2014). This aspect of memory development would seem essential in supporting a transition from fixed patterns to freeing up schematic patterns, for example, allowing to store what is similar (frame) and what is different (slot). More generally this allows decomposing of phonological and syntactic chunks into separate elements, and the flexibility and productivity of language that this brings. In terms of DST, these quantitative changes in one aspect of the system (e.g., the coupling of procedural and declarative memory) can give rise to qualitatively new behaviors (e.g., past-tense productivity) and it moves us beyond the old stability vs change, continuous vs. stage development way of thinking towards a more dynamic systems way of thinking.

By acknowledging that cognition penetrates deep into the linguistic system, it makes some language trajectories more likely than others. The result is a landscape of probabilistic outcomes. 'Probabilistic' because, like the analysis of thermodynamic behavior that DST emerged from, language is a complex adaptive system. It has many interdependent parts whose interactions and dependencies generate emergent behavior that is difficult to model from knowledge of the parts themselves.

Note that this canalization of linguistic possibilities and preferences begins before birth. For example, new-borns are already familiar with their mother's voice from their experience *in utero* and will prefer to listen to the familiar voice rather than the voices of other women (Decasper & Fifer 1980). Newborns also prefer to listen to their native language rather than other languages. In an experiment with 4-day-old babies, Mehler and colleagues presented French babies with two recordings of a bilingual speaker telling the same story – one in French and one in Russian. The babies who had 'overheard' French in the womb showed a clear preference for the French version of the story (Mehler et al. 1988). Mehler and colleagues used the same procedure again, playing tapes to newborns, but then filtered the tapes so that they could no longer tell what words were being spoken with only the general pitch, stress and rhythm of the sound intact. Russian and French have very different prosodies and when Mehler and colleagues ran the same experiment with just prosodic information, the effect of preference for familiarity was replicated.

The multiple cognitive systems in Figure 15 produce coherent behavior in the moment of linguistic use, and those in-the-moment behaviors have consequences that carry forward across the longer time scales of learning and development. Unlike many other complex systems in the natural world, language it is also a cultural one and that means, every generation, a language must be compressed through the cognitive bottleneck of what is learnable (Kirby 1998; Kirby 1999). For example, recall from the early work by Bever (1970), to work on maturational limitations (Newport, 1988; 1990) and the complementary evidence of computational models (Elman, 1993), we saw how memory places various adaptive constraints at various points in development that limit the degrees of freedom on learning. Important in this regard are the downstream consequences of the order in which capacities are introduced upstream. This is where 'when' a developmental milestone is achieved offers less insight than understanding the developmental mechanisms that created it and where DST can provide a useful theoretical framework.

For instance, on their way to learning to toddle, many infants go through a phase where they both crawl and walk. In any given moment they may go from crawling to walking in a matter of seconds but this transition belies a probabilistic landscape that has been changing for months, as the infant edges towards an attractor basin of 'full-time' walking. To understand the forces controlling development therefore, it is less important to define when the infant "has" walking. Rather it is more revealing to uncover the landscape of attractors that makes walking more or less likely in different situations and at different times. So, there is no reason to separate competence from performance in this framework, rather the focus is on how behavior is assembled in the moment in context

(Thelen & Smith, 1994). Likewise with language development, it is sometimes difficult define when a child "has" the productive past tense in English for example, when they over-regularize *go-ed* and double-mark *wented* while at the same time use the correct form *went*. Because language is composed of many agents whose interactions are driven by underlying nonlinear processes, the behavior that emerges from this is best described in probabilistic terms (Holland 1995; Holland 1998; Beckner et al. 2009). And learning mechanisms that incorporate this probabilistic nature into their models have successfully simulated word segmentation and phoneme discrimination (Kuhl, 2000, 2004; Saffran, Newport, & Aslin, 1996).

Lieven and colleagues (Lieven, Salomo, & Tomasello, 2009) found that 78–92 percent of novel multiword utterances spoken by two-year-olds could be traced backed to lexical strings and schemas in their previous utterances (see Bannard, Lieven, & Tomasello, 2009 for a computational implementation of the same idea). The dynamics systems framework suggests a similar approach could be taken to understanding the emergence of meaning. To understand what constructions mean they need to be traced back and understood in terms of the cognitive and social crucibles in which they were formed. To do so is obviously labor-intensive and requires detailed analysis of rich text, audio and visual datasets (Ibbotson et al., 2014 for one example of how this was done for the English progressive construction). But the payoff is that it becomes easier to understand what the social and cognitive landscape looks like in the moment of use and what are the relevant domain-general processes canalizing language development.

This is important as we need to ask 'which are the relevant aspects of general cognition and when are they most important?' To really get traction on this question we need to better understand why we see relationships between language and cognition in some contexts but not in others. For example, sometimes we see cross-sectional and longitudinal correlations between cognitive systems (see Figure 15) and sometimes we do not. Understating this pattern will require tackling the "file-drawer" problem whereby any statistically significant association found between language and cognition is much more likely to be published than those who fail to find an association. Many researchers now use open calls for unpublished datasets and manuscripts to try to address this publication bias and a similar approach is needed for developmental cognitive linguistics. Then, after a comparison between the circumstances under which associations are readily detected (the majority of evidence from this book for example), and those that do not (the result of collecting unpublished research), we will be in a better position to fully address that question. Even before such an analysis, we are in a position to make some tentative predictions about what the relevant factors might be, based on the evidence we have already reviewed. For example, Gathercole and colleagues' (2019) predict cognitive transfer will occur with the creation of novel routines. Their theory was developed to understand when working memory (WM) training would 'spill over' to other domains but the principles behind it are relevant to cognition-to-language transfer in general. Essentially transfer of WM to other capacities will only occur when both the trained and untrained activities impose the same unfamiliar task demands that are not supported by existing WM subsystems. Key is the creation of new routines or mnemonics that are common across both trained and untrained activities and are functionally required by both tasks in order to succeed. For example, using a strategy for chunking items in WM to link them to multi-chunk items in long-term memory for later retrieval is an acquisition of a skill common to both visual-spatial processing and language (Christiansen & Arnon, 2017; Cowan, Rouder, Blume, & Scott Saults, 2012; Miller, 1956). So, cognition-to-language transfer, recycling and reuse should be most evident when creation of new routines are common across both domains; the bridge between domains is functionally required in order to succeed at the task at hand, and the task cannot be accomplished by processes already internal to the system. For example, using a strategy for chunking items in WM to link them to multi-chunk items in long-term memory for later retrieval is an acquisition of a skill common to both visual-spatial processing and language.

Recall that the fact that adults did not show memory to language transfer following training is because the cognitive routines to perform these tasks can be readily accomplished with existing WM processes and mechanisms – no new routines are needed to functionally succeed at this task and so the cognitive architecture for transfer is not created. Thus we saw a similar pattern in the training studies as the correlational studies. Non-verbal working memory and language correlate in populations with wide variance in their linguistic ability but with mixed findings in monolingual non-impaired population. Likewise, training studies have failed to find transfer robust effects between non-verbal WM and language but these populations have been adults where we expect the linguistic elements of WM to be at or near ceiling, again leaving non-verbal WM little variance to work with. So there needs to be enough individual variation in language and cognitive performance to find a correlation (if one exists) and sometimes this means testing at an appropriate age. For example, choosing a young enough age group that still commits a proportion of over-regularization errors so that inhibition errors have some variance to correlate with (Ibbotson & Kearvell-White 2015). Even when there is variance in cognitive and linguistic performance, sometimes linguistic variance is going to be best explained by other linguistic variance. The most obvious example of this is frequency effects and the Frequency Filter tool (Ibbotson, Hartman & Björkenstam 2018) has been designed specifically to tap into social and cognitive drivers of development above and beyond that of input frequency (this is covered in detail in Section 6.3 below). The significance of these language-internal correlations depends on the question we are asking. If one is more interested in processing, then, given the interconnectivity of language, one part of the system may have effects on another and this can reveal something interesting, say the speed at which a morphological marker is understood is dependent on the frequency of another morphological marker. But if one is interested in development, then noting this language-internal association between these morphological markers is not a theory of how either are acquired. Tracing back the social-cognitive history of their use could give a clue (independent of language) as to why one form is easier to process than another and then we are in a position to invoke learning mechanisms that are external to the system we are trying to explain.

This is not to underestimate the challenge of integrating the dynamics of multiple domains of cognition across different time scales in such a way that predict individual differences. Nevertheless, DST is a promising approach in this regard as it has the already developed some of the analytic tools to capture emergent behavior, such as growth models, oscillator models and dynamic neural field models and the statistical tool to describe these patterns (Lewis, Lamey, & Douglas, 1999; Molenaar, Boomsma, & Dolan, 1993; Van Der Maas & Molenaar, 1992).

6.2 A dynamic network analysis of emergent grammar

Here we provide an example of complex dynamic properties in action with a dynamic network analysis of emergent grammar (Ibbotson, Salnikov & Walker 2019). The use of formal tools and computational models have provided a useful complement and challenge to experimental findings, in addition to the greater descriptive rigor and theoretical insight the models themselves can offer (Chomsky, 1975; Pinker, 1979). For example, connectionist-based models, based on parallel systems of artificial neurons, have had success in identifying word boundaries from sequences of phonemes, word classes from sequences of words, and phrase structure and lexical semantics from large usage corpora (Borovsky & Elman, 2006; Christiansen & Chater, 2001; Elman et al., 1996; Elman, 1990, 1993, 1993, 2005; McClelland & Rumelhart, 1988). Some models have been less concerned that they represent any realistic analogue to human cognition and seek to tackle the learnability problem as a mathematical abstraction, for example Klein and Manning state that their solution "makes no claims to modelling human language acquisition," (2005, p.35). Others have been more interested in how the latent structure of natural language interacts with plausible cognitive processing constraints, for example, explicitly modelling how the aspects of memory account for various syntactic phenomena or act as an aid to word learning (Freudenthal et al. 2015; Ibbotson, López & McKane 2018). In this spirit of cognitively-grounded proposals, lexical-based analyses have examined the degree to which the utterances a child produces can be traced to reliable and frequent multi-word patterns in the input (Bannard, Lieven, & Tomasello, 2009; Lieven, Pine, & Baldwin, 1997; Lieven, Salomo, & Tomasello, 2009; Lieven, Behrens, Speares, & Tomasello, 2003). In their model Alishahi and Stevenson (2008) found that constructions gradually emerged through the clustering of different verb-frames as the model learned verb classes and constructions from artificial corpora. A major contribution to this approach was provided by McCauley and Christiansen (2019). Their model essentially tested the idea that the discovery and on-line use of multi-word units – stored in a 'chunkatory' – forms the basis for children's early comprehension and production. High performance was achieved across a large number of different corpora and multiple languages, including capturing many of the features of children's production of complex sentence types. They conclude that the model supports the idea that children's early language can be characterized by item-based learning supported by on-line processing of distributional cues.

Language processing models have varied in the extent to which they have attempted to incorporate semantic information, with some using a supervised neural network to identify the thematic roles associated with words in sentences (Kawamoto and McClelland, 1987) while others have used a broader range of cues, including animacy, sentence position, and the total number of nouns in a sentence to classify nouns as agents or patients (Connor et al. 2008; Connor et al. 2009). Another approach is to consider all the possible structures given in a training corpus, and estimate their likelihood from the data (Bod, Sima'an & Scha 2003). This estimate can then be used to assign a structure to a new utterance by combining sub-trees from the training corpus. In its unsupervised version, this method initially assigns all possible unlabelled binary trees to an un-annotated training set, and then employs a probabilistic model to determine the most likely tree for a new utterance (Bod 2007). In summary, a range of different theoretical models suggest categories can be recovered by distributional data, whether that is via minimum-description length clustering (Cartwright & Brent 1997), clustering based on frequent contexts (Mintz, 2003; Mintz, Newport, & Bever, 2002), or Bayesian approaches (Griffiths & Goldwater 2007; Parisien, Fazly & Stevenson 2010).

What we offer here is a much simpler methodology than many of the models reviewed above (e.g., McCauley & Christiansen, 2019) yet in common with many of them we too make use of the notion that transitional probabilities are important cues for syntactic boundaries. For example, dips in a transitional probability profiles represents likely phrase boundaries and peaks indicate likely groupings of words together (e.g., Thompson & Newport, 2007). Where our approach differs to others, particularly those of a connectionist or neural network orientation, is that patterns are recovered from Child Directed Speech (CDS) unsupervised and with no a priori constraint on the number of hidden layers relevant for the particular learning task. Neither does our approach call for any specific learning biases of word learning models (Golinkoff et al., 1994; Markman, 1994) other than the general capacity to represent words, the transitions between them, and cluster frequently co-occurring words together. While acknowledging semantic information plays an important role in construction formation, this is not formalized into our network as we wanted to purely asses the contribution that distributional properties make to recovering grammatical categories and the dependencies between them. Our approach also uses naturalistic CDS as the input to the model; the raw input out of which children are constructing their language (cf. Reeder, Newport, & Aslin, 2013). The most important aspect of our model is that it offers a representational format that minimally departs from that of both language and the brain – namely a network of interrelated, weighted connections, whose structure evolves over time.

Incremental growth of the network captures something fundamentally developmental and complex (in the sense of many interacting parts) about the process of language acquisition, that neither batch-processing of corpus data nor non-dynamic models of development can. The dynamic networks approach offers a highly plausible psychological medium in which to simulate cognitive processes because, like language, the brain itself is a complex dynamic network (Sporns 2002). Network studies of complex systems have shown that real world networks, such as language, are not random, as was initially assumed (Barabási & Albert 1999; Barabási 2002; Watts & Strogatz 2002). The internal structure and connectivity of the system can have a profound impact upon system dynamics (Newman, Barabási & Watts 2006). Conceptualizing language learning as a Complex Adaptive System (CAS) means that language acquisition research has the potential to benefit from the analytic tools developed to understand CAS in general. The approach can also offer a unified account of various linguistic phenomena, including the probabilistic nature of linguistic behavior; continuous change within agents and across speech communities; the emergence of grammatical regularities from the interaction of agents in language use; and stage-like transitions due to underlying nonlinear processes (Holland

1995; Holland 1998). One such analytic tool developed for CAS analysis is community detection in networks, where network communities form around nodes (words in our case) that are more densely connected with each other than they are with the rest of the network. We explore this idea by instantiating a corpus of early child directed speech (CDS) in to a dynamic network. We allow the network to grow word by word as the mother uses her language, as recorded in a corpus of naturalistic speech. By using CDS, we are interested to know whether organizational properties of the network (i.e., community structure) map onto grammatical patterns in any way that a child could plausibly capitalize on when constructing their language. If such a mapping exists, then community detection could be an important learning mechanism for the child, assuming learners sample words from the input they receive – something they presumably must do as they do not know which language community they are going to be born into.

The network we use is blind to grammatical information and its organization emerges from (a) the frequency of using a word and (b) the probabilities of transitioning from one word to another. We then implement a procedure that measures the density of links inside network communities compared to links between communities, analyze the grammatical composition of these communities and track how they develop over time. We take this approach because many decades of psycholinguistic research have shown how sensitive adults and children are to distributional patterns in language (Bloomfield, 1938, 1973; Cartwright & Brent, 1997; Finch & Chater, 1992, 1994; Goldberg, 2005; Harris, 1954; Mintz, 2003; Mintz, Newport, & Bever, 2002; Redington, Chater, & Finch, 1998; Schütze, 1993; Tomasello, 2003).

If network communities show distinct grammatical characteristics then the dynamic network approach suggests some of language's complexity (grammar) can be an emergent property of how simpler elements (words) interact with one another. It would also suggest that early grammatical patterns can be represented at a level that is grounded in the distributed properties of the network.

All available naturalistic CDS for two children ("Eleanor" and "Fraser") were extracted from the Max Planck-Manchester Corpus (Lieven, Salomo & Tomasello 2009). Utterances were parsed into two-word chunks (bigrams) such that *John liked Mary* became *John → liked, liked → Mary*, which when implemented in a network (Figure 16) represented a total of 6861 unique words for Fraser's CDS (displayed as nodes) and 52,057 links (or edges→) between words. For Eleanor's CDS there were 6184 words with 65,720 links.

When Eleanor's or Fraser's mother said a word for the first time in the corpus a new node was added to the network. As they connect two words for the first time a new edge was added between these two nodes. As they connect the

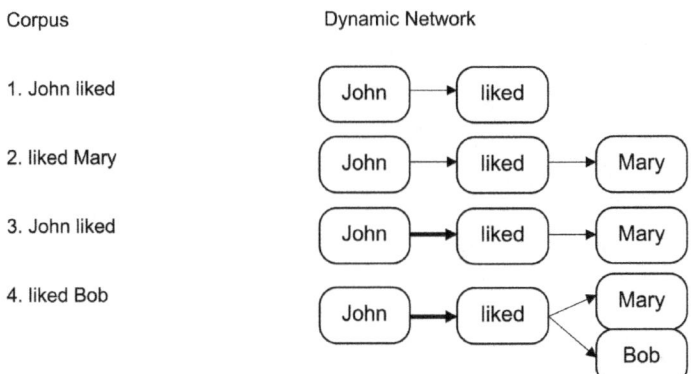

Figure 16: Schematic representation of how the network grows over time (1–4) out of words (nodes) and the relationship between those words (edges) as constructed from naturalistic speech, in this example John liked Mary, John liked Bob. Note the increased weight between repeated connections (e.g., John liked (3)).

same two words as before, the weight of the edge between two nodes was increased proportionate to the frequency that this connection was made. In this manner, the network builds up distributional patterns of use. This procedure is designed to reflect what we know about distributional patterns in naturalistic corpora from other, non-network analyses. For example, in one construction based analysis of child directed speech (Cameron-Faulkner, Lieven & Tomasello 2003), a *What's__X?* frame (Figure 17a) accounted for more than 69% of all of the CDS *What-'is* constructions. The idea is that by instantiating these types of patterns as nodes and edges in a network, it gives community detection a way of mechanistically recovering the kinds of patterns consistent with this frame and slot analysis of early speech (Clark 1974; MacWhinney 1979; Braine 1987). The intuition behind the community detection algorithm is visually displayed in 17b and positioned below purposely to provide a direct comparison with the usage-generated CDS analysis of 17a (Cameron-Faulkner, Lieven & Tomasello 2003).

Informally, network communities form around nodes (words in our case) that are more densely connected with each other than they are with the rest of the network. For example, they may form around the type of *Whats'_X?* collocation in Figure 17a or an adjective-noun phrase or noun-verb-noun pattern or any frequently co-occurring pattern or schema that is more interconnected on average than the rest of the network. Because each word (e.g., *dog*) has grammatical category meta-data attached to it (e.g., noun) in the corpus we could analyze the pattern of grammar not only across the whole network, but also within the communities that formed as the network developed. Importantly the network itself

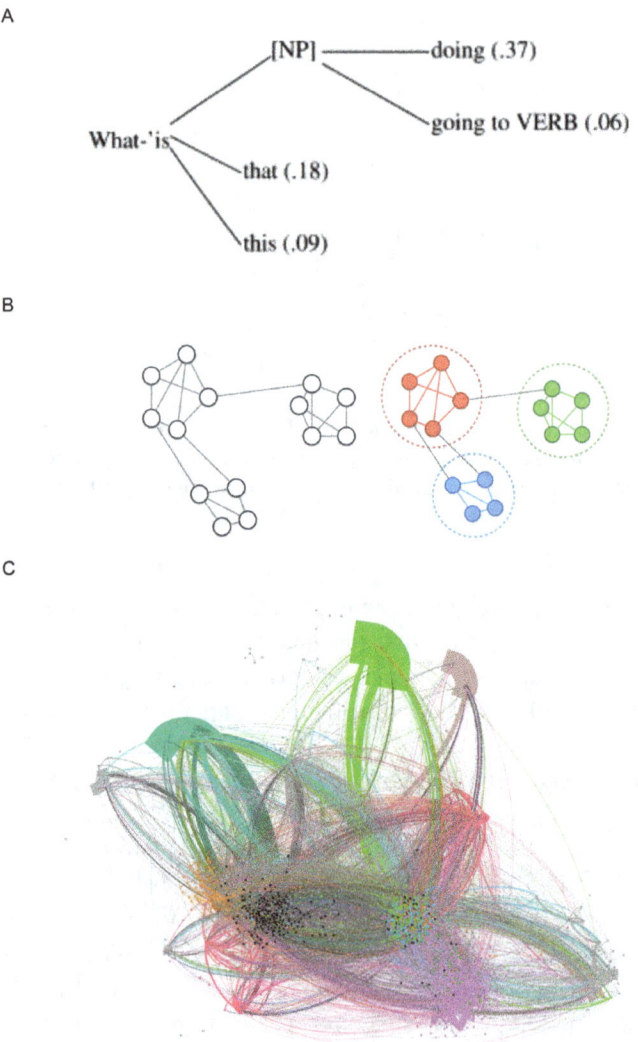

Figure 17: A What's__X frame From Cameron-Faulkner et al. (2003). B visual illustration of how communities are identified (marked by red, green and blue) around densely interconnected nodes. C A whole network visualisation of real CDS from corpus data with commuinties coloured.

was blind to the grammatical information and was only built from the collocations between words that were in CDS, not their grammatical categories. A more formal description of how the model identifies categories is given in the paper on which this summary is based (Ibbotson, Salnikov & Walker 2019).

Within communities we restricted ourselves to analyze grammatical patterns of use across three-word trigrams for the practical reason that strings much longer than this became very difficult to analyze. Figure 18 below gives a close-up of a community identified in the network of Eleanor's CDS. From these trigram maps we characterized some of the most typical grammatical patterns for trigrams within communities, for example, the *preposition → determiner(article) → noun* for the pathway highlighted in red below.

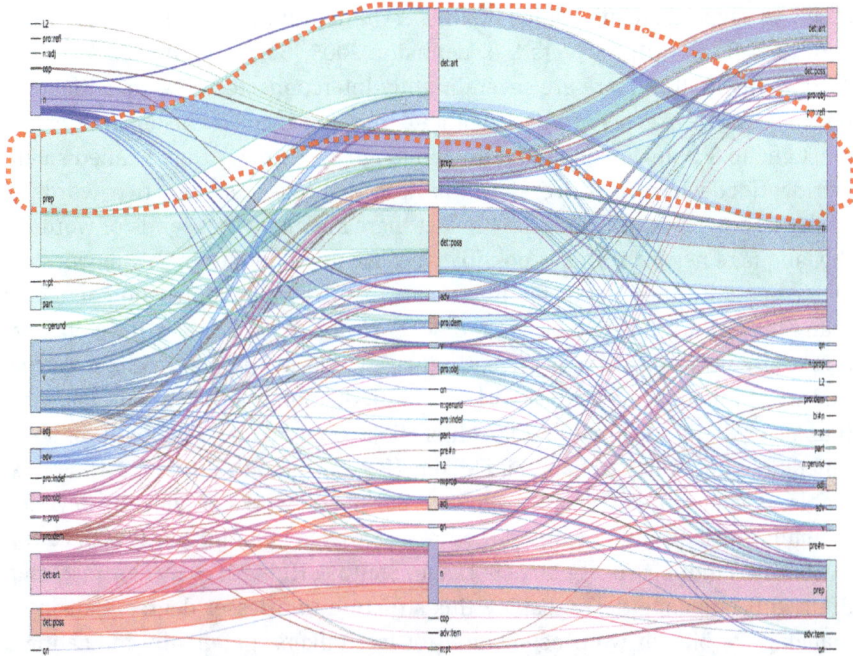

Figure 18: An example of within module trigram grammatical patterns.

To recap, our primary interest concerned whether frequent grammatical (trigram) patterns in the input disassociate by community structure. If they do, then community structure represents an emergent source of grammatical information available to the language learner that is the byproduct of instantiating words and their connections into a dynamic network. First we give an general overview of how the networks developed in line with our expectations – as a sense-check that the community network methodology is working and able to replicate previous findings – and then go on to examine the novel contribution this paper makes, namely, characterizing grammatical patterns within network communities.

As one would expect, by definition of the methodology, the networks become larger and more interconnected over time, as evidenced by the increasing number of nodes and edges as the network grows (a generic feature of dynamic networks widely noted in Banavar, Maritan, & Rinaldo, 1999; Borge-Holthoefer & Arenas, 2010; Cancho & Solé, 2001; Collins & Loftus, 1975; Collins & Quillian, 1969; Hills, Maouene, Maouene, Sheya, & Smith, 2009; Steyvers & Tenenbaum, 2005). Our word-based network displays similar properties to those that focused on semantic relationships (Collins & Quillian 1969; Collins & Loftus 1975; Cancho & Solé 2001; Steyvers & Tenenbaum 2005; Borge-Holthoefer & Arenas 2010), namely, that there are several tightly interconnected clusters with some nodes acting as bridges or hubs to other densely connected clusters. For example, Cancho & Solé demonstrated human language displays the so called small-world effect where the average minimum distance between two words is approximately 2–3 links, despite the fact there are many thousands of words in the language network. This is possible because not all nodes in the network are created equal – there are some hub nodes that are much more interconnected than others. With this combination of local structure combined with global access, these networks become increasingly small-world and approximate a structure that is thought to aid processing and production of efficient language use (Banavar, Maritan & Rinaldo 1999; Hills et al. 2009) and even account for some differences between early and late talkers (Beckage, Smith & Hills 2011). For example, Beckage and colleagues showed that the networks of typically developing children show small world structure as early as 15 months and with as few as 55 words in their vocabulary (Beckage, Smith & Hills 2011). By contrast, children with language delay display this structure to a lesser degree, causing a maladaptive bias in word acquisition for late talkers, potentially indicating a preference for infrequent words. The fact that there is this small-world non-uniform distribution of connectivity allows the community detection algorithm to identify clusters of densely interconnected nodes.

From the grammatical analysis of characteristic pathways through communities, it appears that communities are able to dissociate patterns of grammatical use in CDS. For example, For Fraser's CDs at time point 1, Community 1 contained a *Noun→preposition→noun* frequent pathway, Community 2 *Pronoun(personal)→verb→preposition* and Community 3 *Determiner→adverb→adjective*. For Eleanor's CDS at time point 4 Community 1 identified *Preposition→determiner(article)→noun*, Community 2 *Adjective→noun→adverb,* and Community 3 *Pronoun(interrogative) →Copula→Pronoun(demonstrative)*. Within this general picture, there are interesting individual differences in developmental patterns. For example, for

Eleanor's CDS, the complexity of the plots varies by community size, with the largest communities and smallest communities becoming progressively more complex with each epoch, while the second largest community becomes progressively more skewed, with a small number of strong pathways and a large number of small pathways. For Fraser's CDS, different patterns emerge. The largest community in the final epoch appears more skewed than in the penultimate epoch. The cross-tabulations of Figure 19 summarizes the pattern, showing how the characteristic grammatical pathways disassociate by community structure, that is, one community structure has a different grammatical hub in comparison with another.

The top graph of Figure 19 also shows how the control procedure eventually works to undermine community structure in contrast to the natural community structure growth inherent in language. At the start of the network building there is a period where the control procedure generates more community structure than natural language. At the beginning, the control procedure has lots of sub-communities which are small but meaningless. As the network grows these are subsumed into an ever longer but meaningless string of connected words that is captured by fewer and fewer communities. Natural language shows the opposite pattern with sustained growth in community structure. We know children are sensitive to the kinds of distributional patterns the network instantiates so it seems plausible that community structure could provide an emergent source of information for the learner when constructing their early grammar. Moreover the patterns within communities contained some of the basic grammatical building blocks of English: verbs, nouns, adverbs, adjectives, modals, auxiliaries, and determiners. So, the patterns that are constructed from these units could provide a foothold into the basic *who-did-what-to-whom* that a grammar organizes. Because the grammatical network was tagged with grammatical categories and had the ability to represent transitions between those categories, communities can contain ordered lexical class templates, for example a noun-verb-noun schema able to represent *dog bites man* and *man bites dog*. Grammatical generalizations at an abstraction higher than that level (e.g., Subject- or Agenthood) were not examined here although there is no reason why the same methodology of community detection could not be applied to corpora tagged with that data – the question would be the same in that instance, namely whether community structure can be dissociated by Subjecthood, for example. We chose syntactic class as they represent the least abstracted level away from the words themselves and presumably a level over which ever more abstract categories are later generalized.

Because of some of the analytic complexities involved we focused on the three biggest communities. Just from looking at these three communities though,

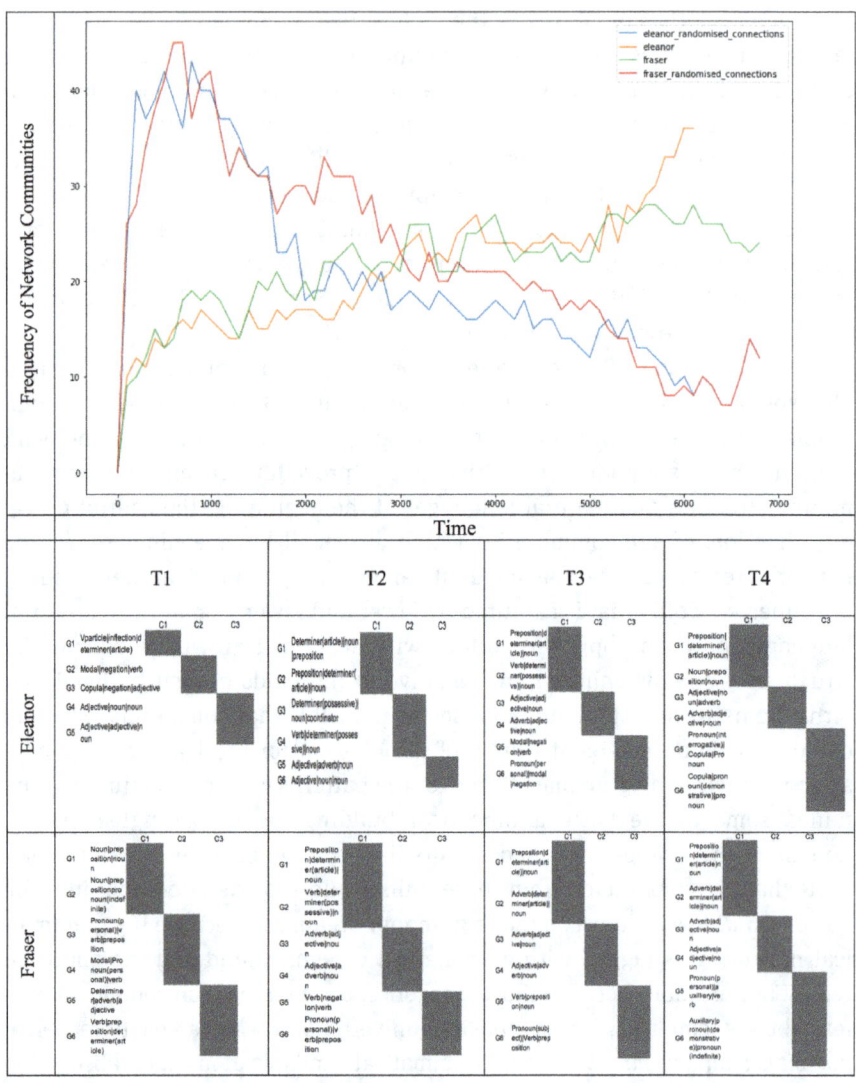

Figure 19: The top graph shows community development for the two networks and their associated randomized controls over time. Beneath the graph is a visual summary of the data presented as cross tabulations and highlights the dissociation between communities (C1-3) and grammatical patterns (G1-6).

it is clear that although there is dissociation across communities at any one time point there is also a fluid characterization of their grammatical pathways within communities across time. For example, the same grammatical pattern is not always the most characteristic of that community across all four time points. To some extent this is to be expected as patterns from smaller communities get subsumed into larger communities as the network grows. Clearly, we need to know more about all the communities for a fuller picture, including whether the communities begin to converge on individual stable grammatical identities after a period of input saturation – something that further investigation could confirm over a larger corpus.

What we hope to offer here is a modest proof-of-concept for the community structure approach to grammatical pattern identification and the potential insight the dynamic network approach can offer. We encourage other researchers to explore the possibilities and limitations of this approach on a larger scale. For example, the scope of this paper was limited to analyzing one language, with two input sources over four time periods and the three largest communities that emerged from that input. A more mechanistic way of recovering characteristic patterns within communities (which was done by hand here) would allow the methodology to be scaled-up to cover more time points, more speakers, more communities and more languages. The cross-linguistic validity of the approach is especially important because, for example, a noun is a noun because of its position relative to its grammatical neighbors: in English, it gets modified an adjective, follows a determiner and precedes a verb. But because the child obviously does not know it is going to be born into an English-speaking community any learning mechanism needs to be robust enough to handle the variation in word order and other aspects of morphosyntactic variation across languages. Because the raw input into the network is words and their transitions (not grammatical categories) it is hopeful that community structure detection would be able to operate with some success cross-linguistically, but it obviously needs to be rigorously tested further. In comparison with previous models (e.g., McCauley & Christiansen, 2019) the architecture of the community detection approach is much simpler and so at present limits the kinds of data we are able to simulate. For example, modelling the trajectory of overgeneralization errors is currently not possible although it is possible to see how network metrics are relevant here too. What the approach loses in its power to demonstrate productivity, it potentially gains in its cognitive plausibility: in a network of interrelated, weighted connections, whose structure evolves over time, it offers a representational format that minimally departs from that of both language and the brain. This, of course, is not a mutually exclusive offer to those more sophisticated models that integrate semantic information or a chunkatory architecture which must surely be part of a more comprehensive story of language acquisition. However, it could be argued that the contribution of this approach is to emphasize how much structure there already is in language when it is presented as a dynamic network of communities, before this information gets fed into these more sophisticated models.

One very interesting way in which the analysis here could be further developed would be to begin to layer the networks and analyze the relationships between layers. The motivation for this is that almost all linguistic theories subscribe to some level of hierarchical organization in language (although they may profoundly disagree where this hierarchy comes from and how detached it becomes from meaning). Most theories admit a role for hierarchy to escape analysis based only on form that, for example, prevents an adequate account of long-distance dependencies or the fact the children readily interpret the novel *the gazer mibbed the toma* as a transitive utterance despite sharing few lexical items with that category in their experience.

In theory community detection offers a way to provide such hierarchical categorization although it has been beyond the scope of the present paper. It would do this by treating the communities that emerge from the CDS (the ones established in the present study) as *the input*, or nodes to second layer of network. The idea here would be that this second layer abstracts away from the form and describes relationships between communities identified at a lower level. The extension to the methodology established here, potentially has important consequences for theories that admit some role for hierarchy. For example, in usage-based approaches to language, grammar is often characterized as a structured inventory of constructions, conceptualized as some sort of organized network of linguistic form and function (Bybee, 2010a; Croft, 2001; Givon, 1995; Goldberg, 2005; Langacker, 1987; Tomasello, 2003). Precisely what this inventory looks like is often not specified in any detail, and where it is, the proposals are often static, highly schematized (viz. hierarchical abstraction) and only partial visualizations of the complete grammatical system. By instantiating language in a dynamic, layered network, we would catch this inventory in the act of being built and visualize what distributional patterns of grammar use might look like for a child acquiring language. In doing so, this approach offers something more concrete, incremental and fleshes out what is meant by the theoretical construct 'structured inventory'.

The communities detected in the CDS examined here are a byproduct of organizing language into a network that is sensitive to the frequency of word use and the transition between words – something that we know adults and children are sensitive to (Bloomfield, 1938, 1973; Braine, 1987; Cartwright & Brent, 1997; Finch & Chater, 1992, 1994; Goldberg, 2005; Harris, 1954; Mintz, 2002, 2003; Mintz et al., 2002; Redington et al., 1998; Schütze, 1993; Tomasello, 2003). It seems plausible to suggest that if this information is available to learner then they might use it as a way of beginning to categorize and organize their grammatical experience. We know language is a classic example of a complex system; with multiple speakers interacting with one another, the way it is adaptive to past behavior and how a speaker's behavior is the consequence of many competing factors that operate on many interrelated time cycles. If some of the complexity of language can be a byproduct of complex dynamic systems, not all of it needs to be actively constructed or organized in advance of experience. That means some of the burden of learning the complexity of language can be outsourced to emergence and the cognitive bandwidth of the children that learn it no longer places the same constraints. In this way, language can sustain intergenerational complexity far beyond the complexity of the learning mechanisms acquiring it.

The average toddler is only just starting to string two words together so at this point in the cultural transmission process the structural complexity of language is almost reduced to zero. In the face of this data compression, it begs the question of how languages have evolved to be complex and how they remain so. The two major theoretical responses addressing this problem have said that either some of the complexity is organized advance of experience (Chomsky, 1957, 1965, 1986, 1993) or that the complexity is actively constructed by the child (Bybee, 2010; Croft, 2001; Givon, 1995; Goldberg, 2005; Langacker, 1987, 1991; Tomasello, 2003). There is a third way to approach this question, compatible with the orthodox dichotomies, that states that some of the complexity in language is an emergent property of many simpler entities interacting with one another, each one of which *is* learnable. In this way, a language can become more complex than it is learnable (e.g., Hopper, 1998, 2015).

A strength of the dynamic network approach is that offers a method of representing language growth that minimally differs from the way language is actually used, and that means the gap between theoretical construct and data is kept small. It also presents a way to ground linguistic representation in a medium that is psychologically plausible, for example, the usage-based proposal that frequently occurring patterns are stored together as templates or schemas can be grounded in the community structure of the network which in turn can be grounded in Hebbian learning principle that neurons that fire together wire together (Hebb, 1949; Lowel & Singer, 1992). Here we formally make this link between distributional learning, the schemas of usage-based theory and the community structure of a network. We hope more researchers from across the linguistic and cognitive theoretical spectrum will find use in this method for visualizing, examining and testing theories about language development.

6.3 Developmental cognitive linguistics, language differences and similarities

We said the horizontal plane of our DST visualization (Figure 15) represents an infinite landscape of possible developmental trajectories for language to develop into and thus an infinite range of possible languages. Here we need to say something about why we see the languages we do see, rather than the ones we could, but don't. When we represent memory, inhibition, attention, categorization, and social cognition as attractor basins in the developmental landscape, they show a gradience of probability, with those at bottom of the basins representing spaces with a strong likelihood of attraction and those on top of the plane representing near impossible outcomes, that is, near impossible languages given the way human cognition works. For example, unlikely outcomes include a language that required syntactic coordination beyond working memory capacity; an inventory of constructions that exceeds procedural memory; a morphological marker that was so subtle as to always fall outside of attention; a regular-irregular pattern that was too powerful for inhibition to control; a category of lexical items that was behaviorally identically to another; a pattern of linguistic use that required anti-normative distributions and so on.

A useful analogy with linguistic sound systems might be the following. The International Phonetic Alphabet (Figure 20) maps all unique sounds in

International Phonetic Alphabet (IPA)   ˌɪntəˈnæʃn·l fəˈnɛtɪk ˈælfəˌbɛt

Consonants (pulmonic)

	Bilabial	Labio-dental	Dental	Alveolar	Post-alveolar	Retroflex	Palatal	Velar	Uvular	Pharyngeal	Glottal
Plosive	p b			t d		ʈ ɖ	c ɟ	k g	q ɢ		ʔ
Nasal	m	ɱ		n		ɳ	ɲ	ŋ	ɴ		
Trill	ʙ			r					ʀ		
Tap or flap		ⱱ		ɾ		ɽ					
Fricative	ɸ β	f v	θ ð	s z	ʃ ʒ	ʂ ʐ	ç ʝ	x ɣ	χ ʁ	ħ ʕ	h ɦ
Lateral fricative				ɬ ɮ							
Approximant		ʋ		ɹ		ɻ	j	ɰ			
Lateral approximant				l		ɭ	ʎ	ʟ			

Figure 20: The International Phonetic Alphabet.

every language to one symbol and one symbol to a unique sound, a one-to-one correspondence system. When the consonant sounds are plotted with place of articulation (top row) against and the manner of articulation (left column) they describe a space of theoretically possible sounds. The cells with symbols in them have been attested by typologists in languages across the world – these are the sounds we know people use. The cells that do not have a symbol in are thought to be possible, but we have not found a language that uses them . . . yet. When we discover a new one, it is added to the chart, as last happened in 2005 when the labiodental flap was introduced – a sound attested in seventy African languages and fully incorporated into the phonological system of at least twenty. The cells that are shaded are thought to be impossible, given the human articulatory capacity. A velar trill would require a flap of skin loose enough to vibrate at the back of your mouth or a lateral glottal would somehow require letting air around the sides of your tongue half way down your throat. These are the easy ones to explain: we do not see them because we cannot use them.

What about the ones we could see but don't? As indicated, this is more a matter of history, with new instances filling the niches when they are coined and others disappearing when a language dies. From generation to generation cultural inheritance is exploring the bounds of what the human articulation system can do. Fricatives seem like linguistically popular solutions and can be thought of as the attractor basins of our dynamic landscape. The flat plain of the dynamic landscape is equivalent to the dark areas of the phonetic alphabet – with near-zero percent probability. The analogy to developmental cognitive linguistics is this. What we have tried to show is that the rows and columns of our social and cognitive makeup define a space of possible languages in the same way that the place and manner of articulation limit the space of possible human sounds. Note the gap between what is impossible and what is attested – the possible but unattested. This can be thought of as the difference between cognition *permitting* a particular language vs. cognition *entailing* a particular language (Ibbotson 2013b). The impossible sounds are a matter of our biology; the possible sounds are a matter of our biology *and* history. The impossible syntax is a matter of our cognition; the possible syntax is a matter of our cognition *and* history.

Because languages need to evolve through the bottleneck of what is cognitively possible to learn, every generation, the same forces that constrain language development for the child are the same ones that constrain language evolution over generations. For example, the typological popularity for local structure (e.g., sounds are grouped into words, morphological markers usually modify adjacent elements, adjacent words clump into phrases) is because the languages that failed to adapt to the cognitive niche of the Now-Or-Never general processing constraint are not around to be learned (Christiansen & Chater, 2016).

Word order provides another good example. The world's languages can be categorized on the basis of how they order the basic constituents of a sentence which function to coordinate who did what to whom. Over historical time frames the serial position becomes grammaticalized into subject, verb, and object position, hence (Givón, 1979, p.208–209) aphorism "today's syntax is yesterday's pragmatic discourse." Of the six logically possible word orders this creates, some are much more prevalent than others. A survey of 402 languages reveals that the majority of languages favor either SOV (44.78%) or SVO (41.79%) with the other possibilities – VSO (9.20%), VOS (2.99%), OVS (1.24%), or OSV (0.00%) – significantly less popular (Tomlin, 1986). There are several mechanisms that could be at work here to create this typological distribution. For example, we know there is a cross-linguistic preference to speak of given information before information that is new to the discourse (Bock & Irwin, 1980; Ferreira & Yoshita, 2003; MacWhinney & Bates, 1978; Prat-Sala & Branigan, 2000), a preference for shorter dependency length (Hawkins 1994; Hawkins 2007) and a preference for efficient information transfer (Maurits, Perfors & Navarro 2010). Christiansen (2000; Christiansen & Devlin, 1997) presented converging evidence from connectionist simulations, typological language analyses, and artificial language learning in normal adults and aphasic patients, that basic cognitive constraints on sequential learning explains a large proportion of the distribution we see in basic word orders across the world.

What about the languages that are possible, given the way cognition works, yet will still don't see (or haven't seen yet)? Here is where we need to consider how languages have evolved over time – "a linguist who asks "Why?" must be a historian" (Haspelmath, 1999, p.205). Dunn and colleagues (2011) used computational phylogenetics to show that typological variation in word order could be explained as a function of the iterated learning processes of cultural evolution. Croft and colleagues (2011) provide criticism of their methodology – the absence of any Type II error analysis to assess the rate of false negatives, the absence of contact effects and the nature of the phylogenies used – although they are in favor of the general approach. These criticisms do not undermine the wider point though, namely, that popularity of word orders across languages can be explained in terms of general cognitive principles (e.g., pressure for iconicity of form and function, or concise representation of salient/frequent concepts). *Why any particular language* has come to the combination of solutions it has, needs reference to its historical antecedents/evolution (Bybee 2010b).

In the context of historical antecedents, an analogy with biological evolution may be informative. Evolution has to work with what it's got, cumulatively tinkering with solutions to problems that have worked well enough for previous generations, but which might not be considered "ideal" if one could start afresh (e.g., the backward installed retina in humans). An evolutionary biologist could ask the question *Why do we only see the mammals we do given all the possible mammals that could exist but don't?* For the biologist, today's mammals could be thought of as a living record of competing motivations, that have over time explored some of the space of what is physiological plausible for a mammal to be. For a particular feature of the animal's development, for example the skeleton, a bat could be thought of as occupying one corner of this space while an elephant skeleton is in another – extreme variations on an underlying theme. Different languages are also a history of competing motivations that have explored some of the space of what is communicatively and cognitively possible. Over time languages have radiated to different points in this space. For a particular feature of the language development, for example the sound system, in one corner there might be a three-vowel system (e.g., Greenlandic, an Eskimo-Aleut language) while in another corner is a language with 24 vowels (e.g., !Xu, a Khoisan language). Importantly, as language is a complex adaptive system, evolving toward an extreme in one direction will have functional consequences for the system as a whole. Just as a bat skeleton will place certain functional demands on the rest of its physiology, so it is with language. In languages with freer word order, the communicative work that is done by a fixed word order in other languages must be picked up by other aspects of the system, e.g., morphology and pragmatic inference. The analogy with biological evolution might be useful in another way. The eye has independently evolved in several different species, converging on a similar solution to a similar engineering problem. The major nuts and bolts of grammar (e.g., word-order, case-agreement, tense-aspect) that appear time after time in the world's languages could be thought of as historically popular solutions to similar communicative and coordination problems, such as sharing, requesting, and informing. What this means is that the cognitive constraints can rule out some languages and permit a possible space of languages but might not entail any particular language in the absence of an historical perspective – the boundaries of the space of cognition do not make contact with that of language in way that allows those predictions.

6.4 'Doing' developmental cognitive linguistics

At its heart, this approach is about the relationship between domains of the mind therefore it is natural that many of the sources of evidence have come from correlational designs (development of cognitive aspect x shapes, constrains, predicts language ability y) although we have also seen evidence from other sources such as longitudinal designs and training studies of cognitive transfer. When looking for such relationships it is important to control for factors that might be masking the social and cognitive drivers shaping language development. One such aspect is the effect of frequency in language.

Over recent decades, the availability of online, densely sampled, longitudinal corpora have given researchers a much clearer picture of what child language looks like: the frequency with which children say things, what kinds of errors they make and when they acquire words and phrases. What has become evident is that the nature of the language they hear around them – particularly the frequency distribution of words and phrases – is a reliable predictor of the frequency distribution in the child language forms (Ambridge, Kidd, Rowland, & Theakston, 2015; Diessel, 2007; Tomasello, 2003). For example, in a hierarchical regression analysis by Naigles and Hoff-Ginsberg (1998) input frequency accounted for around 90% of the variance in the frequency of verb use in child speech. Similar patterns have been found for adjectives (Blackwell, 2005) and nouns (Goodman, Dale & Li 2008). The way children use verbs (as either transitives, intransitives, or both) is strongly related to the way their mothers used those particular verbs (Theakston et al. 2001). Whether children mark verbs for tense and agreement is related to the way they hear those same verbs used – marked infinite clauses or unmarked in non-finite clauses–by their mothers (Pine et al. 2005). Children's acquisition of some particular grammatical morphemes in English (e.g. past tense *–ed*, plural *–s*, progressive *–ing*) is facilitated when mothers use these morphemes as immediate recasts of the child's utterances that are missing them (Farrar 1990; Farrar 1992). The acquisition order of *wh*-questions is predicted by the frequency with which particular wh-words and verbs occur in children's input (Rowland & Pine, 2000; Rowland, Pine, Lieven, & Theakston, 2003). Children's proportional use of *me-for-I* errors (e.g., *me do it*) correlates with their caregivers' proportional use of me in 1st person singular preverbal contexts (e.g., *let me do it*). Further-more, the verbs that children produce in *me*-error utterances appear in complex sentences containing *me* in the input more often than verbs that do not appear in *me-for-I* errors in the children's speech (Kirjavainen, Theakston & Lieven 2009). The pattern of negator emergence (*no* → *not* →' *nt*) follows the frequency of negators in the input, i.e. negators used frequently in the input are the first to emerge in the child's speech (Cameron-Faulkner, Lieven & Theakston 2007).

The null-hypothesis or default position that follows from this body of work is that, all other things being equal, the frequency with which a child hears a piece of language is reflected in the frequency they produce that piece of language. However, even if input frequency effects explained all of the child frequency variance it would contribute little to the explanatory adequacy of any theory of language acquisition–the why and how of language acquisition. First, distributions are not a theory of acquisition themselves but a manifestation of the mechanisms that created them. An example of this is the robust finding that in any large corpus, including Child Speech (CS) and Child Directed Speech (CDS), most word types and word combinations are used relatively infrequently and a few are used very frequently (Zipf 1935). This Zipfian distribution may point to deeper principles at work, (e.g., "least effort" Cancho & Sole, 2003) but it is not itself a learning mechanism. Moreover, similarities between child and adult speech can arise from a variety of sources including fully abstract representations (e.g. Noun Verb Noun), partially specified schemas (e.g., *She hits* Noun) or memorized lexical chunks (e.g., *That's right*; cf. Pine, Freudenthal, Krajewski, & Gobet, 2013 and Yang, 2013 on determiner use). So noting coordination between CS and CDS does not in itself shed light on the acquisition process, much less so why these correlations should occur in humans but not in other species.

Second, all other things are not equal. As much of Part II of this book demonstrated, there are social, cognitive and linguistic factors that operate above and beyond the effects of frequency. These include processing factors such how easy a word is to segment from the speech stream and articulate (Christophe & Dupoux 1996; Monaghan & Christiansen 2010; Vihman & Vihman 2011); semantic factors such as the word's imageability, semantic transparency or grammatical class (Bird, Franklin, & Howard, 2001; Gentner, 1982; Narasimhan & Gullberg, 2011); social pragmatic factors such as whether there is an easily identifiable referent (Gentner, 1982); whether the word occurs during episodes of joint-attention (Tomasello & Farrar, 1986); is directed to the child rather than overheard in speech (Shneidman & Goldin-Meadow 2012; Weisleder & Fernald 2013) and how knowledgeable the speaker is (Sabbagh & Baldwin 2001). These factors have been shown to influence how learnable a word is, which has consequences for how frequently that word is produced by the child. For example, if there are inherent semantic properties of nouns that make them a conceptually easier category to learn than verbs (e.g., Gentner, 1982) then we would expect the child's frequency distribution of nouns and verbs to reflect this.

The variance not explained by input frequency can tell us more about why and how children are constructing their language because it acts as a window into the social and cognitive biases that drive development. To the extent that we all share common elements of the developmental path of our cognitive and social faculties, we should see evidence of these supra-frequency effects manifesting themselves across different languages, albeit using different linguistic resources to do so. What is needed then, is a standardized method for partialling out the variance attributable to frequency so that we can see what might be driving the shape of language development. Ibbotson and colleagues created the Frequency Filter to address this need by (Ibbotson, Hartman & Björkenstam 2018) simultaneously combining data from the child, the care-giver, multiple languages, across multiple time points. We then apply it in three different linguistic contexts and conclude what the likely relevant social and cognitive biases are that the filter reveals. We make the code that implements the filter publicly available as an R-Package (with notes) for other researchers to use here https://github.com/rosemm/FrequencyFilter

The Frequency Filter begins by counting the frequency of items that occur both in CS and CDS. For example, the word *me* might be said 15 times by the child and it might be heard 25 times in CDS. Note that because the goal is to assess frequency of use (rather than simply if a word occurs at all, as may be the case for studies of age of acquisition (e.g., Roy, Frank, DeCamp, Miller, & Roy, 2015), the only forms included in the analyses are words that occur in both child and caregiver speech. As an example, Figure 21(A) shows the result of plotting frequency counts of pronouns for one month of development from the Thomas corpus (Lieven, Salomo, & Tomasello, 2009; MacWhinney, 2000).

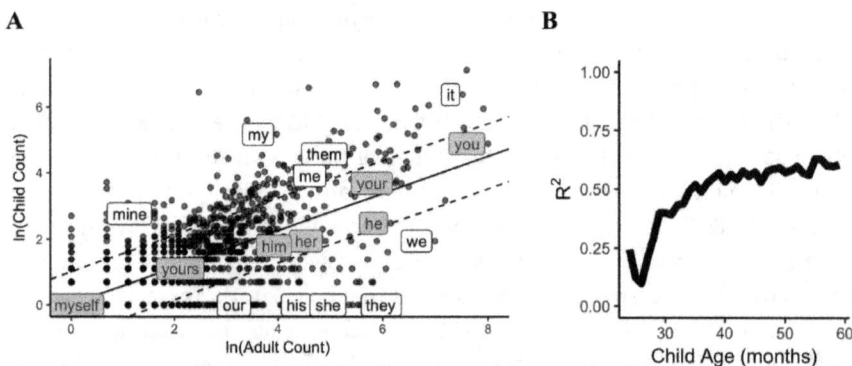

Figure 21: (A) An example of the relationship between the frequency of items in CS and CDS plotted as a regression line for child Thomas at 33 months. Labels are provided to highlight the pronouns, with those falling more than 1 SD from the regression line shown in white and those closer to the regression line in grey. As would be expected, the distribution profile is Zipfian so the results are shown on a log-log scale. (B) Percent variance in CS log frequencies that can be attributed to CDS log frequency (squared Pearson Correlation Coefficient) as a function of age for one child (Thomas).

Figure 21(A) is a static, vertical slice of the corpus summarizing the relationship between CS and CDS for one period of time. When we repeat this process for the entire corpus it is possible to lay these vertical slices end to end and produce a dynamic plot of how the strength of the relationship changes over time, Figure 21(B). As we would expect, the proportion of variance in CS that is explained by CDS increases as the child's use of items begins to approximate that of the use that they hear around them. As well as showing the strength of association (R^2) in the frequency distribution of Child Directed Speech and Child Speech, it is possible to describe the extent to which each word deviates from the line of best fit by calculating its residual as displayed in Figure 22. This gives us a continuous measure of the extent to which frequency in CS differs from that which we would expect given the frequency in CDS.

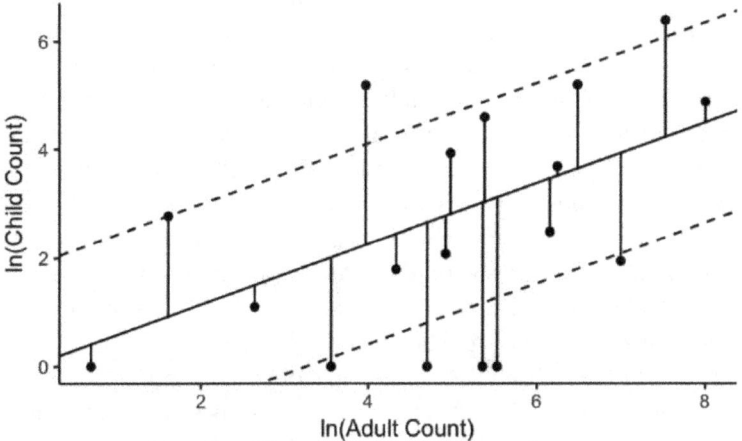

Figure 22: An example showing positive and negative residuals from the regression between CS and CDS for child Thomas at 33 months. Points represent words, with vertical lines showing the difference between each word's log CS count and the log CS count that would be predicted from the log CDS count, shown as a solid regression line with dashed lines showing +−1SD.

Assuming CDS is on x-axis and CS is plotted on the y-axis, those items that are above the line of best fit have positive residual values and are defined as overrepresented in CS. These items are produced by the child more frequently than we would expect given how much they hear them. Those items that are below the line of best fit have negative residual values and are defined as underrepresented in CS. These items are produced by the child less frequently than we would expect given how much they hear them. To facilitate comparison, the R-code in the Frequency Filter package includes the option to standardize residuals within each child's current age (i.e. each item's residual is divided by the standard deviation of the residuals for all items for that child at that age point, expressing it as a Z score). As we have stated, a wide range of corpus work suggests that the null-hypothesis is that the frequency with which a child hears a piece of language predicts the frequency at which they produce that piece of language (Ambridge et al., 2015; Diessel, 2007; Tomasello, 2003). The residuals give us a continuous way to measure child language use that deviates substantially from that null hypothesis. Patterns in which words are over- versus under-represented in child speech indicate a process at work that is above and beyond that of frequency and so may be a candidate for a cognitive or social developmental process.

Ibbotson demonstrated how the tool works in three domains of language learning and across six languages. The results demonstrate the usefulness of this approach as well as providing deeper insight into three areas of language production and acquisition: egocentric language use, the learnability of nouns versus verbs, and imageability. Specifically they found that in the case of the English and Swedish Pronoun system, that remaining variance may be explained with respect to the communicative goals of the child and their developing cognitive and social world. In the case of noun and verb use in English and Japanese, that remaining variance may be explained by the relative ease-of-acquisition of nouns versus verbs early on in development. And in the case of noun use, some that variance is explained by how imageable that noun is for English, French, Japanese, Italian and Spanish.

To take one of the experiments as an example of the tool in use, study two looked at noun and verb use in English and Japanese. We chose verbs and nouns because there is a long-standing debate in the child acquisition literature as to whether nouns represent a conceptually easier category to learn than verbs (Au, Dapretto, & Song, 1994; Bornstein et al., 2004; Choi & Gopnik, 1995; Gentner, 1982; Kim, McGregor, & Thompson, 2000; Tardif, 1996; Tardif, Gelman, & Xu, 1999; Tardif, Shatz, & Naigles, 1997). The idea is that the world-to-word mapping for verbs is just more difficult for children to learn than it is for nouns. Nouns have more clearly individuated, concrete referents in perception whereas verbs include only part of the available relational information and vary more so across languages (e.g., Bowerman & Choi, 2003; Casad & Langacker, 2005; Levinson, 1996; Slobin, 1996; Talmy, 1985). If learning nouns is easier for these reasons, it should be a universal fact of acquisition, and we should see this advantage manifest across different languages. To the extent that nouns are easier to learn, nouns should be relatively overrepresented in CS when compared to verbs. It could also be that properties of individual languages make the acquisition of nouns or verbs more or less difficult. For example, Gentner (1982) tested specific input factors, including word order, verb final, relative morphological transparency, and patterns of language teaching that resulted in a "verb-friendliness" score for each of the six languages considered. On this scale, Japanese was rated as more "verb-friendly" than English.

However, Gentner concluded that, while linguistic input factors do influence the degree of the noun advantage, they do not outweigh the semantic-conceptual advantage of nouns mapping to objects. A purely input-driven explanation would predict no universal advantage to noun learning once the cross-linguistic effects had been taken into account. Nouns tend to be acquired earlier and represent a larger proportion of children's vocabulary. This finding has been replicated for German, Mandarin, Kaluli, Japanese, Turkish (Gentner, 1982), Spanish (Jackson-Maldonado et al. 1993), French (Bassano 2000), Dutch, Hebrew and Korean (Bornstein et al., 2004). However, none of these studies controlled for levels of nouns and verbs in CDS in the way we do here. Of those studies that have considered CDS, some have not paired the CDS with CS (Fernald & Morikawa 1993; Gopnik, Choi & Baumberger 1996) or they did pair CDS with CS but they did so for one language–therefore limiting the cognitive universality of any claims–or the time periods were collapsed–so could not provide any picture of developmental change (Goldfield, 1993; Huttenlocher, Haight, Bryk, Seltzer, & Lyons, 1991; Kim et al., 2000; Naigles & Hoff-Ginsberg, 1998; Tardif et al., 1997). Choi and Gopnik (1995) did pair CDS with CS but not the same child-caregiver dyads, and so not controlling for inter-parent variability, while Au et al. (1994) collected data under different conditions for different language groups. As part of a wider set of experiments Tardif et al. (1999) compared the ratio of verbs to nouns spoken by mothers in Mandarin and English, which was then compared to the verb/noun ratio that children spoke in a session of pretend play. They concluded a significant noun bias when the ratio differed statistically from chance – a 50/50 noun/verb ratio. We argue that in this case the null hypothesis and baseline should have been the noun/verb ratio in *CDS*. If this criterion was adopted they may well have found stronger evidence for a significant noun advantage not only for English but for Mandarin as well. Apart from this analytical difference, our study differs in that it uses a much larger corpus, it explicitly lays out a generalized procedure for controlling for CDS frequency, and includes a developmental dimension rather than one time frame. Some authors (e.g., Au et al., 1994; Caselli et al., 1995; Cheng, 1994; Choi & Gopnik, 1995; Tardif, 1996) have argued that spontaneous speech samples are not an appropriate measure because they oversample children's use of highly frequent items, which disproportionately affects verbs because of their low type-token frequencies in adult speech. However, in our procedure, this over/under sampling issue no longer represents the same concern as each CDS word acts as control for its CS pair. Gentner (1982, p.317) notes that "Without precise descriptions of the parents' input to children, we cannot definitively rule out the possibility that these early nouns are simply the words spoken most frequently to children". Because online corpora have been made available since this was written we can now provide the description Genter called for.

Our analysis (Figure 23) confers with other studies showing an early noun bias (Au et al., 1994; Bornstein et al., 2004; Choi & Gopnik, 1995; Gentner, 1982; Kim et al., 2000; Tardif, 1996; Tardif et al., 1999, 1997). However, unlike these previous studies, we found this bias with a methodology that rules out some confounding explanations. Because the Frequency Filter used CDS-CS pairs that were caregiver-child dyads across languages, we could control for input frequency and language-specific explanations as causes of this bias. Furthermore, we have been able to show a more fine-grained, dynamic picture by revealing how this noun-preference attenuates and eventually reverses overtime. The fact that the analytic tool can be applied at multiple time points is an important strength of the tool. The analysis collapsing across time points obscures the developmental effect between nouns and verb use as the early positive residuals cancel out the later negative ones and vice versa.

We make the Frequency Filter openly available as an R-package in the hope that other researchers will take the work forward and adapt this tool to study their own questions regarding language development. This could be as exploratory research with no *a priori* assumptions about the nature of over- and underrepresented categories to generate hypothesis for further corpus or experimental investigation, or it could be used to test existing hypotheses, such as was the case in our studies. An interesting avenue would be to move beyond the lexical items considered here to consider morphosyntactic phenomena and argument structure constructions. Whether one approaches the questions of language development from a nativist or constructionist perspective, all theories seeking descriptive and explanatory adequacy need a method of accounting for frequency effects – to that end the tool we propose here will be of utility across the theoretical spectrum. To answer some of the tough questions of language development we need to attack the problem from multiple perspectives. The Frequency Filter does this by allowing researchers to simultaneously combine data from the child, the caregiver, multiple languages, across multiple time points to make inferences about what might be driving the shape of language development.

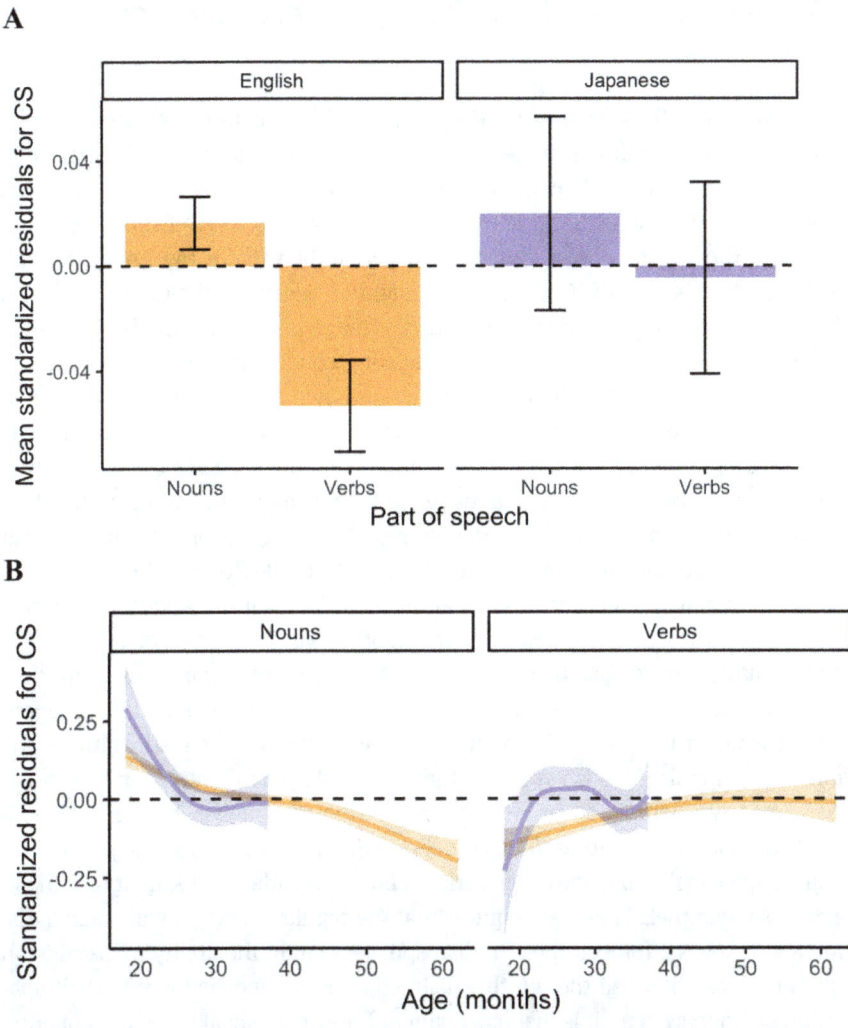

Figure 23: (A). Standardized residuals for noun and verb use CS in English and Japanese, collapsing across age. Positive values indicate overrepresentation in CS relative to CDS, and negative values indicate underrepresentation. Error bars are 95% CI. (B) Standardized residuals over developmental time for nouns and verbs in English and Japanese. The lines are Loess smoothed curves with the 95% CI.

6.5 Language constraining the degrees of freedom on cognition

Most of the book has focused on the ways in which cognition narrows the degrees of freedom of linguistic generalizations for conceptual and historical reasons. But the interaction between cognition and language means the information flows in both directions, and the idea that language has a significant role in determining thought has been most intensively studied under the linguistic relatively hypothesis (Whorf 1956). In their insightful review on the topic, Wolff and Holmes find no support for the idea that language determines the basic categories of thought or that it overwrites pre-existing conceptual distinctions. On empirical and conceptual grounds they rule-out two versions of the Whorfian hypothesis, namely that language and thought are the same thing or that there is a one-to-one mapping between language and thought. Instead they argue that the evidence points towards language making some distinctions difficult to avoid – language as a 'spotlight' on cognition – as well as for the proposal that language can augment certain types of thinking (Wolff & Holmes 2011).

If the language you use is constantly requiring you to carve the semantic space of the world in one way rather than another way it could have been carved, then it makes sense that these distinctions themselves become foregrounded, privileged and easier to access in memory, attention and categorization, independent of whether language is being used to reason about these distinctions at the time. For example, Turkish requires the speaker to take a stance on whether a past event was witnessed or not witnessed whereas English does not (Slobin 1996). Obviously the witness/not witness distinction is not made impossible to English speakers by not speaking Turkish, but it is made more salient to Turkish speakers when their language requires that the regularly engage with such a distinction. Likewise, for example, English speakers retain the ability to distinguish tight and loose fit, even though this distinction is not encoded within their spatial preposition system, it is just more salient for Korean speakers who frequently must encode it (Hespos & Spelke 2004).

The permeable boundary between cognition and language also predicts that when the two conceptual systems align with each other, the speed and accuracy of judgments improve, and when they are in conflict, they reduce (Winawer et al. 2007). Boroditsky (2003) and her colleagues found support for this 'language as meddler' idea by showing that Spanish and German speakers' ability to learn associations between proper and common nouns (e.g., Tom and apple) showed interference when the grammatical gender of the common noun differed from the biological gender of the proper noun's referent. Recall from our examination of event cognition in Chapter 3 that Papafragou found significant differences in the eye-movements of native Greek and English speakers that corresponded to the differences in the way their language encoded manner and path. But when they watched the same videos with no expectation to engage their language the eye-movements were largely the same (Papafragou, Hulbert & Trueswell 2008).

Language can also push the boundaries of what cognition can do, for example there is evidence to suggest that exact magnitude calculation requires language (Dehaene et al. 1999; Gordon 2004; Frank et al. 2008; Gordon 2010) as opposed to the numerosity that merely discriminates large and small quantities and that is present pre-linguistically and in non-human species (Dehaene, 1997; Gallistel, 1990; Wynn, 1995). Language may also have a crucial role in exercising the mindreading ability to higher levels of flexibility. For example de Villiers and colleagues have found that the language delays of deaf children have a very significant impact on their false belief reasoning even when the tasks are nonverbal: the more impoverished their language, the later is their false belief understanding with some children not passing the false belief until 8 years old (de Villiers, 2005; de Villiers & de Villiers, 2000; Peterson & Siegal, 1995; Woolfe, Want, & Siegal, 2002).

So, what does this mean for Developmental Cognitive Linguistics? First, these findings are consistent with the idea of significant interaction between language and cognition and that the regular use of language can lead people to prefer one construal of the world over others. None of the findings imply that people are unable to use certain conceptual distinctions that are not afforded to them by their language. This means the conceptual playing field is wider than the area that language occupies – not the other way around (see above on the difference between cognition *permitting* vs. *entailing* language). Second, note that for all the areas of cognition where language has been found to meddle with, highlight or augment cognition – spatial categorization, intention-reading, color perception – they are all beginning to emerge before language. It is language that first must accommodate to the landscape of cognition even if language then immediately responds by making future cognitive decisions more or less likely. That is why our focus has been on memory, inhibition, attention, categorization and analogy because they emerge earlier in development than does language, and so they have the greatest effect on canalizing the course of language development. Language internal processes (e.g., syntactic and semantic bootstrapping; language as spotlight, augmenter and meddler) can only occur once language is "off the ground", and that is why we have spent more space in this book devoted to the cognitive and social prerequisites that makes language possible.

Again, the best hope for understanding such complex interactions seems to be through theoretical frameworks like that of the dynamic systems approach. Recall from the Memory chapter the debate as to whether increases in short term verbal memory allow for greater vocabulary development (Adams & Gathercole, 1995; Avons, Wragg, Cupples, & Lovegrove, 1998; Baddeley, Gathercole, & Papagno, 1998; Leclercq & Majerus, 2010) or vocabulary growth expands the boundaries of what short-term memory can do (Fowler 1991; Metsala 1999; Bowey 2006). Likewise, this kind of transactional modelling (Figure 24 below) is evident in the social/cognition/language interface: higher levels of perspective-taking motivate more sophisticated use of mental-state language and in turn, an expanding repertoire of mental state language repeatedly highlights different psychological perspectives.

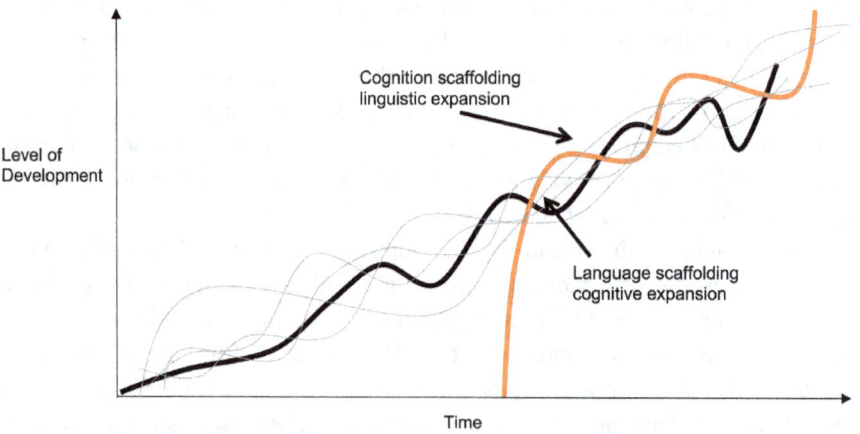

Figure 24: By the time language emerges, general cognition has a "head start". Dark black line represents the average cognitive growth of individual capacities such as memory, categorization, social cognition, attention and inhibition, faint grey lines. By the time language emerges, the structures, processes and biases of general cognition are there for language to use. Thereafter sometimes language scaffolds some cognitive expansion or increased efficacy and sometimes the reverse.

6.6 A test of the directionality of cognitive transfer

By now you might be in broad acceptance of the idea that domain-general cognition plays a significant role in shaping language acquisition, comprehension and production. Even by that admission, there is still a huge amount of research needed in order for us to pin down the precise dynamics of the relationship. To understand more about the directionality of this interaction, PhD candidate Ernesto Roque-Gutierrez examined whether working memory training could improve syntactic ability and/or vice versa. Recall that the cognitive linguistics approach is a hypothesis about the relationship between domains of the mind and it is therefore expected that many of the sources of evidence are correlational in nature: development of cognitive aspect *x* shapes, constrains, predicts language ability *y*. A more powerful demonstration of the causal interaction between the two would be shown if by *training* someone on ability *x* they became better at ability *y*. Not only this, but by creating randomly assigned language-only, memory-only training groups (and a control) we could begin unpick which way around the interaction runs, Figure 25.

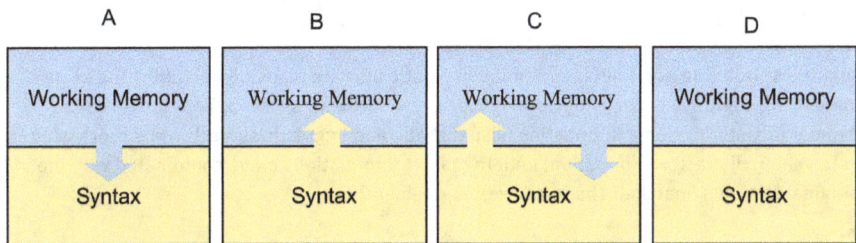

Figure 25: Four hypotheses regarding the relationship between syntax and working memory. Improved working memory performance will transfer into improved syntactic ability, but not the other way around (A); improved syntactic ability will transfer into working memory performance, but not the other way around (B); interactions between working memory and syntax will run in both directions (C); interactions will run in neither direction (D).

Important in this exploration would be selecting a (non-linguistic) working memory task that plausibly engages the kinds of cognitive operations thought to be at work in particular syntactic operations, for example, the kind of long-distance dependencies we first encountered in Chapter 1. Recall Gathercole and colleagues' (2019) predicted cognitive transfer relied on the creation of novel routines that are common across both trained and untrained activities and that are functionally required by both tasks in order to succeed. Applying this reasoning to working memory and syntax in this study Figure 26 shows the functional analogy between the non-linguistic and linguistic tasks.

Using a pre- post-test randomized control trial with 104 Spanish-speaking children learning English (Mean age 7;8), we assigned them to one of four counterbalanced groups [1] memory-only training using the N-back test [2] training on Spanish subject-verb agreement [3] training on English subject-verb agreement [4] control with tuition as normal. (We were also interested the effect of second language learning but this is subsidiary to the main point we are making here). After 6.5 weeks of language or memory training (16 sessions*6.67 hours) each group was given the same tests of working memory and syntactic ability post-

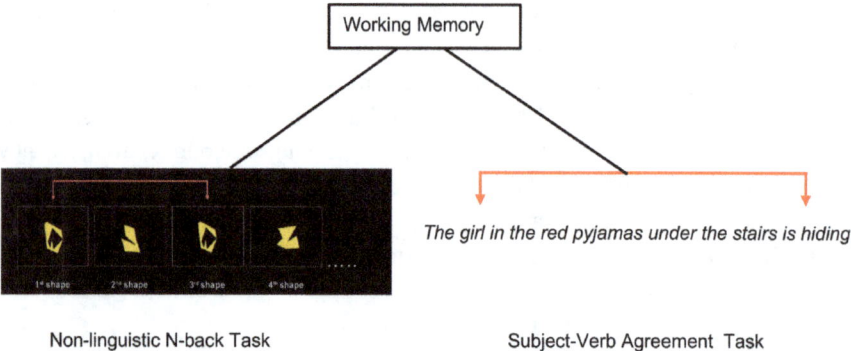

Figure 26: Both the non-linguistic and the linguistic task are plausibly recruiting the same underlying cognitive capacity of working memory. In order to succeed, both tasks require temporarily storing some information (visual shape and linguistic subject) while processing intervening distractor information, until the target information can be coordinated with the original stimulus (matched shape and verb-agreement).

test as they were pre-test. We found working memory training significantly improved children's syntactic performance ([1] vs.[4]) and moreover that working memory training was *as effective* as language training in improving syntactic ability (no significant difference [1] vs. [2]). The effect was less pronounced in the second-language learning condition ([1] vs. [3]) but followed the same pattern. Importantly, the reverse was not true: training children on syntax had no measurable effect on their short-term memory abilities. So, overall we were able to support hypothesis A (Figure 25) as a model of language-cognition interaction and to our knowledge this is the first demonstration that there is cognitive transfer from memory to syntax but not vice versa. It was as if training was able to transfer up the left hand branch of Figure 26 and down the right hand branch but not the reverse. Again, these results fit the general theme of the data bought together for this book: the primacy of general-cognition over language and the deep interconnection between the two.

6.7 Conclusions

In 'Language as an Adaptation to the Cognitive Niche', Pinker states (2010, p.21)

> One alternative is that language is not an adaptation itself, but a manifestation of more general cognitive abilities, such as 'general intelligence', 'a symbolic capacity', 'cultural learning', 'mimesis', or 'hierarchically organized behavior' . . . If so, these more general

cognitive capacities would be the adaptation. These alternatives are difficult to evaluate, because no one has spelled out a mechanistic theory of 'general intelligence' or 'cultural learning' that is capable of acquiring human language.

Hopefully the evidence presented here has shown that we have moved beyond notions of 'general intelligence' and presented a degree of mechanistic detail that shows how human language is made possible because of its deep integration with cognition. Where we have examined how language recycles and repurposes the structure and processes written through cognition, these examples have come from the heart of the language system, for example prototype categorization effects for the transitive construction (Ibbotson et al. 2012); attentional grounding of Subjecthood (Ibbotson, Lieven & Tomasello 2013); inhibitory control for verb morphology (Ibbotson & Kearvell-White 2015). So cognition interacts with language not just at the periphery but at its core and moreover, the kinds of linguistic systems it interacts with are typologically widespread. Given language is a permeable system, always losing some information and gaining some information from other mental systems, that means there are behaviors internal to the language system that can never be explained by rules unique to that system. It also means there are going to be a set of language problems that will never fall if a language-internal analysis is the only one that is pursued. This gives us reason to think we should shift the burden of proof onto showing how the development of a linguistic ability cannot be explained in terms of the development of a deeper, more general cognitive ability first.

Something in our human nature allows language to happen and whatever that turns out to be, it is of significance because it answers two of the most stubborn and non-trivial problems in developmental science: the generation of syntactic generalizations and the mechanism that constrain them. The hope is that other researchers will entertain linguistic-internal accounts for language phenomena only after they have ruled-out the possibility they are manifestations of deeper, wider and simpler principles of cognition, and as such, general-cognitive explanations will come to represent the default first line of enquiry. Some recurrent themes have proved particularly important in this story:

- Examples from memory, attention, inhibition and categorization show human maturational constraints, developmental bottlenecks, and biases of cognition are adaptive for language learning and have created the fitness landscape against which language had to adapt. Moreover, the sequence with which these capacities unfold, and the incremental exposure to data that creates, is important for dampening the combinatorial possibilities of what language can be.
- Because learning constrains and shapes what kind of thing language can be, understanding development get us closer to understanding what language

is. As these cognitive forces are prior to language in ontogeny and phylogeny it is language that has adapted to what cognition will allow.
- Linguistic meaning is constructed through action and interaction, novel problems are solved by analogy to experience of the way the world works and means-ends solutions that have been successful in the past. The world is then carved into categories that are meaningful in light of experience and these categories can be used as rules-of-thumb to predict behavior in the future.
- The cognitive cost of creating new linguistic categories has to be offset by the predictive benefit of owning and maintaining a category. How non-linguistic categories behave, what they can do and not just what they look like deeply canalizes the possibilities over which children generalize linguistic categories. Words and constructions are not always given by the structure of the world but invitations to share our perspective on an object, event or process.
- The motivations, beliefs and knowledge of others; the dynamics of event-cognition; the normative expectations of people; their attentional and inhibitory resources are not represented as an infinite landscape of possibilities, so if language significantly interacts with general cognition, cooperative motivations and the way the world works, linguistic generalizations are not equipotent in every direction either.

We of course need more studies that further explore the nature of the cognition-language interface and speaking to the growing interest in this area there are several planned special issues in journals dedicated to the topic, including . . .
- "The Interplay between Language Acquisition and Cognitive Development" in *Infant Behaviour and Development*
- "The interplay of language and emotion" in *Affective Science*

. . . which unfortunately will not available by the time this book goes to press but will be of interest to anyone wanting to take the ideas presented here further.

In the end, it was the sheer cross-linguistic diversity that defeated any purely-linguistic component of a module which would be helpful to a learner in narrowing the degrees of freedom on generalizations. Cognition stands a much better chance of being universalized to all languages because (a) children around the world share a common (but not identical) path of cognitive development and (b) domain-general properties of cognition, for example memory, have not been subject to the same cultural forces of change that act on language. The difference between the standard endowment of French-speakers' memory and Japanese-speakers' memory is less than the difference between French and Japanese. For this reason language is in a worse off position to be universalized than is general cognition because specific linguistic biases that act in favour of learning one language often work against learning the next, or else the specific language structure needs to be stated at such a general level it either is of no advantage to the learner or unlikely to be specific to language.

The idea that novel cultural cognitive processes can invade cortical domains areas devoted to different but similar functions has been explored under the Neuronal Recycling Hypothesis (Dehaene, 2004; Dehaene & Cohen, 2007). The original proposal was made with respect to reading, where there is widespread agreement this has to have emerged too recently (~5400 years ago) to result in a cognitive adaptation with its own dedicated cortical area (Dehaene, 2010). However, the assumptions about neural recycling could equally apply to what we have explored about developmental cognitive linguistics as well:

Assumption 1: The organization of the human brain is subject to anatomical constraints from evolution and is not infinitely plastic. Neural maps are present in infancy which biases subsequent learning. *These biases are the attractor spaces of social and cognitive adaptations represented in Figure 15 of our dynamic systems landscape.*

Assumption 2: The original organization of the cerebral cortex is never fully erased once these cultural tools invade the cortical areas. Instead, these initial neural constraints exert a powerful influence on what can be learned. *Again this fits with the developmental psychology literature we have reviewed here: an individual obviously still has (non-linguistic) memory, attention, categorization and so on after language is acquired, but that these deeply channel the possibilities of subsequent language learning.*

The consequences of this neuronal and cognitive recycling are that (a) cultural variability regarding the acquired cognitive processes are limited due to neural constraints; from a cognitive and social perspective why languages look similar in some respects and (b) the speed and ease of cultural acquisitions are predictable based on the amount and complexity of the recycling required; from a cognitive and social perspective why the developmental trajectory of language acquisition looks similar across cultures. So, the idea is that language finds its neuronal niche by invading those areas whose function serve similar ends and that are plastic enough to be co-opted towards the same ends (cf. Figure 1B).

The possibilities for language are thus biased before learning begins as not all cognitive areas are as useful or plastic as language requires them to be.

For me at least, the idea that language is made possible by the recycling, repurposing and sharing of existing cognitive structure and processes is no less stimulating than the idea that language gets its own encapsulated module, with content organized in advance of experience and particular to that domain. It is also in line with a move for language science to catch up with other disciplines and get serious about integration (Christiansen & Chater, 2016; Christiansen & Chater, 2017). It is an approach that has clearly testable claims – such as the intertwined developmental trajectories of language and other cognitive faculties, many examples of which we have come across in this book. It is possible to imagine a adult human that has memory, attention, inhibition, categorization, analogy and social cognition, who does not have language – indeed one does not need to wander very far from the human branch of the evolutionary tree to see this in many non-human apes. What is more difficult to imagine is human language existing without these cognitive capacities and the cooperative impetus to share, inform and request information. Language is special not because of the content of a Narrow Language Faculty or some encapsulated module impenetrable and hived-off form the rest of cognition. It is special because of the forms it can take rather than the parts it is made of; it is special because these forms have been driven into existence by a uniquely human motivation to turn cooperative cognition into cooperative action; and it is special because it could be nature's finest example of cognitive recycling and reuse.

About the Author

Dr. Paul Ibbotson is a lecturer in Developmental Psychology at The Open University. His interests and expertise lie at the intersection between language and cognition. He has applied this interest to understanding how children learn language. His work reveals the deep connections between the linguistic system and general psychological processes such as attention, inhibition and memory. The aim is that we can build better models of child language development if we integrate their developing social and cognitive worlds as well. By developing this line of research, he has been an advocate of the 'developmental cognitive linguistics' approach. This is revealing some fresh insights into how and why language develops the way it does. Paul has contributed to this by providing conceptual, analytical and methodological innovations. For example, using *Google Ngram* to answer questions about historical linguistics; developing an open-access child language analytic tool; providing models of how cognitive and social processes narrow the degrees of freedom on linguistic generalizations. He has communicated his research and the research of colleagues in his field to a general audience in popular science writing in *The Guardian* and *Scientific American*.

References

Abbot-Smith, Kirsten & Michael Tomasello. 2006. Exemplar-learning and schematization in a usage-based account of syntactic acquisition. *Linguistic Review* 23(3). 275–290. doi:10.1515/TLR.2006.011.

Adams, Anne-Marie & Susan E Gathercole. 1995. Phonological working memory and speech production in preschool children. *Journal of Speech & Hearing Research* 38(2). 403–414. doi:10.1044/jshr.3802.403.

Adams, Anne-Marie & Susan Elizabeth Gathercole. 2000. Limitations in working memory: implications for language development. *International Journal of Language & Communication Disorders* 35(1). 95–116. doi:10.1080/136828200247278.

Adams, Rick A., Karl J. Friston & Andre M. Bastos. 2015. Active inference, predictive coding and cortical architecture. In Manuel Casanova & Ioan Opris (eds.), *Recent Advances On The Modular Organization Of The Cortex*, 97–121. doi:10.1007/978-94-017-9900-3_7.

Adamson, Lauren B. & Janet E. Frick. 2003. The still face: A history of a shared experimental paradigm. *Infancy* 4(4). 451–473. doi:10.1207/S15327078IN0404_01.

Adolph, Karen E. & John M. Franchak. 2017. The development of motor behavior. *Wiley Interdisciplinary Reviews: Cognitive Science* 8(1–2). e1430. doi:10.1002/wcs.1430.

Aissen, Judith. 1999. Markedness and subject choice in optimality theory. *Natural Language and Linguistic Theory* 17. 637–711. doi:10.1023/A:1006335629372.

Akhtar, Nameera, Malinda Carpenter & Michael Tomasello. 1996. The Role of Discourse Novelty in Early Word Learning. *Child Development*. 67(2). 635–645. doi:10.1111/j.1467-8624.1996.tb01756.x.

Alishahi, Afra & Suzanne Stevenson. 2008. A computational model of early argument structure acquisition. *Cognitive Science: A Multidisciplinary Journal* 32(5), 789–834. doi: 10.1080/03640210801929287

Allan, Keith. 1977. Classifiers. *Language* 53(2), 285–311.

Allen, Shanley E. M. & Martha B. Crago. 2008. Early passive acquisition in Inuktitut. *Journal of Child Language* 23(1). 129–155. doi:10.1017/s0305000900010126.

Altmann, Gerry T. M. & Jelena Mirković. 2009. Incrementality and prediction in human sentence processing. *Cognitive Science* 33(4). 583–609. doi:10.1111/j.1551-6709.2009.01022.x.

Ambridge, Ben & Elena V. M. Lieven. 2011. *Child Language Acquisition: Contrasting Theoretical Approaches*. Cambridge: Cambridge University Press.

Ambridge, Ben, Evan Kidd, Caroline F. Rowland & Anna L. Theakston. 2015. The ubiquity of frequency effects in first language acquisition. *Journal of Child Language* 42(2). 239–273. doi:10.1017/S030500091400049X.

Ambridge, Ben, Julian M. Pine & Caroline F. Rowland. 2011. Children use verb semantics to retreat from overgeneralization errors: A novel verb grammaticality judgment study. *Cognitive Linguistics* 22(2). 303–323. doi:10.1515/COGL.2011.012.

Ambridge, Ben, Julian M. Pine & Caroline F. Rowland. 2012. Semantics versus statistics in the retreat from locative overgeneralization errors. *Cognition* 123(2). 260–79. doi:10.1016/j.cognition.2012.01.002.

Ambridge, Ben, Julian M. Pine, Caroline F. Rowland & Franklin Chang. 2012. The roles of verb semantics, entrenchment, and morphophonology in the retreat from dative argument-structure overgeneralization errors. *Language* 88(1). 45–81. doi:10.1353/lan.2012.0000.

Ambridge, Ben, Julian M. Pine, Caroline F. Rowland, Franklin Chang & Amy Bidgood. 2013. The retreat from overgeneralization in child language acquisition: Word learning, morphology, and verb argument structure. *Wiley Interdisciplinary Reviews: Cognitive Science* 4. 47–62. doi:10.1002/wcs.1207.

Amster, Guy & Guy Sella. 2016. Life history effects on the molecular clock of autosomes and sex chromosomes. *Proceedings of the National Academy of Sciences* 113(6). 1588–1593. doi:10.1073/pnas.1515798113.

Andersen, RW & Yasuhiro Shirai. 1996. The Primacy of Aspect in First and Second Language Acquisition: The Pidgin-Creole Connection. In William C. Ritchie & Tej K. Bhatia (eds.), *Handbook of Second Language Acquisition*, 527–570. San Diego, CA: Academic Press.

Ando, Shinki. 2002. Luminance-induced shift in the apparent direction of gaze. *Perception* 31(6). 657–674. doi:10.1068/p3332.

Andre-Thomas, Y. & S. Autgaerden. 1966. *Locomotion from pre- to postnatal life*. Lavenham, Suffolk, England: Spastics Society Medical Education and Information Unit and William Heinemann Medical Books.

Applebee, Arthur N. 1978. *The child's concept of story: Ages two to seventeen*. University of Chicago Press.

Aslin, Richard. 1987. Visual and auditory development in infancy. In Joy D. Osoksky (ed.), *Handbook of infant development*, 5–97. New York: Wiley.

Aslin, Richard N., Jenny R. Saffran & Elissa L. Newport. 1998. Computation of conditional probability statistics by 8-month-old infants. *Psychological Science* 9(4). 321–324. doi:10.1111/1467-9280.00063.

Asoh, Hideki, Yoichi Motomura, Futoshi Asano, Isao Hara, Satoru Hayamizu, Katsunobu Itou, Takio Kurita, Toshihiro Matsui, Roland Bunschoten & Ben Krose. 2001. Jijo-2: An Office Robot That Communicates and Learns. *IEEE Intelligent Systems* 16(5). 46–55. doi:10.1109/MIS.2001.956081.

Atkins, Paul. & Alan Baddeley. 1998. Working memory and distributed vocabulary learning. *Applied Psycholinguistics* 19(4). 537–552. doi:10.1017/S0142716400010353.

Atran, Scott. 1998. Folk biology and the anthropology of science: Cognitive universals and cultural particulars. *Behavioral and Brain Sciences* 21(4). 547–569. doi:10.1017/S0140525X98001277.

Audrey L.H. van der Meer, Marte Ramstad, F.R. (Ruud) van der Weel. 2008. Choosing the shortest way to mum: Auditory guided rotation in 6-to 9-month-old infants, Infant Behavior and Development, Volume 31(2), 207–216.

Au, Terry Kit Fong, Mirella Dapretto & You Kyung Song. 1994. Input Vs Constraints: Early Word Acquisition in Korean and English. *Journal of Memory and Language* 33(5). 567–582. doi:10.1006/jmla.1994.1027.

Aureli, Filippo & Kerrie Yates. 2010. Distress prevention by grooming others in crested black macaques. *Biology Letters* 6(1). 27–29. doi:10.1098/rsbl.2009.0513.

Avons, Steve E., Christopher A. Wragg, Wragg L. Cupples & William J. Lovegrove. 1998. Measures of phonological short-term memory and their relationship to vocabulary development. *Applied Psycholinguistics* 19(4). 583–601. doi:10.1017/S0142716400010377.

Axer, Hubertus, Carsten M. Klingner & Andreas Prescher. 2013. Fiber anatomy of dorsal and ventral language streams. *Brain and Language* 127(2). 192–204. doi:10.1016/j.bandl.2012.04.015.

Azumagakito, Tsubasa, Reiji Suzuki & Takaya Arita. 2018. An integrated model of gene-culture coevolution of language mediated by phenotypic plasticity. *Scientific Reports* 8. 8025. doi:10.1038/s41598-018-26233-7.

Baaren, Rick B. Van, Rob W. Holland, Kerry Kawakami & Ad Van Knippenberg. 2004. Mimicry and Prosocial Behavior. *Psychological Science* 15(1). 71–74. doi:10.1111/j.0963-7214.2004.01501012.x.

Baars, Bernard J. & Nicole M. Gage. 2010. Learning and memory. In *Cognition, Brain, and Consciousness* (Second edition), 304–343. Academic Press. doi:10.1016/B978-0-12-375070-9.00009-7. https://www.sciencedirect.com/science/article/pii/B9780123750709000097 (21 January, 2019).

Baddeley, Alan. 1992. Working Memory. *Science* 255(5044). 556–559. doi:10.1126/science.1736359.

Baddeley, Alan, Susan Gathercole & Costanza Papagno. 1998. The Phonological Loop as a Language Learning Device. *Psychological Review* 105(1). 158–173. doi:10.1037/0033-295X.105.1.158.

Baddeley, Alan & Graham Hitch. 1974. Working memory. *Psychology of Learning and Motivation* 8, 47–89. doi: 10.1037/0894-4105.8.4.485.

Baddeley, Alan, Robert Logie, Ian Nimmo-Smith & Neil Brereton. 1985. Components of fluent reading. *Journal of Memory and Language* 24(1). 119–131. doi:10.1016/0749-596X(85)90019-1.

Baird, Abigail A., Jerome Kagan, Thomas Gaudette, Kathryn A. Walz, Natalie Hershlag & David A. Boas. 2002. Frontal lobe activation during object permanence: Data from near-infrared spectroscopy. *NeuroImage* 16(4). 1120–1126. doi:10.1006/nimg.2002.1170.

Bakeman, Roger & Lauren B. Adamson. 1984. Coordinating Attention to People and Objects in Mother-Infant and Peer-Infant Interaction. *Child Development* 55(4). 1278–1289. doi:10.2307/1129997.

Baldwin, Dare A. 1995. Understanding the link between joint attention and language. In Chris Moore & Philip J. Dunham (eds.), *Joint attention: Its origins and role in development*, 131–158. Hillsdale, NJ: Lawrence Erlbaum.

Baldwin, Dare A. 1991. Infants' Contribution to the Achievement of Joint Reference. *Child Development* 62(5). 875–890. doi:10.1111/j.1467-8624.1991.tb01577.x.

Baldwin, Dare A. 1993. Early Referential Understanding: Infants' Ability to Recognize Referential Acts for What They Are. *Developmental Psychology* 29(5). 832–843. doi:10.1037/0012-1649.29.5.832.

Baldwin, Dare A., Jodie A. Baird, Megan M. Saylor & M. Angela Clark. 2001. Infants parse dynamic action. *Child Development* 72(3). 708–717. doi:10.1111/1467-8624.00310.

Baldwin, Dare A. & Louis J. Moses. 2001. Links between social understanding and early word learning: Challenges to current accounts. *Social Development* 10(3). 309–329. doi:10.1111/1467-9507.00168.

Banavar, Jayanth R., Amos Maritan & Andrea Rinaldo. 1999. Size and form in efficient transportation networks. *Nature* 399. 130–132. doi:10.1038/20144.

Bannard, Colin, Elena Lieven & Michael Tomasello. 2009. Early grammatical development is piecemeal and lexically specific. *Proceedings of the National Academy of Science* 106(41). 17284–17289.

Bannard, Colin, Elena Lieven & Michael Tomasello. 2009. Modeling children's early grammatical knowledge. *Proceedings of the National Academy of Sciences of the United States of America*. doi:10.1073/pnas.0905638106.

Bar, Moshe. 2007. The proactive brain: using analogies and associations to generate predictions. *Trends in Cognitive Sciences* 11(7). 280–289. doi:10.1016/j.tics.2007.05.005.

Bar, Moshe. 2009. The proactive brain: Memory for predictions. *Philosophical Transactions of the Royal Society B: Biological Sciences* 364(1521). doi:10.1098/rstb.2008.0310.

Barabási, Albert-László. 2002. *Linked: The new science of networks*. Cambridge, MA: Perseus Books.

Barabási, Albert-László & Réka Albert. 1999. Emergence of scaling in random networks. *Science* 286(5439). 509–512. doi:10.1126/science.286.5439.509.

Bard, Chantal, Laurette Hay & Michelle Fleury. 1990. Timing and accuracy of visually directed movements in children: Control of direction and amplitude components. *Journal of Experimental Child Psychology* 50(1). 102–118. doi:10.1016/0022-0965(90)90034-6.

Baron-Cohen, Simon, Ruth Campbell, Annette Karmiloff-smith, Julia Grant & Jane Walker. 1995. Are children with autism blind to the mentalistic significance of the eyes? *British Journal of Developmental Psychology* 13(4). 379–398. doi:10.1111/j.2044-835X.1995.tb00687.x.

Baron-Cohen, Simon. 1994. How to build a baby that can read minds: Cognitive mechanisms in mindreading. *Cahiers de Psychologie Cognitive [Current Psychology of Cognition]* 13, 513–552.

Baron-Cohen, Simon. 1998. Does the study of autism justify minimalist innate modularity? *Learning and Individual Differences* 10(3). 179–191. doi:10.1016/S1041-6080(99)80129-0.

Barr, Rachel & Harlene Hayne. 2000. Age-related changes in imitation: Implications for memory development. In Carolyn Rovee-Collier, Lewis P. Lipsitt & Harlene Hayne (eds.), *Progress in infancy research* Volume 1, 21–67. Mahwah, NJ: Lawrence Erlbaum Associates.

Barr, Rachel, Anne Dowden & Harlene Hayne. 1996. Developmental changes in deferred imitation by 6- to 24-month-old infants. *Infant Behavior and Development* 19(2). 159–170. doi:10.1016/S0163-6383(96)90015-6.

Barsalou, Lawrence W. 1999. Perceptual symbol systems. *Behavioral and Brain Sciences* 22(4). 577–660. doi:10.1017/S0140525X99002149.

Barsalou, Lawrence W. 2007. Grounded Cognition. *Annual Review of Psychology* 59(1). 617–645. doi:10.1146/annurev.psych.59.103006.093639.

Bartsch, Karen & Henry M. Wellman. 1995. *Children Talk about the Mind*. New York: Oxford University Press.

Bassano, Dominique. 2000. Early development of nouns and verbs in French: Exploring the interface between lexicon and grammar. *Journal of Child Language* 27(3). 521–559. doi:10.1017/S0305000900004396.

Basu, Debarchana & Ronnie Wilbur. 2010. Complex predicates in Bangla: an event-based analysis. *Rice Working Papers in Linguistics 2*.

Bauer, Patricia J. 2006. Constructing a past in infancy: a neuro-developmental account. *Trends in Cognitive Sciences* 10(4). 175–181. doi:10.1016/j.tics.2006.02.009.

Baumeister, Roy F. & Mark R. Leary. 1995. The Need to Belong: Desire for Interpersonal Attachments as a Fundamental Human Motivation. *Psychological Bulletin* 117(3). 497–529. doi:10.1037/0033-2909.117.3.497.

Baumgartner, Heidi A. & Lisa M. Oakes. 2013. Investigating the relation between infants' manual activity with objects and their perception of dynamic events. *Infancy* 18(6). 983–1006. doi:10.1111/infa.12009.

Beckage, Nicole, Linda Smith & Thomas Hills. 2011. Small worlds and semantic network growth in typical and late talkers. *PLoS ONE* 6(5). e19348. doi:10.1371/journal.pone.0019348.

Becker, Misha. 2014. *The Acquisition of Syntactic Structure: Animacy and Thematic Alignment.* Cambridge: Cambridge University Press.

Becker, Misha. & Bruno Estigarribia. 2013. Harder words: How children learn abstract verbs with opaque syntax. *Language Learning and Development* 9(3). 211–244. doi: 10.1080/15475441.2013.753798.

Becker, Misha. 2005. Learning verbs without arguments: The problem of raising verbs. *Journal of Psycholinguistic Research* 34. 173–199. doi:10.1007/s10936-005-3637-2.

Becker, Misha. 2006. There began to be a learnability puzzle. *Linguistic Inquiry* 37(3). 441–456. doi:10.1162/ling.2006.37.3.441.

Becker, Misha. 2009. The role of NP animacy and expletives in verb learning. *Language Acquisition* 16(4). 283–296. doi:10.1080/10489220903178997.

Becker, Misha. 2015. Animacy and the Acquisition of Tough Adjectives. *Language Acquisition* 22(1). 68–103. doi:10.1080/10489223.2014.928298.

Beckner, Clay, Richard Blythe, Joan Bybee, Morten H. Christiansen, William Croft, Nick C. Ellis, John Holland, Jinyun Ke, Diane Larsen-Freeman & Tom Schoenemann. 2009. Language is a complex adaptive system: Position paper. *Language Learning* 59(s1). 1–26. doi:10.1111/j.1467-9922.2009.00533.x.

Behne, Tanya, Malinda Carpenter, Josep Call & Michael Tomasello. 2005. Unwilling versus unable: Infants' understanding of intentional action. *Developmental Psychology* 41(2). 328–337. doi:10.1037/0012-1649.41.2.328.

Bell, Martha Ann & Stephanie E. Adams. 1999. Comparable performance on looking and reaching versions of the A-not-B task at 8 months of age. *Infant Behavior and Development* 22(2). 221–235. doi:10.1016/S0163-6383(99)00010-7.

Bell, Martha Ann & Nathan A. Fox. 1992. The Relations between Frontal Brain Electrical Activity and Cognitive Development during Infancy. *Child Development* 63(5). 1142–1163. doi:10.1111/j.1467-8624.1992.tb01685.x.

Bellugi, Ursula, Paul P. Wang & Terry L. Jernigan. 1994. Williams syndrome: An unusual neuropsychological profile. In Sarah H. Broman & Jordan H. Grafman (eds.), Atypical cognitive deficits in developmental disorders: Implications for brain function, 23–56. Hillsdale NJ: Lawrence Erlbaum Associates.

Belpaeme, Tony & Joris Bleys. 2005. Explaining universal color categories through a constrained acquisition process. *Adaptive Behavior* 13(4). 293–310. doi:10.1177/105971230501300404.

Benasich, April A. & Paula Tallal. 2002. Infant discrimination of rapid auditory cues predicts later language impairment. *Behavioural Brain Research* 136(1). 31–49. doi:10.1016/S0166-4328(02)00098-0.

Beran, Michael J. 2015. Chimpanzee Cognitive Control. *Current Directions in Psychological Science* 24(5). 352–357. doi:10.1177/0963721415593897.

Berger, Andrea. 2011. *Self-regulation: Brain, cognition, and development.* Washington, DC, USA: American Psychological Association. doi.org/10.1037/12327-000

Bergman Nutley, Sissela, Stina Söderqvist, Sara Bryde, Lisa B. Thorell, Keith Humphreys & Torkel Klingberg. 2011. Gains in fluid intelligence after training non-verbal reasoning in 4-year-old children: A controlled, randomized study. *Developmental Science* 14(3). 591–601. doi:10.1111/j.1467-7687.2010.01022.x.

Berman, Ruth & Dan Slobin. 1994. *Relating Events in Narrative: A Crosslinguistic Developmental Study*. Hillsdale, NJ, Lawrence Erlbaum.

Bernstein, Nikolai A. 1967. *The Coordination and Regulation of Movements*. Oxford: Pergamon Press.

Bertenthal, Bennett I. & Joseph J. Campos. 1990. A systems approach to the organizing effects of self-produced locomotion during infancy. In Carolyn Rovee-Collier & Lewis P. Lipsitt (eds.), *Advances in Infancy Research* 6, 1–60. Norwood, NJ: Ablex Publishing.

Bever, Thomas. 1970. The Cognitive Basis for Linguistic Structures. In John R. Hayes (ed.), *Cognition and the development of language*, 279–352. New York: Wiley.

Bhatt, Ramesh & Carolyn Rovee-Collier. 1994. Perception and 24-hour retention of feature relations in infancy. Developmental Psychology, 30, 142–150.

Bialystok, Ellen, Fergus I. M. Craik, Cheryl Grady, Wilkin Chau, Ryouhei Ishii, Atsuko Gunji & Christo Pantev. 2005. Effect of bilingualism on cognitive control in the Simon task: Evidence from MEG. *NeuroImage* 24(1). 40–49. doi:10.1016/j.neuroimage.2004.09.044.

Binder, Jeffrey R. 2015. The Wernicke area: Modern evidence and a reinterpretation. *Neurology* 85(24). 2170–2175. doi:10.1212/WNL.0000000000002219.

Bird, Helen, Sue Franklin & David Howard. 2001. Age of acquisition and imageability ratings for a large set of words, including verbs and function words. *Behavior Research Methods, Instruments, and Computers* 33. 73–79. doi:10.3758/BF03195349.

Blackwell, Aleka. 2005. Acquiring the English adjective lexicon: relationships with input properties and adjectival semantic typology. *Journal of Child Language* 32(3). 535–562. doi:10.1017/s0305000905006938.

Blair, Clancy. 2002. School readiness: Integrating cognition and emotion in a neurobiological conceptualization of children's functioning at school entry. *American Psychologist* 57(2). 111–127. doi:10.1037/0003-066X.57.2.111.

Bloomfield, Leonard. 1938. Language or Ideas? *Language* 12(2). 89–95. doi:10.2307/408751.

Bloomfield, Leonard. 1973. *Language*. London: George Allen & Unwin.

Bock, Kathryn & David Irwin. 1980. Syntactic effects of information availability in sentence production. *Journal of Verbal Learning and Verbal Behavior* 19, 467–484. doi:10.1016/s0022-5371(80)90321-7.

Bod, Rens. 2007. Is the End of Supervised Parsing in Sight? *Proceedings of the 45th Annual Meeting of the Association of Computational Linguistics, Prague, Czech Republic*, 400–407. Association for Computational Linguistics.

Bod, Rens, Khalil Sima'an & Remko Scha. 2003. *Data-Oriented Parsing*. Stanford: CSLI Publications,.

Bogartz, Richard S. 1994. The future of dynamic systems models in developmental psychology in the light of the past. *Journal of Experimental Child Psychology* 58(2). 289–319. doi:10.1006/jecp.1994.1036.

Bogen, Joseph E. & G. M. Bogen. 1976. Wernicke's region—Where is it? *Annals of the New York Academy of Sciences* 280, 834–843.

Bomba, Paul C. & Einar R. Siqueland. 1983. The nature and structure of infant form categories. *Journal of Experimental Child Psychology* 35(2). 294–328. doi:10.1016/0022-0965(83)90085-1.

Borge-Holthoefer, Javier & Alex Arenas. 2010. Semantic Networks: Structure and Dynamics. *Entropy* 12. 1264–1302. doi:10.3390/e12051264.

Bornkessel-Schlesewsky, Ina, Matthias Schlesewsky, Steven L. Small & Josef P. Rauschecker. 2015. Neurobiological roots of language in primate audition: Common computational properties. *Trends in Cognitive Sciences* 19(3). 142–150. doi:10.1016/j.tics.2014.12.008.

Bornstein, Marc H. & Marian D. Sigman. 1986. Continuity in mental development from infancy. *Child development* 57(2). 251–274. doi:10.1111/j.1467-8624.1986.tb00025.x.
Bornstein, Marc H., Linda R. Cote, Sharone Maital, Kathleen Painter, Sung Yun Park, Liliana Pascual, Marie Germaine Pêcheux, Josette Ruel, Paola Venuti & Andre Vyt. 2004. Crosslinguistic analysis of vocabulary in young children: Spanish, Dutch, French, Hebrew, Italian, Korean, and American English. *Child Development* 75(4). 1115–1139. doi:10.1111/j.1467-8624.2004.00729.x.
Bornstein, Marc H., Chun Shin Hahn, Clare Bell, O. Maurice Haynes, Alan Slater, Jean Golding & Dieter Wolke. 2006. Stability in cognition across early childhood a developmental cascade. *Psychological Science* 17(2). 151–158. doi:10.1111/j.1467-9280.2006.01678.x.
Boroditsky, Lera, Lauren A. Schmidt & Webb Phillips. 2003. Sex, syntax, and semantics. In Dedra Gentner & Susan Goldin-Meadow (eds.), *Language in Mind: Advances in the Study of Language and Thought*, 61–79. Cambridge, MA: MIT Press.
Borovsky, Arielle & Jeff Elman. 2006. Language input and semantic categories: A relation between cognition and early word learning. *Journal of Child Language* 33(4). 759–790. doi:10.1017/S0305000906007574.
Borovsky, Arielle, Jeffrey L. Elman & Anne Fernald. 2012. Knowing a lot for one's age: Vocabulary skill and not age is associated with anticipatory incremental sentence interpretation in children and adults. *Journal of Experimental Child Psychology* 114(2). 371–73. doi:10.1016/j.jecp.2012.01.005.
Bowerman, Melissa & Soonja Choi. 2003. Space under construction: Language-specific special categorization in first language acquisition. In Dedra Gentner & Susan Goldin-Meadow (eds.), *Language in Mind: Advances in the Study of Language and Thought*, 387–427. Cambridge, MA: MIT Press.
Bowey, Judith A. 2006. Clarifying the phonological processing account of nonword repetition. *Applied Psycholinguistics* 27(4). 548–552. doi:10.1017.S0142716406060401.
Boyd, Jeremy K. & Adele E. Goldberg. 2009. Input effects within a constructionist framework. *Modern Language Journal* 93. 418–429. doi:10.1111/j.1540-4781.2009.00899.x.
Boyd, Robert, Herbert Gintis, Samuel Bowles & Peter J. Richerson. 2003. The evolution of altruistic punishment. *Proceedings of the National Academy of Sciences* 100(6). 3531–3535. doi:10.1073/pnas.0630443100.
Boyd, Robert & Peter J. Richerson. 1992. Punishment allows the evolution of cooperation (or anything else) in sizable groups. *Ethology and Sociobiology* 13(3). 171–195. doi:10.1016/0162-3095(92)90032-Y.
Braine, Martin D. S. 1987. What is Learned in Acquiring Word Classes – A Step Toward an Acquisition Theory. In Brian MacWhinney (ed.), *Mechanisms of language acquisition*, 65–87. Lawrence Erlbaum Associates.
Braine, Martin, Patricia Brooks, Nelson Cowan, Mark Samuels & Catherine Tamis-LeMonda. 1993. The Development of categories at the semantics/syntax interface. *Cognitive Development* 8(4). 465–494. doi:10.1016/S0885-2014(05)80005-X.
Braine, Martin D. S. & Patricia J. Brooks. 1995. Verb argument structure and the problem of avoiding an overgeneral grammar. In Michael Tomasello & William E. Merriman (eds.), *Beyond names for things: Young children's acquisition of verbs*, 353–376. Lawrence Erlbaum Associates.
Brass, Marcel, Harold Bekkering & Wolfgang Prinz. 2001. Movement observation affects movement execution in a simple response task. *Acta Psychologica* 106(1–2). 3–22. doi:10.1016/S0001-6918(00)00024-X.

Brass, Marcel, Harold Bekkering, Andreas Wohlschläger & Wolfgang Prinz. 2000. Compatibility between observed and executed finger movements: Comparing symbolic, spatial, and imitative cues. *Brain and Cognition* 44(2). 124–143. doi:10.1006/brcg.2000.1225.

Brock, Jon. 2007. Language abilities in Williams syndrome: A critical review. *Development and Psychopathology* 19(1). 97–127. doi:10.1017/S095457940707006X.

Bronson, Gordon W. 1994. Infants' Transitions toward Adult-like Scanning. *Child Development* 65(5). 1243–1261. doi:10.1111/j.1467-8624.1994.tb00815.x.

Brooks, Patricia J. & Michael Tomasello. 1999. Young children learn to produce passives with nonce verbs. *Developmental Psychology* 35(1). 29–44. doi:10.1037/0012-1649.35.1.29.

Brooks, Rechele & Andrew N. Meltzoff. 2005. The development of gaze following and its relation to language. *Developmental Science* 8(6). 535–543. doi:10.1111/j.1467-7687.2005.00445.x.

Bruin, Angela de, Barbara Treccani & Sergio Della Sala. 2015. Cognitive Advantage in Bilingualism: An Example of Publication Bias? *Psychological Science* 26(1). 99–107. doi:10.1177/0956797614557866.

Burger, Joanna, Michael Gochfeld & Bertram G. Murray. 1992. Risk discrimination of eye contact and directness of approach in black iguanas (Ctenosaura similis). *Journal of Comparative Psychology* 106(1). 97–101. doi:10.1037/0735-7036.106.1.97.

Burghardt, Gordon M. & Harry W. Greene. 1988. Predator simulation and duration of death feigning in neonate hognose snakes. *Animal Behaviour* 36(6). 1842–1844. doi:10.1016/S0003-3472(88)80127-1.

Butler, Judith & Carolyn Rovee-Collier. 1989. Contextual gating of memory retrieval. *Developmental Psychobiology* 22(6). 533–552. doi:10.1002/dev.420220602.

Bybee, Joan. 1985. *Morphology: A study of the Relation between meaning and form*. Amsterdam: John Benjamins Publishing Company.

Bybee, Joan. 2010. Language, Usage and Cognition. Cambridge: Cambridge University Press.

Bybee, Joan. 2010a. *Frequency of Use and the Organization of Language. Frequency of Use and the Organization of Language*. Oxford: Oxford University Press. doi:10.1093/acprof:oso/9780195301571.001.0001.

Bybee, Joan. 2010b. *Language, Usage and Cognition*. Cambridge: Cambridge University Press. doi:10.1017/CBO9780511750526

Bybee, Joan & James L. McClelland. 2005. Alternatives to the combinatorial paradigm of linguistic theory based on domain general principles of human cognition. *Linguistic Review* 22(2–4). 381–410. doi:10.1515/tlir.2005.22.2-4.381.

Calkins, Susan D. & Nathan A. Fox. 2002. Self-regulatory processes in early personality development: A multilevel approach to the study of childhood social withdrawal and aggression. *Development and Psychopathology* 14(3). 477–498. doi:10.1017/S0954579402003057.

Calkins, Susan D. & Robin B. Howse. 2004. Individual differences in self-regulation: Implications for childhood adjustment. In Robert S. Feldman & Pierre Philippot (eds.), *The regulation of emotion*, 307–332. Mahwah, NJ: Lawrence Erlbaum Associates.

Call, Josep & Michael Tomasello. 2008. Does the chimpanzee have a theory of mind? 30 years later. *Trends in cognitive sciences* 12(5). 187–192. doi:10.1016/j.tics.2008.02.010.

Cameron-Faulkner, Thea, Elena Lieven & Anna Theakston. 2007. What part of no do children not understand? A usage-based account of multiword negation. *Journal of Child Language* 34(2). 251–282. doi:10.1017/S0305000906007884.

Cameron-Faulkner, Thea, Elena Lieven & Michael Tomasello. 2003. A construction based analysis of child directed speech. *Cognitive Science* 27(6). 843–873. doi:10.1016/j.cogsci.2003.06.001.

Campbell, Ruth, Charles A. Heywood, Alan Cowey, Marianne Regard & Théodor Landis. 1990. Sensitivity to eye gaze in prosopagnosic patients and monkeys with superior temporal sulcus ablation. *Neuropsychologia* 28(11). 1123–1142. doi:10.1016/0028-3932(90)90050-X.

Cancho, Ramon F. i. & Ricard V. Solé. 2003. Least effort and the origins of scaling in human language. *Proceedings of the National Academy of Sciences* 100(3). 788–791. doi:10.1073/pnas.0335980100.

Cancho, Ramon Ferrer i & Ricard V Solé. 2001. The small-world of human language. *Proceedings of the Royal Society B* 268 (1482). doi:10.1098/rspb.2001.1800

Cangelosi, Angelo, Emmanouil Hourdakis & Vadim Tikhanoff. 2006. Language Acquisition and Symbol Grounding Transfer with Neural Networks and Cognitive Robots. *The 2006 IEEE International Joint Conference on Neural Network Proceedings*, 1576–1582. Vancouver, BC. doi:10.1109/IJCNN.2006.246621.

Carpenter, Malinda, Nameera Akhtar & Michael Tomasello. 1998. Fourteen- through 18-month-old infants differentially imitate intentional and accidental actions. *Infant Behavior and Development* 21(2). 315–330. doi:10.1016/S0163-6383(98)90009-1.

Carpenter, Malinda, Josep Call & Michael Tomasello. 2002. Understanding "prior intentions" enables two-year-olds to imitatively learn a complex task. *Child Development* 73(5). 1431–1441. doi:10.1111/1467-8624.00481.

Carpenter, Malinda, Josep Call & Michael Tomasello. 2005. Twelve- and 18-month-olds copy actions in terms of goals. *Developmental Science* 8(1). F13–F20. doi:10.1111/j.1467-7687.2004.00385.x.

Carpenter, Malinda, Katherine Nagell, Michael Tomasello, George Butterworth & Chris Moore. 1998. Social Cognition, Joint attention, and Communicative Competence from 9 to 15 Months of Age. *Monographs of the Society for Research in Child Development* 63(4). i–174. doi:10.2307/1166214

Cartwright, Timothy A. & Michael R. Brent. 1997. Syntactic categorization in early language acquisition: Formalizing the role of distributional analysis. *Cognition* 63(2). 121–170. doi:10.1016/S0010-0277(96)00793-7.

Casad, Eugene H. & Ronald W. Langacker. 2005. "Inside" and "Outside" in Cora Grammar. *International Journal of American Linguistics* 51(3). 247–281. doi:10.1086/465872.

Casasola, Marianella. 2005. When less is more: How infants learn to form an abstract categorical representation of support. *Child Development* 76(1). 279–290. doi:10.1111/j.1467-8624.2005.00844.x.

Caselli, Maria Cristina, Elizabeth Bates, Paola Casadio, Judi Fenson, Larry Fenson, Lisa Sanderl & Judy Weir. 1995. A cross-linguistic study of early lexical development. *Cognitive Development* 10(2). 159–199. doi:10.1016/0885-2014(95)90008-X.

Casenhiser, Devin & Adele E. Goldberg. 2005. Fast mapping between a phrasal form and meaning. *Developmental Science* 8(6). 500–508. doi:10.1111/j.1467-7687.2005.00441.x.

Chang, Franklin, Gary S. Dell & Kathryn Bock. 2006. Becoming syntactic. *Psychological Review* 113(2). 234–272. doi:10.1037/0033-295X.113.2.234.

Charman, Tony, Simon Baron-Cohen, John Swettenham, Gillian Baird, Antony Cox & Auriol Drew. 2000. Testing joint attention, imitation, and play as infancy precursors to language and theory of mind. *Cognitive Development* 15(4). 481–498. doi:10.1016/S0885-2014(01)00037-5.

Chartrand, Tanya L. & John A. Bargh. 1999. The chameleon effect: The perception-behavior link and social interaction. *Journal of Personality and Social Psychology* 76(6). 893–910. doi:10.1037/0022-3514.76.6.893.

Chater, Nick, Florencia Reali & Morten H. Christiansen. 2009. Restrictions on biological adaptation in language evolution. *Proceedings of the National Academy of Sciences* 106(4). 1015–1020. doi:10.1073/pnas.0807191106.

Chechik, Gal, Isaac Meilijson & Eytan Ruppin. 1998. Synaptic Pruning in Development: A Computational Account. *Neural Computation* 10(7). 1759–1777. doi:10.1162/089976698300017124.

Cheng, S.-W. 1994. Beginning words of three children acquiring Mandarin Chinese. Manuscript in preparation, National Chung Cheng University, Taiwan, as cited in Caselli et al.,1995.

Chi, Michelene. 1978. Knowledge structures and memory development. In R.S. Siegler (Ed.), Children's thinking: What develops? Hillsdale, NJ: Lawrence Erlbaum Associates Inc.

Childers, Jane B. & Michael Tomasello. 2003. Children extend both words and non-verbal actions to novel exemplars. *Developmental Science* 6(2). 185–90. doi:10.1111/1467-7687.00270.

Choi, Soonja & Melissa Bowerman. 1991. Learning to express motion events in English and Korean: The influence of language-specific lexicalization patterns. *Cognition* 41(1–3). doi:10.1016/0010-0277(91)90033-Z.

Choi, Soonja & Alison Gopnik. 1995. Early acquisition of verbs in Korean: A cross-linguistic study. *Journal of Child Language* 22(3). 497–529. doi:10.1017/S0305000900009934.

Choi, Youngon & John C. Trueswell. 2010. Children's (in)ability to recover from garden paths in a verb-final language: Evidence for developing control in sentence processing. *Journal of Experimental Child Psychology* 106(1). 41–61. doi:10.1016/j.jecp.2010.01.003.

Chomsky, Noam. 1957. *Syntactic Structures*. The Hague: Mouton

Chomsky, Noam. 1965. *Aspects of the Theory of Syntax*. Cambridge MA: MIT Press.

Chomsky, Noam. 1975. *The logical structure of linguistic theory*. New York: Springer US.

Chomsky, Noam. 1977. On WH-movement. In Adrian Akmajian, Peter Culicover & Thomas Wasow (eds.), *Formal Syntax*, 71–133. New York: Academic Press.

Chomsky, Noam. 1980. Rules and representations. *Behavioral and Brain Sciences* 3(1). 1–15. doi:10.1017/S0140525X00001515.

Chomsky, Noam. 1986. *Knowledge of Language*. Westport CT: Praeger.

Chomsky, Noam. 1993. A Minimalist Program for Linguistic Theory. In Kenneth Hale & Samuel Jay Keyser (eds.), *The View From Building 20: Essays in Linguistics in Honor of Sylvain Bromberger*. Cambridge MA: MIT Press.

Chomsky, Noam. 2011. Language and other cognitive systems. What is special about language? *Language Learning and Development* 7(4). 263–278. doi:10.1080/15475441.2011.584041.

Christiansen, Morten H. 2000. Using artificial language learning to study language evolution: Exploring the emergence of word order universals. Paper presented at the Third Conference on the Evolution of Language, Paris, France.

Christiansen, Morten H. & Joseph T. Devlin. 1997. Recursive Inconsistencies Are Hard to Learn: A Connectionist Perspective on Universal Word Order Correlations. *Proceedings of the 19th Annual Cognitive Science Society Conference*, 113–118. Mahwah, NJ: Lawrence Erlbaum Associates.

Christiansen, Morten H. & Nick Chater. 2016. *Creating language: Integrating evolution, acquisition, and processing*. Cambridge MA: MIT Press.

Christiansen, Morten H. & Inbal Arnon. 2017. More Than Words: The Role of Multiword Sequences in Language Learning and Use. *Topics in Cognitive Science* 9(3). 542–551. doi:10.1111/tops.12274.

Christiansen, Morten H. & Nick Chater. 2001. Connectionist psycholinguistics: Capturing the empirical data. *Trends in Cognitive Sciences* 5(2). 82–88. doi:10.1016/S1364-6613(00)01600-4.

Christiansen, Morten H. & Nick Chater. 2016. The Now-or-Never bottleneck: A fundamental constraint on language. *Behavioral and Brain Sciences* 39. E62. doi:10.1017/S0140525X1500031X.

Christiansen, Morten H. & Nick Chater. 2017. Towards an integrated science of language. *Nature Human Behaviour* 1(1–3). 0163. doi:10.1038/s41562-017-0163.

Christiansen, Morten H., Florencia Reali & Nick Chater. 2011. Biological Adaptations for Functional Features of Language in the Face of Cultural Evolution. *Human Biology* 83(2). 247–259. doi:10.3378/027.083.0206.

Christiansen, Morten H. & Nick Chater. 2008. Language as shaped by the brain. *Behavioral and brain sciences* 31(5). 489–509. doi:10.1017/S0140525X08004998.

Christophe, Anne & Emmanuel Dupoux. 1996. Bootstrapping lexical acquisition: The role of prosodic structure. *Linguistic Review* 13(3–4). 383–412. doi:10.1515/tlir.1996.13.3-4.383.

Chudek, Maciej & Joseph Henrich. 2011. Culture-gene coevolution, norm-psychology and the emergence of human prosociality. *Trends in cognitive sciences* 15(5). 218–226. doi:10.1016/j.tics.2011.03.003.

Chung, Sandra. 1983. The ECP and government in Chamorro. *Natural Language and Linguistic Theory* 1(2). 207–244. doi:10.1007/BF00154831.

Clark, Andy. 2013. Whatever next? Predictive brains, situated agents, and the future of cognitive science. *Behavioral and brain sciences* 36(3). 181–204. doi:10.1017/S0140525X12000477.

Clark, Herbert H. 1982. The relevance of common ground: Comments on Sperber and Wilson. In Neilson V. Smith (ed.), *Mutual knowledge*, 124–127. New York: Academic Press.

Clark, Herbert H. 1985. Language use and language users. In Gardner Lindzey & Elliot Aronson (eds.), *Handbook of social psychology* 3rd ed., 179–231. New York: Random House.

Clark, Ruth. 1974. Performing without competence. *Journal of Child Language* 1(1). 1–10. doi:10.1017/S0305000900000040.

Cochran, Kathryn & J. Kent Davis. 1987. Individual differences in inference processes. *Journal of Research in Personality*. 21(2). 197–210. doi:10.1016/0092-6566(87)90007-9.

Cohn, Neil, Martin Paczynski & Marta Kutas. 2017. Not so secret agents: Event-related potentials to semantic roles in visual event comprehension. *Brain and Cognition* 119. 1–9. doi:10.1016/j.bandc.2017.09.001.

Collins, Allan M. & Elizabeth F. Loftus. 1975. A spreading-activation theory of semantic processing. *Psychological Review* 82(6). 407–428. doi:10.1037/0033-295X.82.6.407.

Collins, Allan M. & M. Ross Quillian. 1969. Retrieval time from semantic memory. *Journal of Verbal Learning and Verbal Behavior* 8(2). 240–247. doi:10.1016/S0022-5371(69)80069-1.

Colombo, John. 1993. *Infant cognition: Predicting later intellectual functioning*. Newbury Park, CA : Sage.

Colombo, John. 2002. The Development of Visual Attention in Infancy. *Annual Review of Psychology* 52. 337–367. doi:10.1146/annurev.psych.52.1.337.

Colombo, John, Laura J. Freeseman, Jeffrey T. Coldren & Janet E. Frick. 1995. Individual differences in infant fixation duration: Dominance of global versus local stimulus properties. *Cognitive Development* 10(2). 271–285. doi:10.1016/0885-2014(95)90012-8.

Colombo, John, W. Allen Richman, D. Jill Shaddy, Andrea Follmer Greenhoot & Julie M. Maikranz. 2001. Heart rate-defined phases of attention, look duration, and infant performance in the paired-comparison paradigm. *Child Development* 72(6). 1605–1616. doi:10.1111/1467-8624.00368.

Colombo, John, D. Jill Shaddy, W. Allen Richman, Julie M. Maikranz & Otilia M. Blaga. 2004. The developmental course of habituation in infancy and preschool outcome. *Infancy* 5(1). 1–38. doi:10.1207/s15327078in0501_1.

Comrie, Bernard. 1989. *Language Universals and Linguistic Typology*. Chicago: University of Chicago Press.

Connor, Michael, Yael Gertner, Cynthia Fisher & Dan Roth. 2008. Baby SRL: Modeling Early Language Acquisition. *CoNLL 2008 – Proceedings of the Twelfth Conference on Computational Natural Language Learning*, 81–88. Stroudsburg, PA: Association for Computational Linguistics. doi:10.3115/1596324.1596339.

Connor, Michael, Yael Gertner, Cynthia Fisher & Dan Roth. 2009. Minimally supervised model of early language acquisition. *CoNLL '09: Proceedings of the Thirteenth Conference on Computational Natural Language Learning*, 84–92. Stroudsburg, PA: Association for Computational Linguistics. doi:10.3115/1596374.1596391.

Corrigan, Roberta. 1988. Children's identification of actors and patients in prototypical and nonprototypical sentence types. *Cognitive Development* 3(3). 285–297. doi:10.1016/0885-2014(88)90013-5.

Cosmides, Leda & John Tooby. 2008. Can a General Deontic Logic Capture the Facts of Human Moral Reasoning? How the Mind Interprets Social Exchange Rules and Detects Cheaters. In Walter Sinnott-Armstrong (ed.), *Moral psychology, Vol. 1. The evolution of morality: Adaptations and innateness*, 53–119. Cambridge MA: MIT Press.

Courage, Mary L., Greg D. Reynolds & John E. Richards. 2006. Infants' attention to patterned stimuli: Developmental change from 3 to 12 months of age. *Child Development* 77(3). 680–695. doi:10.1111/j.1467-8624.2006.00897.x.

Cowan, Nelson, Jeffrey N. Rouder, Christopher L. Blume & J. Scott Saults. 2012. Models of verbal working memory capacity: What does it take to make them work? *Psychological Review* 119(3). 480–99. doi:10.1037/a0027791.

Croft, William. 2001. Radical Construction Grammar. *Oxford Oxford University Press*. doi:10.1093/acprof:oso/9780198299554.001.0001.

Croft, William. 2003. *Typology and universals* (Second edition). Cambridge: Cambridge University Press.

Croft, William, Tanmoy Bhattacharya, Dave Kleinschmidt, D. Eric Smith & T. Florian Jaeger. 2011. Greenbergian universals, diachrony, and statistical analyses. *Linguistic Typology* 15(2). 433–453. doi:10.1515/lity.2011.029.

Crosson, Bruce. 2013. Thalamic mechanisms in language: a reconsideration based on recent findings and concepts. *Brain and language* 126(1). 73–88. doi:10.1016/j.bandl.2012.06.011.

Cuevas, Kimberley, Amy Giles, & Carolyn Rovee-Collier. 2009, March. Sensory preconditioning and second-order conditioning at 6 and 9 months of age. Poster presented at the meeting of the Eastern Psychological Association, Pittsburgh, PA.

Cuevas, Kimberly & Adam Sheya. 2019. Ontogenesis of learning and memory: Biopsychosocial and dynamical systems perspectives. *Developmental Psychobiology* 61(3). 402–415. doi:10.1002/dev.21817.

Cuevas, Kimberly, Margaret M. Swingler, Martha Ann Bell, Stuart Marcovitch & Susan D. Calkins. 2012. Measures of frontal functioning and the emergence of inhibitory control processes at 10 months of age. *Developmental Cognitive Neuroscience* 2(2). 235–43. doi:10.1016/j.dcn.2012.01.002.

Cummins, Denise Dellarosa. 1996a. Evidence of deontic reasoning in 3- and 4-year-old children. *Memory and Cognition* 24. 823–829. doi:10.3758/BF03201105.

Cummins, Denise Dellarosa. 1996b. Evidence for the innateness of deontic reasoning. *Mind and Language* 11(2). 160–190. doi:10.1111/j.1468-0017.1996.tb00039.x.

D'Entremont, Barbara, Aimee Yazbeck, Amanda Morgan & Sarah MacAulay. 2007. Early gaze-following and the understanding of others. In Ross Flomm, Kang Lee & Darwin Muir (eds.), *Gaze-following: Its development and significance*, 77–94. Mahwah: Lawrence Erlbaum Associates.

Dabrowska, Ewa, Caroline Rowland & Anna Theakston. 2009. The acquisition of questions with long-distance dependencies. *Cognitive Linguistics* 20(3). 571–597. doi:10.1515/COGL.2009.025.

Dahl, Östen & Kari Fraurud. 1996. Animacy in grammar and discourse. In Thorstein Fretheim & Jeanette K. Gundel (eds.), *Reference and referent accessibility*, 47–64. John Benjamins Publishing Company.

Dale, Karen L. & Roy F. Baumeister. 1999. Self-regulation and psychopathology. In Mark R. Leary & Robin M. Kowalski (eds.), *The social psychology of emotional and behavioral problems: Interfaces of social and clinical psychology.*, 139–166. Washington, DC: American Psychological Association.

Dally, Joanna M., Nathan J. Emery & Nicola S. Clayton. 2006. Food-caching western scrub-jays keep track of who was watching when. *Science* 312(5780). 1662–1665. doi:10.1126/science.1126539.

Daneman, Meredyth. 1987. Reading and working memory. In John Beech & Anne Colley (eds.), *Cognitive Approaches to Reading*, 57–86. Chichester, UK: Wiley.

Daneman, Meredyth. 1991. Working memory as a predictor of verbal fluency. *Journal of Psycholinguistic Research* 20. 445–464. doi:10.1007/BF01067637.

Daneman, Meredyth & Patricia A. Carpenter. 1980. Individual differences in working memory and reading. *Journal of Verbal Learning and Verbal Behavior* 19(4). 450–466. doi:10.1016/S0022-5371(80)90312-6.

Daneman, Meredyth & Patricia A. Carpenter. 1983. Individual differences in integrating information between and within sentences. *Journal of Experimental Psychology: Learning, Memory, and Cognition* 9(4). 561–584. doi:10.1037/0278-7393.9.4.561.

Daneman, Meredyth & Ian Green. 1986. Individual differences in comprehending and producing words in context. *Journal of Memory and Language* 25(1). 1–18. doi:10.1016/0749-596X(86)90018-5.

Darwin, Charles. 1874. *The descent of man and selection in relation to sex*. London: John Murray. doi:10.1017/CBO9780511703829.

Daum, Moritz M., Wolfgang Prinz & Gisa Aschersleben. 2009. Means-end behavior in young infants: The interplay of action perception and action production. *Infancy* 14(6). 613–640. doi:10.1080/15250000903263965.

Daum, Moritz M., Maria T. Vuori, Wolfgang Prinz & Gisa Aschersleben. 2009. Inferring the size of a goal object from an actor's grasping movement in 6- and 9-month-old infants. *Developmental Science* 2(6). 854–862. doi:10.1111/j.1467-7687.2009.00831.x.

Davis, Janet M. & Carolyn K. Rovee-Collier. 1983. Alleviated forgetting of a learned contingency in 8-week-old infants. *Developmental Psychology* 19(3). 353–365. doi:10.1037/0012-1649.19.3.353.

Dawkins, Richard. 1976. *The Selfish Gene*. Oxford: Oxford University Press. doi:10.4324/9781912281251.

de Bruin, Angela., Barbara Treccani, & Sergio Della Sala. 2015. Cognitive Advantage in Bilingualism: An Example of Publication Bias? *Psychological Science*, 26(1), 99–107. https://doi.org/10.1177/0956797614557866.

Decasper, Anthony J. & William P. Fifer. 1980. Of human bonding: Newborns prefer their mothers' voices. *Science* 208(4448). 1174–1176. doi:10.1126/science.7375928.

Dehaene, Stanislas. 1997. *The Number Sense*. New York: Oxford University Press.

Dehaene, Stanislas, Michel Kerszberg & Jean-Pierre Changeux. 1998. A neuronal model of a global workspace in effortful cognitive tasks. *Proceedings of the National Academy of Sciences* 95(24). 14529–14534. doi:10.1073/pnas.95.24.14529.

Dehaene, Stanislas, Elizabeth Spelke, Philippe Pinel, Ruxandra Stanescu & Sanna Tsivkin. 1999. Sources of mathematical thinking: Behavioral and brain-imaging evidence. *Science* 284(5416). 970–974. doi:10.1126/science.284.5416.970.

Dehaene, Stanislas. 2004. Evolution of human cortical circuits for reading and arithmetic : The "neuronal recycling" hypothesis. In Stanislas Dehaene, Jean-René Duhamel, Marc D. Hauser and Giacomo Rizzolatti (eds.), *From Monkey Brain to Human Brain*, 133–157. Cambridge, MA: MIT Press.

Dehaene, Stanislas. 2010. *Reading in the Brain. The Science and Evolution of a Human Invention*. New York: Viking.

Dehaene, Stanislas & Laurent Cohen. 2007. Cultural recycling of cortical maps. *Neuron* 56(2). 384–398. doi:10.1016/j.neuron.2007.10.004.

DeLancey, Scott & Bernard Comrie. 1983. Language Universals and Linguistic Typology: Syntax and Morphology. *Language* 59(2). 406–411. doi:10.2307/413584.

Delaney, Peter F., Peter P. J. L. Verkoeijen & Arie Spirgel. 2010. Spacing and Testing Effects: A Deeply Critical, Lengthy, and At Times Discursive Review of the Literature. *Psychology of Learning and Motivation – Advances in Research and Theory* 53. 63–147. doi:10.1016/S0079-7421(10)53003-2.

Delvaux, Véronique & Alain Soquet. 2007. The influence of ambient speech on adult speech productions through unintentional imitation. *Phonetica* 64. 145–173. doi:10.1159/000107914.

Denny, John P. 1976. What are noun classifiers good for? In Salikoko S. Mufwene, Carol A. Walker & Sanford B. Steever (eds.), *Papers from the Twelfth Regional Meeting, Chicago Linguistic Society, April 23–25*, 122–132. Chicago Linguistic Society, Chicago.

DeWall, C. Nathan, Geoff MacDonald, Gregory D. Webster, Carrie L. Masten, Roy F. Baumeister, Caitlin Powell, David Combs, David R. Schurtz, Tyler F. Stillman, Dianne M. Tice & Naomi I. Eisenberger. 2010. Acetaminophen reduces social pain: Behavioral and neural evidence. *Psychological Science* 21(7). 931–937. doi:10.1177/0956797610374741.

Diamond, Adele. 1985. Development of the ability to use recall to guide action, as indicated by infants' performance on AB. *Child development* 56(4). 868–83. doi:10.2307/1130099.

Diamond, Adele. 1990. Developmental Time Course in Human Infants and Infant Monkeys, and the Neural Bases of, Inhibitory Control in Reaching. *Annals of the New York Academy of Sciences* 608(1). 637–676. doi:10.1111/j.1749-6632.1990.tb48913.x.

Diamond, Adele. 2002. Normal development of prefrontal cortex from birth to young adulthood: Cognitive functions, anatomy, and biochemistry. In Donald T. Stuss & Robert T. Knight (eds.), *Principles of frontal lobe function*, 466–503. New York, NY: Oxford University Press.

Diamond, Adele & Patricia S. Goldman-Rakic. 1989. Comparison of human infants and rhesus monkeys on Piaget's AB task: evidence for dependence on dorsolateral prefrontal cortex. *Experimental Brain Research* 74. 24–40. doi:10.1007/BF00248277.

Diamond, Adele, Stuart Zola-Morgan & Larry R. Squire. 1989. Successful Performance by Monkeys With Lesions of the Hippocampal Formation on AB and Object Retrieval, Two Tasks That Mark Developmental Changes in Human Infants. *Behavioral Neuroscience* 103(3). 526–537. doi:10.1037/0735-7044.103.3.526.

Dick, Anthony, Byron Bernal & Pascale Tremblay. 2014. The language connectome: New pathways, new concepts. *Neuroscientist* 20(5). 453–467. doi:10.1177/1073858413513502.

Dick, Anthony & Pascale Tremblay. 2012. Beyond the arcuate fasciculus: Consensus and controversy in the connectional anatomy of language. *Brain* 35(12). 3529–3550. doi:10.1093/brain/aws222.

Dick, Frederic, Elizabeth Bates, Jennifer Aydelott Utman, Beverly Wulfeck, Nina Dronkers & Morton Ann Gernsbacher. 2001. Language deficits, localization, and grammar: Evidence for a distributive model of language breakdown in aphasic patients and neurologically intact individuals. *Psychological Review* 108(4). 759–788. doi:10.1037/0033-295X.108.4.759.

Diessel, Holger. 2007. Frequency effects in language acquisition, language use, and diachronic change. *New Ideas in Psychology* 25(2). 108–127. doi:10.1016/j.newideapsych.2007.02.002.

Diessel, Holger & Michael Tomasello. 2005. A New Look at the Acquisition of Relative Clauses. *Language* 81. 882–906. doi:10.1353/lan.2005.0169.

Dijksterhuis, Ap & John A. Bargh. 2004. The perception-behavior expressway: Automatic effects of social perception on social behavior. *Advances in Experimental Social Psychology* 33. 1–40. doi:10.1016/s0065-2601(01)80003-4.

Dorval, Bruce, Carol O. Eckerman & Susan Ervin-Tripp. 1984. Developmental Trends in the Quality of Conversation Achieved by Small Groups of Acquainted Peers. *Monographs of the Society for Research in Child Development* 49(2). 1–91. doi:10.2307/1165872.

Dowty, David. 1991. Thematic proto-roles and argument selection. *Language* 67(3). 547–619. doi:10.2307/415037.

Dronkers, Nina F. 2000. The Pursuit of Brain–Language Relationships. *Brain and Language* 71(1). 59–61. doi:10.1006/brln.1999.2212.

Duguid, Shona, Emily Wyman, Anke F. Bullinger, Katharina Herfurth-Majstorovic & Michael Tomasello. 2014. Coordination strategies of chimpanzees and human children in a Stag Hunt game. *Proceedings of the Royal Society B: Biological Sciences* 281. doi:10.1098/rspb.2014.1973.

Dunn, Michael, Simon J. Greenhill, Stephen C. Levinson & Russell D. Gray. 2011. Evolved structure of language shows lineage-specific trends in word-order universals. *Nature* 473. 79–82. doi:10.1038/nature09923.

Ebert, Kerry Danahy. 2014. Role of auditory non-verbal working memory in sentence repetition for bilingual children with primary language impairment. *International Journal of Language and Communication Disorders* 49(5). 631–636. doi:10.1111/1460-6984.12090.

Eichenbaum, Howard & Neal J. Cohen. 2008. *From Conditioning to Conscious Recollection: Memory systems of the brain.* New York: Oxford University Press doi:10.1093/acprof:oso/9780195178043.001.0001.

Eisenberg, Michelle L, Jeffrey M Zacks & Shaney Flores. 2018. Dynamic Prediction During Perception of Everyday Events. *bioRxiv.* doi:10.1101/348946.

Eisenberg, Sarita L., Ling-Yu Guo & Mor Germezia. 2012. How Grammatical Are 3-Year-Olds? *Language, Speech, and Hearing Services in Schools* 43(1). 36–52. doi:10.1044/0161-1461(2011/10-0093).

Eisenberger, Naomi I., Matthew D. Lieberman & Kipling D. Williams. 2003. Does rejection hurt? An fMRI study of social exclusion. *Science* 302(5643). 290–292. doi:10.1126/science.1089134.

Ejiri, Keiko & Nobuo Masataka. 2001. Co-occurrence of preverbal vocal behavior and motor action in early infancy. *Developmental Science* 4(1). 40–48. doi:10.1111/1467-7687.00147.

Elio, Renee & John R. Anderson. 1984. The effects of information order and learning mode on schema abstraction. *Memory & Cognition* 12. 20–30. doi:10.3758/BF03196994.

Ellefson, Michelle R. & Morten H. Christiansen. 2000. Subjacency constraints without universal grammar: Evidence from artificial language learning and connectionist modeling. *The Proceedings of the 22nd Annual Cognitive Science Society Conference*, 645–50. Mahwah NJ: Lawrence Erlbaum Associates.

Ellis, Rod. 1991. Grammaticality Judgments And Second Language Acquisition. *Studies in Second Language Acquisition* 13(2). 161–186. doi:10.1017/S0272263100009931.

Elman, Jeffrey L. 1990. Finding structure in time. *Cognitive Science* 14(2). 179–211. doi:10.1016/0364-0213(90)90002-E.

Elman, Jeffrey L. 1993. Learning and development in neural networks: the importance of starting small. *Cognition* 48(1). 71–99. doi:10.1016/0010-0277(93)90058-4.

Elman, Jeffrey L. 2005. Connectionist models of cognitive development: Where next? *Trends in Cognitive Sciences* 9(3).112–117. doi:10.1016/j.tics.2005.01.005.

Elman, Jeffrey, Elizabeth A. Bates, Mark H. Johnson, Annette Karmiloff-Smith, Domenico Parisi & Kim Plunkett. 1996. *Rethinking Innateness: A Connectionist Perspective on Development. Rethinking Innateness: A Connectionist Perspective on Development.* Cambridge, MA: MIT Press. doi:10.1016/S0001-6918(97)00029-2.

Emery, Nathan J. & Nicola S. Clayton. 2001. Effects of experience and social context on prospective caching strategies by scrub jays. *Nature* 414. 443–446. doi:10.1038/35106560.

Emery, Nathan J. & Nicola S. Clayton. 2004. The mentality of crows: Convergent evolution of intelligence in corvids and apes. *Science* 306(5703). 1903–1907. doi:10.1126/science.1098410.

Eppler, Marion A. 1995. Development of manipulatory skills and the deployment of attention. *Infant Behavior and Development* 18(4). 391–405. doi:10.1016/0163-6383(95)90029-2.

Erickson, Thomas D. & Mark E. Mattson. 1981. From words to meaning: A semantic illusion. *Journal of Verbal Learning and Verbal Behavior* 20(5). 540–551. doi:10.1016/S0022-5371(81)90165-1.

Ericsson, K. Anders, William G. Chase & Steve Faloon. 1980. Acquisition of a memory skill. *Science* 208(4448). 1181–1182.

Evans, Nicholas & Stephen C. Levinson. 2009. The myth of language universals: Language diversity and its importance for cognitive science. *Behavioral and Brain Sciences* 32(5). 429–448. doi:10.1017/S0140525X0999094X.

Everett, Daniel. 2012. *Language: The Cultural Tool*. London: Profile Books.

Fagan, Joseph F. 1984. The relationship of novelty preferences during infancy to later intelligence and later recognition memory. *Intelligence* 8(4). 339–346. doi:10.1016/0160-2896(84)90016-3.

Falck-Ytter, Terje, Gustaf Gredebäck & Claes Von Hofsten. 2006. Infants predict other people's action goals. *Nature Neuroscience* 9(7). 878–879. doi:10.1038/nn1729.

Fantz, Robert L. 1963. Pattern vision in newborn infants. *Science* 140(3564). 296–297. doi:10.1126/science.140.3564.296.

Fantz, Robert L. 1964. Visual experience in infants: Decreased attention to familiar patterns relative to novel ones. *Science* 146(3644). 668–670. doi:10.1126/science.146.3644.668.

Farrar, Michael Jeffrey. 1990. Discourse and the acquisition of grammatical morphemes. *Journal of Child Language* 17(3). 607–624. doi:10.1017/s0305000900010904.

Farrar, Michael Jeffrey. 1992. Negative Evidence and Grammatical Morpheme Acquisition. *Developmental Psychology* 28(1). 90–98. doi:10.1037/0012-1649.28.1.90.

Farroni, Teresa, Gergely Csibra, Francesca Simion & Mark H. Johnson. 2002. Eye contact detection in humans from birth. *Proceedings of the National Academy of Sciences* 99(14). 9602–9605. doi:10.1073/pnas.152159999.

Farroni, Teresa, Mark H. Johnson & Gergely Csibra. 2004. Mechanisms of eye gaze perception during infancy. *Journal of Cognitive Neuroscience* 16(8). 1320–1326. doi:10.1162/0898929042304787.

Farroni, Teresa, Stefano Massaccesi, Enrica Menon & Mark H. Johnson. 2007. Direct gaze modulates face recognition in young infants. *Cognition* 102(3),396–404. doi:10.1016/j.cognition.2006.01.007.

Farroni, Teresa, Stefano Massaccesi, Donatella Pividori & Mark H. Johnson. 2004. Gaze following in newborns. *Infancy* 5(1). 39–60. doi:10.1207/s15327078in0501_2.

Feldman, Jerome & Srinivas Narayanan. 2004. Embodied meaning in a neural theory of language. *Brain and Language* 89(2). 385–392. doi:10.1016/S0093-934X(03)00355-9.

Fernald, Anne & Hiromi Morikawa. 1993. Common Themes and Cultural Variations in Japanese and American Mothers' Speech to Infants. *Child Development* 64(3). 637–656. doi:10.1111/j.1467-8624.1993.tb02933.x.

Fernald, Anne, Kirsten Thorpe & Virginia A. Marchman. 2010. Blue car, red car: Developing efficiency in online interpretation of adjective-noun phrases. *Cognitive Psychology* 60(3). 190–217. doi:10.1016/j.cogpsych.2009.12.002.

Fernald, Anne, Renate Zangl, Ana Luz Portillo & Virginia A. Marchman. 2008. Looking while listening: Using eye movements to monitor spoken language comprehension in infants and young children. In Irina A. Sekerina, Eva M. Fernández, & Harald Clahsen (Eds.), *Language acquisition and language disorders: Vol. 44. Developmental psycholinguistics: On-line methods in children's language processing*, 97–135. Amsterdam: John Benjamins Publishing Company. doi:10.1075/lald.44.06fer

Ferreira, Fernanda & John M. Henderson. 2004. *The Interface of Language, Vision, and Action: Eye Movements and the Visual World*. New York: Psychology Press. doi:10.4324/9780203488430.

Ferreira, Victor S. & Hiromi Yoshita. 2003. Given-new ordering effects on the production of scrambled sentences in Japanese. *Journal of Psycholinguistic Research* 32(6). 669–692. doi:10.1023/A:1026146332132.

Fillmore, Charles J. 1976. Frame semantics and the nature of language. *Annals of the New York Academy of Sciences* 280(1). 20–32. doi:10.1111/j.1749-6632.1976.tb25467.x.

Fillmore, Charles J., Paul Kay & Mary Catherine O'Connor. 1988. Regularity and Idiomaticity in Grammatical Constructions: The Case of Let Alone. *Language* 64(3). 501–538. doi:10.2307/414531.

Finch, Steven & Nick Chater. 1992. Bootstrapping Syntactic Categories. In Walter Daelmans and David Powers (eds.), *Background and Experiments in Machine Learning of Natural Language*, 229–235. Institute for Language Technology and Artificial Intelligence, Tilburg University.

Finch, Steven & Nick Chater. 1994. Distributional Bootstrapping: From Word Class to Proto-Sentence. *Proceedings of the Sixteenth Annual Conference of the Cognitive Science Society*, 301–306. Hillsdale NJ: Lawrence Erlbaum Associates.

Fiser, József & Richard N. Aslin. 2002. Statistical Learning of Higher-Order Temporal Structure from Visual Shape Sequences. *Journal of Experimental Psychology: Learning Memory and Cognition* 28(3). 458–467. doi:10.1037/0278-7393.28.3.458.

Fisher, Cynthia. 2002. Structural limits on verb mapping: The role of abstract structure in 2.5-year-olds' interpretations of novel verbs. *Developmental Science* 5(1). 55–64. doi:10.1111/1467-7687.00209.

Flanagan, J. Randall & Roland S. Johansson. 2003. Action plans used in action observation. *Nature* 424(6950). 769–771. doi:10.1038/nature01861.

Flecken, Monique, Panos Athanasopoulos, Jan Rouke Kuipers & Guillaume Thierry. 2015. On the road to somewhere: Brain potentials reflect language effects on motion event perception. *Cognition* 141. 41–51. doi:10.1016/j.cognition.2015.04.006.

Flecken, Monique, Christiane Von Stutterheim & Mary Carroll. 2014. Grammatical aspect influences motion event perception: findings from a cross- linguistic non-verbal recognition task. *Language and Cognition* 6(1). 45–78. doi:10.1017/langcog.2013.2.

Flege, James Emil. 1984. The detection of French accent by American listeners. *The Journal of the Acoustical Society of America* 76. 692–707. doi:10.1121/1.391256.

Flombaum, Jonathan I. & Laurie R. Santos. 2005. Rhesus monkeys attribute perceptions to others. *Current Biology* 15(5):447–452. doi:10.1016/j.cub.2004.12.076.

Fodor, Jerry A. 1983. *Modularity of Mind: An Essay on Faculty Psychology*. Cambridge, MA: MIT Press.

Fowler, Anne E. 1991. How early phonological development might set the stage for phoneme awareness. In Susan A. Brady & Donald P. Shankweiler (eds.), *Phonological processes in literacy: A tribute to Isabelle Y. Liberman*, 97–117. Lawrence Erlbaum Associates.

Frank, Michael C., Daniel L. Everett, Evelina Fedorenko & Edward Gibson. 2008. Number as a cognitive technology: Evidence from Pirahã language and cognition. *Cognition* 108(3). 819–24. doi:10.1016/j.cognition.2008.04.007.

Frank, Michael C., Noah D. Goodman & Joshua B. Tenenbaum. 2009. Using speakers' referential intentions to model early cross-situational word learning: Research article. *Psychological Science* 20(5). 578–585. doi:10.1111/j.1467-9280.2009.02335.x.

Franks, Jeffery J. & John D. Bransford. 1971. Abstraction of visual patterns. *Journal of Experimental Psychology* 90(1). 65–74. doi:10.1037/h0031349.

Freire, Alejo, Michelle Eskritt & Kang Lee. 2004. Are eyes windows to a deceiver's soul? Children's use of another's eye gaze cues in a deceptive situation. *Developmental Psychology* 40(6). 1093–1104. doi:10.1037/0012-1649.40.6.1093.
Freudenthal, Daniel, Julian M. Pine, Gary Jones & Fernand Gobet. 2015. Simulating the cross-linguistic pattern of Optional Infinitive errors in children's declaratives and Wh-questions. *Cognition* 143. 61–76. doi:10.1016/j.cognition.2015.05.027.
Friederici, Angela D. & Wolf Singer. 2015. Grounding language processing on basic neurophysiological principles. *Trends in Cognitive Sciences* 9(6). 329–38. doi:10.1016/j.tics.2015.03.012.
Friedman, Naomi P. & Akira Miyake. 2017. Unity and diversity of executive functions: Individual differences as a window on cognitive structure. *Cortex* 86. 186–204. doi:10.1016/j.cortex.2016.04.023.
Friend, Margaret & Amy Pace. 2011. Beyond event segmentation: Spatial- and social-cognitive processes in verb-to-action mapping. *Developmental Psychology* 47(3). 867–876. doi:10.1037/a0021107.
Friston, Karl & Stefan Kiebel. 2009. Predictive coding under the free-energy principle. *Philosophical Transactions of the Royal Society B: Biological Sciences*, 364(1521). 1211–1221. doi:10.1098/rstb.2008.0300.
Fuertes, Jairo N., William H. Gottdiener, Helena Martin, Tracey C. Gilbert & Howard Giles. 2012. A meta-analysis of the effects of speakers' accents on interpersonal evaluations. *European Journal of Social Psychology* 42. 120–133. doi:10.1002/ejsp.862.
Fujimori, Atsushi. 2012. The association of sound with meaning. The case of telicity. In Anna Maria Di Sciullo (ed.), *Towards a Biolinguistic Understanding of Grammar: Essays on Interfaces*, 141–166. Amsterdam: John Benjamins Publishing Company.
Fujita, Kazuo & Tetsuro Matsuzawa. 1990. Delayed figure reconstruction by a chimpanzee (Pan troglodytes) and humans (Homo sapiens). *Journal of Comparative Psychology* 104(4). 345–351. doi:10.1037/0735-7036.104.4.345.
Gagne, Jeffrey R. & Kimberly J. Saudino. 2016. The development of inhibitory control in early childhood: A twin study from 2-3 years. *Developmental Psychology* 52(3). 391–399. doi:10.1037/dev0000090.
Gallistel, Charles R. 1990. *The Organization of Learning*. Cambridge, MA: MIT Press.
Gandolfi, Elena & Paola Viterbori. 2020. Inhibitory Control Skills and Language Acquisition in Toddlers and Preschool Children. *Language Learning*. doi:doi:10.1111/lang.12388.
Gangopadhyay, Ishanti, Meghan M. Davidson, Susan Ellis Weismer & Margarita Kaushanskaya. 2016. The role of nonverbal working memory in morphosyntactic processing by school-aged monolingual and bilingual children. *Journal of Experimental Child Psychology* 142. 171–194. doi:10.1016/j.jecp.2015.09.025.
Garvey, Catherine. 1984. *Children's Talk*. Cambridge, MA: Harvard University Press.
Gathercole, Susan E., Darren L. Dunning, Joni Holmes & Dennis Norris. 2019. Working memory training involves learning new skills. *Journal of Memory and Language* 105. 19–42. doi:10.1016/J.JML.2018.10.003.
Gaulin, Cynthia A. & Thomas F. Campbell. 1994. Procedure for assessing verbal working memory i n normal school-age children: some preliminary data. *Perceptual and Motor Skills* 79(1-1). 55–64. doi:10.2466/pms.1994.79.1.55.
Gebhart, Andrea L., Elissa L. Newport & Richard N. Aslin. 2009. Statistical learning of adjacent and nonadjacent dependencies among nonlinguistic sounds. *Psychonomic Bulletin and Review* 16. 486–490. doi:10.3758/PBR.16.3.486.

Geert, Paul Van. 2011. Nonlinear complex dynamical systems in developmental psychology. In Stephen Guastello, Matthijs Koopmans, & David Pincus (eds.), *Chaos and Complexity in Psychology: The Theory of Nonlinear Dynamical Systems*, 242–281. Cambridge: Cambridge University Press. doi:10.1017/CBO9781139058544.009.

Gelman, Susan A. & Melissa A. Koenig. 2001. The role of animacy in children's understanding of "move". *Journal of child language* 28(3). 683–701. doi:10.1017/S0305000901004810.

Gennari, Silvia P., Steven A. Sloman, Barbara C. Malt & W. Tecumseh Fitch. 2002. Motion events in language and cognition. *Cognition* 3(1). 49–79. doi:10.1016/S0010-0277(01)00166-4.

Gentner, Dedre. 1982. Why nouns are learned before verbs: Linguistic relativity versus natural partitioning. *Language* 2. 301–334.

Gentner, Dedre & Arthur B. Markman. 1993. Analogy-watershed or Waterloo? Structural alignment and the development of connectionist models of cognition. In Steven J. Hanson, Jack D. Cowan & C. Lee Giles (eds.), *Advances in neural information processing systems*, 855–862. 5th ed. San Mateo, CA: Kaufmann.

Gentner, Dedre & Arthur B. Markman. 1994. Structural alignment in comparison: No Difference Without Similarity. *Psychological Science* 5(3). 152–158. doi:10.1111/j.1467-9280.1994.tb00652.x.

Gentner, Dedre & Arthur B. Markman. 1995. Similarity Is Like Analogy: Structural Alignment in Comparison. In Cristina Cacciari (ed.), *Similarity in language, thought and perception*, 111–147. Brussels: Brepols.

Gentner, Dedre & Arthur B. Markman. 1997. Structure Mapping in Analogy and Similarity. *American Psychologist* 52(1). 45–56. doi:10.1037/0003-066X.52.1.45.

Gentner, Dedre & José Medina. 1998. Similarity and the development of rules. *Cognition* 65(2-3). 263–297. doi:10.1016/S0010-0277(98)00002-X.

Gentner, Dedre, Mary Jo Rattermann & Kenneth D. Forbus. 1993. The Roles of Similarity in Transfer: Separating Retrievability From Inferential Soundness. *Cognitive Psychology* 5(4). 524–575. doi:10.1006/cogp.1993.1013.

Gergely, György, Harold Bekkering, Ildikó Király & I Kiraldy. 2002. Rational imitation in preverbal infant. *Nature* 415(6873). 755. doi:10.1038/415755a

Gibson, Eleanor J., Karen E. Adolph, Steven M. Boker, Bennett I. Bertenthal & Eugene C. Goldfield. 2006. Learning in the Development of Infant Locomotion. *Monographs of the Society for Research in Child Development* 62(3). i–162. doi:10.2307/1166199.

Gierhan, Sarah M. E. 2013. Connections for auditory language in the human brain. *Brain and Language* 127(2). 205–21. doi:10.1016/j.bandl.2012.11.002.

Gilby, Ian C. 2006. Meat sharing among the Gombe chimpanzees: Harassment and reciprocal exchange. *Animal Behaviour* 71(4). 953–963. doi:10.1016/j.anbehav.2005.09.009.

Giles, Amy, & Carolyn Rovee-Collier. 2011. Infant long-term memory for associations formed during mere exposure. Infant Behavior and Development, 34, 327–338. doi:10.1016/j.infbeh.2011.02.004.

Giles, Howard & Andrew Billings. 2004. Assessing language attitudes. In Alan Davies and Catherine Elder (eds.), *Handbook of Applied Linguistics*, 187–209. Oxford: Blackwell.

Giles, Howard, Justine Coupland & Nikolas Coupland (eds.). 1991. *Contexts of accommodation: Developments in applied sociolinguistics. Contexts of accommodation: Developments in applied sociolinguistics.* Cambridge: Cambridge University Press. doi:10.1017/CBO9780511663673.

Gintis, Herbert. 2011. Gene-culture coevolution and the nature of human sociality. *Philosophical Transactions of the Royal Society B: Biological Sciences* 366(1566). 878–888. doi:10.1098/rstb.2010.0310.

Givón, Talmy. 1979. *On Understanding Grammar*. New York: Academic Press.

Givón, Talmy. 1992. The grammar of referential coherence as mental processing instructions. *Linguistics* 30(1). 5–55. doi:10.1515/ling.1992.30.1.5.

Givón, Talmy. 1995. *Functionalism and Grammar*. Amsterdam: John Benjamins Publishing Company. doi:10.1075/z.74.

Gleick, James. 1998. *Chaos: Making a New Science*. New York: Penguin.

Gleitman, Lila. 1990. The Structural Sources of Verb Meanings. *Language Acquisition* 1(1). 3–55. doi:10.1207/s15327817la0101_2.

Gleitman, Lila R., David January, Rebecca Nappa & John C. Trueswell. 2007. On the give and take between event apprehension and utterance formulation. *Journal of Memory and Language* 57(4). 544–569. doi:10.1016/j.jml.2007.01.007.

Glenberg, Arthur M. 2012. Language and action: Creating sensible combinations of ideas. In M. Gareth Gaskell (ed.), *The Oxford Handbook of Psycholinguistics*, 361–370. New York: Oxford University Press. doi:10.1093/oxfordhb/9780198568971.013.0021.

Glenberg, Arthur M. & Michael P. Kaschak. 2002. Grounding language in action. *Psychonomic Bulletin and Review* 9(3). 558–565. doi:10.3758/BF03196313.

Gobet, Fernand, Peter C. R. Lane, Steve Croker, Peter C. H. Cheng, Gary Jones, Iain Oliver & Julian M. Pine. 2001. Chunking mechanisms in human learning. *Trends in Cognitive Sciences* 5(6). 236–243. doi:10.1016/S1364-6613(00)01662-4.

Göksun, Tilbe, Kathy Hirsh-Pasek & Roberta M. Golinkoff. 2008. Foundations for learning relational terms: What is in an event? Paper presented at *Figure and ground: Conceptual primitives for processing events*. Symposium conducted at the Eleventh International Congress for the Study of Child Language, Edinburgh, Scotland.

Göksun, Tilbe, Kathy Hirsh-Pasek & Roberta Golinkoff. 2010. Trading spaces: Carving up events for learning language. *Perspectives on Psychological Science* 5(1). 33–42. doi:10.1177/1745691609356783.

Goldberg, Adele E. 1995. *Constructions: A construction grammar approach to argument structure*. Chicago: University of Chicago Press.

Goldberg, Adele E. 2005. *Constructions at Work: The Nature of Generalization in Language. Constructions at Work: The Nature of Generalization in Language*. New York: Oxford University Press. doi:10.1093/acprof:oso/9780199268511.001.0001.

Goldberg, Adele E. 2007. *Constructions at Work. Constructions at Work*. Oxford Scholarship Online. doi:10.1093/acprof:oso/9780199268511.001.0001.

Goldberg, Adele E. 2019. *Explain Me This: Creativity, Competition, and the Partial Productivity of Constructions*. Princeton: Princeton University Press.

Goldberg, Adele E., Devin M. Casenhiser & Nitya Sethuraman. 2004. Learning argument structure generalizations. *Cognitive Linguistics* 15(3). 289–316. doi:10.1515/cogl.2004.011.

Goldfield, Beverly A. 1993. Noun bias in maternal speech to one-year-olds. *Journal of Child Language* 20(1). 85–99. doi:10.1017/S0305000900009132.

Goldinger, Stephen D. 1998. Echoes of Echoes? An Episodic Theory of Lexical Access. *Psychological Review* 105(2). 251–279. doi:10.1037/0033-295X.105.2.251.

Goldsmith, John A. 2010. Segmentation and Morphology. *The Handbook of Computational Linguistics and Natural Language Processing*. Chichester: Wiley-Blackwell. doi:10.1002/9781444324044.ch14.

Goldstone, Robert L. 1994. The role of similarity in categorization: providing a groundwork. *Cognition* 52(2). 125–157. doi:10.1016/0010-0277(94)90065-5.

Goldstone, Robert L. & Douglas L. Medin. 1994. Interactive activation, similarity, and mapping: An overview. In Keith J. Holyoak & John A. Barnden (eds.), *Advances in connectionist and neural computation theory, Vol. 2. Analogical connections*, 321–362. Bristol: Intellect Ltd.

Goldstone, Robert L., Douglas L. Medin & Dedre Gentner. 1991. Relational similarity and the nonindependence of features in similarity judgments. *Cognitive Psychology* 23(2). 222–262. doi:10.1016/0010-0285(91)90010-L.

Golinkoff, Roberta, He Len Chung, Kathy Hirsh-Pasek, Jing Liu, Bennett Bertenthal, Rebecca Brand, Mandy Maguire & Elizabeth Hennon. 2002. Young children can extend motion verbs to point-light displays. *Developmental Psychology* 38(4). 604–614. doi:10.1037/0012-1649.38.4.604.

Golinkoff, Roberta, Carol G. Harding, Vicki Carlson & Miriam E. Sexton. 1984. The infant's perception of causal events: the distinction between animate and inanimate objects. In Lewis P. Lipsitt & Carolyn Rovee-Collier (eds.), *Advances in Infancy Research* 3. 145–151. Norwood, NJ: Ablex Publishing.

Golinkoff, Roberta Michnick, Carolyn B. Mervis & Kathryn Hirsh-Pasek. 1994. Early Object Labels: The Case for a Developmental Lexical Principles Framework. *Journal of Child Language* 21(1). 125–155. doi:10.1017/S0305000900008692.

Gomes, Cristina M., Roger Mundry & Christophe Boesch. 2009. Long-term reciprocation of grooming in wild West African chimpanzees. *Proceedings of the Royal Society B: Biological Sciences* 276. 699–706. doi:10.1098/rspb.2008.1324.

Goodglass, Harold. 1993. *Understanding Aphasia*. San Diego: Academic Press.

Goodman, Judith C., Philip S. Dale & Ping Li. 2008. Does frequency count? Parental input and the acquisition of vocabulary. *Journal of Child Language* 35(3). 515–531. doi:10.1017/S0305000907008641.

Goodwyn, Susan W., Linda P. Acredolo & Catherine A. Brown. 2000. Impact of symbolic gesturing on early language development. *Journal of Nonverbal Behavior* 24(2). 81–103. doi:10.1023/A:1006653828895.

Gopnik, Alison, Soonja Choi & Therese Baumberger. 1996. Cross-linguistic differences in early semantic and cognitive development. *Cognitive Development* 11(2). 197–227. doi:10.1016/S0885-2014(96)90003-9.

Gordon, Peter. 2004. Numerical cognition without words: Evidence from Amazonia. *Science* 306(5695). 496–499. doi:10.1126/science.1094492.

Gordon, Peter. 2010. Worlds without Words: Commensurability and Causality in Language, Culture, and Cognition. In Barbara Malt & Phillip Wolff (eds.), *Words and the Mind: How Words Capture Human Experience*, 199–218. New York: Oxford University Press. doi:10.1093/acprof:oso/9780195311129.003.0011.

Gould, Stephen Jay & Elisabeth S. Vrba. 1982. Exaptation – a Missing Term in the Science of Form. *Paleobiology* 8(1). 4–15. doi:10.1017/S0094837300004310.

Greco, Carolyn, Carolyn Rovee-Collier, Harlene Hayne, Pamela Griesler & Linda Earley. 1986. Ontogeny of early event memory: I. Forgetting and retrieval by 2- and 3-month-olds. *Infant Behavior and Development* 9(4). 441–460. doi:10.1016/0163-6383(86)90017-2.

Greenberg, Jeff, Sheldon Solomon & Tom Pyszczynski. 1997. Terror Management Theory of Self-Esteem and Cultural Worldviews: Empirical Assessments and Conceptual

Refinements. *Advances in Experimental Social Psychology* 29, 61–139. doi:10.1016/S0065-2601(08)60016-7.

Griffin, Zenzi M. & Kathryn Bock. 2000. What the eyes say about speaking. *Psychological Science* 11(4). 274–279. doi:10.1111/1467-9280.00255.

Griffiths, Thomas L. & Sharon Goldwater. 2007. A fully Bayesian approach to unsupervised part-of-speech tagging. *Proceedings of the 45th Annual Meeting of the Association of Computational Linguistics*, 744–751.

Grossmann, Tobias, Tricia Striano & Angela D. Friederic. 2006. Crossmodal integration of emotional information from face and voice in the infant brain. *Developmental Science* 9. 309–315. doi:10.1111/j.1467-7687.2006.00494.x.

Gruter, Margaret & Roger D. Masters. 1986. Ostracism as a social and biological phenomenon: An introduction. *Ethology and Sociobiology* 7(3-4). 149–158. doi:10.1016/0162-3095(86)90043-9.

Hafri, Alon, Anna Papafragou & John C. Trueswell. 2013. Getting the gist of events: Recognition of two-participant actions from brief displays. *Journal of Experimental Psychology: General* 142(3). 880–905. doi:10.1037/a0030045.

Hafri, Alon, John C. Trueswell & Brent Strickland. 2018. Encoding of event roles from visual scenes is rapid, spontaneous, and interacts with higher-level visual processing. *Cognition* 175. 36–52. doi:10.1016/j.cognition.2018.02.011.

Hahn, Erin R. & Lisa Gershkoff-Stowe. 2010. Children and adults learn actions for objects more readily than labels. *Language Learning and Development* 6(4). 283–308. doi:10.1080/15475441003635315.

Haith, Marshall. 1980. *Rules that babies look by: The organization of newborn visual activity*. Hillsdale, NJ: Lawrence Erlbaum Associates.

Haith, Marshall M., Cindy Hazan & Gail S. Goodman. 1988. Expectation and anticipation of dynamic visual events by 3.5-month-old babies. *Child development* 59(2). 467–479. doi:10.1111/j.1467-8624.1988.tb01481.x.

Halliday, Michael. 1985. *An introduction to functional grammar*. London: Edward Arnold.

Hamilton, Antonia, Daniel Wolpert & Uta Frith. 2004. Your own action influences how you perceive another person's action. *Current Biology* 4(6). 493–498. doi:10.1016/j.cub.2004.03.007.

Hamrick, Phillip. 2014. Recognition memory for novel syntactic structures. *Canadian Journal of Experimental Psychology* 68(1). 2–7. doi:10.1037/cep0000002.

Hanafiah, Zaliyana Mohd, Chizu Yamazaki, Akio Nakamura & Yoshinori Kuno. 2004. Understanding inexplicit utterances using vision for helper robots. *Proceedings – International Conference on Pattern Recognition* 4. 925–928. doi:10.1109/ICPR.2004.1333924.

Hanna, Elizabeth & Andrew N. Meltzoff. 1993. Peer Imitation by Toddlers in Laboratory, Home, and Day-Care Contexts: Implications for Social Learning and Memory. *Developmental Psychology* 29(4). 701–710. doi:10.1037/0012-1649.29.4.701.

Hannon, Erin E. & Sandra E. Trehub. 2005a. Metrical categories in infancy and adulthood. *Psychological Science* 16(1). 48–55. doi:10.1111/j.0956-7976.2005.00779.x.

Hannon, Erin E. & Sandra E. Trehub. 2005b. Tuning in to musical rhythms: Infants learn more readily than adults. *Proceedings of the National Academy of Sciences of the United States of America* 102(35). 12639–12643. doi:10.1073/pnas.0504254102.

Harris, Paul L. & María Núñez. 1996. Understanding of Permission Rules by Preschool Children. *Child Development* 67: 1572–1591. doi:10.1111/j.1467-8624.1996.tb01815.x.

Harris, Zellig S. 1954. Distributional Structure. *WORD* 10(2-3) 146–162. doi:10.1080/00437956.1954.11659520.

Hartshorn, Kristin, Carolyn Rovee-Collier, Peter Gerhardstein, Ramesh S. Bhatt, Pamela J. Klein, Fiamma Aaron, Teresa L. Wondoloski & Nathaniel Wurtzel. 1998. Developmental changes in the specificity of memory over the first year of life. *Developmental Psychobiology* 33. 61–78. doi:10.1002/(SICI)1098-2302(199807)33:1<61::AID-DEV6>3.0.CO;2-Q.

Haspelmath, M. 1999. Optimality and diachronic adaptation. *Zeitschrift für Sprachwissenschaft* 18(2). 180–205.

Hasson, Uri, Giovanna Egidi, Marco Marelli & Roel M. Willems. 2018. Grounding the neurobiology of language in first principles: The necessity of non-language-centric explanations for language comprehension. *Cognition* 180. 135–157. doi:10.1016/j.cognition.2018.06.018.

Hauser, Marc D., Noam Chomsky & W. Tecumseh Fitch. 2002. The Faculty of Language: What Is It, Who Has It, and How Did It Evolve? *Science* 298. 1569–1579. doi: 10.1126/science.298.5598.1569

Hawkins, John A. 1994. *A Performance Theory of Order and Constituency*. Cambridge: Cambridge University Press.

Hawkins, John A. 2007. Processing typology and why psychologists need to know about it. *New Ideas in Psychology* 25(2). 87–107. doi:10.1016/j.newideapsych.2007.02.003

Hay, Dale F. 1979. Cooperative interactions and sharing between very young children and their parents. *Developmental Psychology* 5(6). 647–653. doi:10.1037/0012-1649.15.6.647.

Hay, Dale F. & Patricia Murray. 1982. Giving and requesting: Social facilitation of infants' offers to adults. *Infant Behavior and Development* 5(3). 301–310. doi:10.1016/S0163-6383(82)80039-8.

Hayhoe, Mary & Dana Ballard. 2005. Eye movements in natural behavior. *Trends in Cognitive Sciences* 9(4). 188–194. doi:10.1016/j.tics.2005.02.009.

Hayne, Harlene, Joanne Boniface & Rachel Barr. 2000. The development of declarative memory in human infants: Age-related changes in deferred imitation. *Behavioral Neuroscience* 114(1). 77–83. doi:10.1037/0735-7044.114.1.77.

Hayne, Harlene, Carolyn Greco, Linda Earley, Pamela Griesler & Carolyn Rovee-Collier. 1986. Ontogeny of early event memory: II. Encoding and retrieval by 2- and 3-month-olds. *Infant Behavior and Development* 9(4). 461–472. doi:10.1016/0163-6383(86)90018-4.

Hayne, Harlene, Shelley MacDonald & Rachel Barr. 1997. Developmental changes in the specificity of memory over the second year of life. *Infant Behavior and Development* 20(2), 233–245. doi: https://doi.org/10.1016/S0163-6383(97)90025-4.

Heathcote, Andrew, Scott Brown & Douglas J. K. Mewhort. 2000. The power law repealed: The case for an exponential law of practice. *Psychonomic Bulletin and Review* 7(2). 185–207. doi:10.3758/BF03212979.

Hebb, Adam O. & George A. Ojemann. 2013. The thalamus and language revisited. *Brain and Language* 126(1). 99–108. doi:10.1016/j.bandl.2012.06.010.

Hebb, Donald O. 1949. *The Organization of Behavior*. New York: Wiley. doi:10.2307/1418888.

Heimann, Mikael & Andrew N. Meltzoff. 1996. Deferred imitation in 9- and 14-month-old infants: A longitudinal study of a Swedish sample. *British Journal of Developmental Psychology* 14(1). 55–64. doi:10.1111/j.2044-835X.1996.tb00693.x.

Heimann, Mikael, Karin Strid, Lars Smith, Tomas Tjus, Stein Erik Ulvund & Andrew N. Meltzoff. 2006. Exploring the relation between memory, gestural communication, and the emergence of language in infancy: A longitudinal study. *Infant and Child Development* 15. 233–249. doi:10.1002/icd.462.

Heiser, Marc, Marco Iacoboni, Fumiko Maeda, Jake Marcus & John Mazziotta. 2003. The essential role of Broca's area in imitation. *European Journal of Neuroscience* 17. 1123–1128. doi:10.1046/j.1460-9568.2003.02530.x.

Henke, Katharina. 2010. A model for memory systems based on processing modes rather than consciousness. *Nature Reviews Neuroscience* 11. 523–532. doi:10.1038/nrn2850.

Henrich, Joseph & Robert Boyd. 2001. Why people punish defectors: Weak conformist transmission can stabilize costly enforcement of norms in cooperative dilemmas. *Journal of Theoretical Biology* 208(1). 79–89. doi:10.1006/jtbi.2000.2202.

Henshilwood, Christopher, Francesco D'Errico, Royden Yates, Zenobia Jacobs, Chantal Tribolo, Geoff A.T. Duller, Norbert Mercier, Judith C. Sealy, Helene Valladas, Ian Watts & Ann G. Wintle. 2002. Emergence of modern human behavior: Middle stone age engravings from South Africa. *Science* 295(5558). 1278–1280. doi:10.1126/science.1067575.

Henshilwood, Christopher & Benoit Dubreuil. 2009. Reading the artifacts: gleaning language skills from the Middle Stone Age in southern Africa. In Rudolf Botha & Chris Knight (eds.), *The Cradle of Language*, 41–60. Oxford: Oxford University Press. doi:10.1002/9780470561119.socpsy001017.

Herrmann, Esther & Michael Tomasello. 2015. Focusing and shifting attention in human children (Homo sapiens) and Chimpanzees (Pan troglodytes). *Journal of Comparative Psychology* 129(3). 268–274. doi:10.1037/a0039384.

Hespos, Susan J. & Renée Baillargeon. 2006. Décalage in infants' knowledge about occlusion and containment events: Converging evidence from action tasks. *Cognition* 99(2). B31–B41. doi:10.1016/j.cognition.2005.01.010.

Hespos, Susan J. & Elizabeth S. Spelke. 2004. Conceptual precursors to language. *Nature* 430(6998). 453–456. doi:10.1038/nature02634.

Heuven, Walter J. B. van, Kathy Conklin, Emily L. Coderre, Taomei Guo & Ton Dijkstra. 2011. The influence of cross-language similarity on within- and between-language Stroop effects in trilinguals. *Frontiers in Psychology* 2. 374. doi:10.3389/fpsyg.2011.00374.

Hickmann, Maya. 2002. *Children's discourse: person, space and time across languages*. Cambridge studies in linguistics. Cambridge: Cambridge University Press.

Hicks, Glyn. 2009. Tough-Constructions and their derivation. *Linguistic Inquiry* 40(4). 535–566. doi:10.1162/ling.2009.40.4.535.

Hicks, Julie M. & John E. Richards. 1998. The effects of stimulus movement and attention on peripheral stimulus localization by 8- to 26-week-old infants. *Infant Behavior and Development* 21(4). 571–589. doi:10.1016/S0163-6383(98)90030-3.

Hill, Wendy L., Dianne Borovsky & Carolyn Rovee-Collier. 1988. Continuities in infant memory development. *Developmental Psychobiology* 21(1). 43–62. doi:10.1002/dev.420210104.

Hills, Thomas T., Mounir Maouene, Josita Maouene, Adam Sheya & Linda Smith. 2009. Categorical structure among shared features in networks of early-learned nouns. *Cognition* 112(3). 381–396. doi:10.1016/j.cognition.2009.06.002.

Hirsh-Pasek, Kathryn A. & Roberta Michnick Golinkoff. 2010. *Action Meets Word: How Children Learn Verbs*. Oxford: Oxford University Press. doi:10.1093/acprof:oso/9780195170009.001.0001.

Holland, John H. 1995. *Hidden order: How adaption builds complexity*. Reading, MA: Addison Wesley.

Holland, John H. 1998. *Emergence: From chaos to order*. Oxford: Oxford University Press.

Holmboe, Karla, Arielle Bonneville-Roussy, Gergely Csibra & Mark H. Johnson. 2018. Longitudinal development of attention and inhibitory control during the first year of life. *Developmental Science* 21(6). e12690. doi:10.1111/desc.12690.

Holmboe, Karla, R. M. Pasco Fearon, Gergely Csibra, Leslie A. Tucker & Mark H. Johnson. 2008. Freeze-Frame: A new infant inhibition task and its relation to frontal cortex tasks during infancy and early childhood. *Journal of Experimental Child Psychology* 100(2). 89–114. doi:10.1016/j.jecp.2007.09.004.

Holmboe, Karla, Zsofia Nemoda, R. M. Pasco Fearon, Gergely Csibra, Maria Sasvari-Szekely & Mark H. Johnson. 2010. Polymorphisms in Dopamine System Genes Are Associated With Individual Differences in Attention in Infancy. *Developmental Psychology* 46(2). 404–416. doi:10.1037/a0018180.

Holyoak, Keith J. & Kyunghee Koh. 1987. Surface and structural similarity in analogical transfer. *Memory & Cognition* 15(4). 332–340. doi:10.3758/BF03197035.

Hood, Bruce M. 1995. Shifts of visual attention in the human infant: A neuroscientific approach. In Carolyn Rovee-Collier & Lewis P. Lipsitt (eds.), *Advances in Infancy Research* 10. 163–216. New York: Ablex Publishing.

Hood, Bruce M., J. Douglas Willen & Jon Driver. 1998. Adult's eyes trigger shifts of visual attention in human infants. *Psychological Science* 9(2). 131–134. doi:10.1111/1467-9280.00024.

Hood, Bruce M., C. Neil Macrae, Victoria Cole-Davies & Melanie Dias. 2003. Eye remember you: The effects of gaze direction on face recognition in children and adults. *Developmental Science* 6. 67–71. doi:10.1111/1467-7687.00256.

Hopper, Paul. 1998. Emergent grammar. In Michael Tomasello. (ed.), *The new psychology of language: Cognitive and functional approaches to language structure*, 155–175. Mahwah, NJ: Lawrence Erlbaum Associates.

Hopper, Paul. 2015. Emergent Grammar. *Proceedings of the Thirteenth Annual Meeting of the Berkeley Linguistics Society*,139–157. doi:10.3765/bls.v13i0.1834.

Hopper, Paul J. & Sandra A. Thompson. 1980. Transitivity in Grammar and Discourse. *Language* 56(2). 251–299. doi:10.2307/413757.

Hout, Angelique van. 2001. Event semantics in the lexicon-syntax interface. In Carol Tenny & James Pustejovsky (eds.), *Events as grammatical objects*, 239–282. Stanford, CA: CSLI Publications.

Hsu, Vivian C. 2010. Time windows in retention over the first year-and-a-half of life: Spacing effects. *Developmental Psychobiology* 52. 764–774. doi:10.1002/dev.20472.

Hughes, Claire. 1998. Executive function in preschoolers: Links with theory of mind and verbal ability. *British Journal of Developmental Psychology* 16. 233–253. doi:10.1111/j.2044-835X.1998.tb00921.x.

Hunter, Michael A. & Elinor W. Ames. 1988. A multifactor model of infant preferences for novel and familiar stimuli. In Carolyn Rovee-Collier & Lewis P. Lipsitt (eds.), *Advances in Infancy Research* 5, 69–95. Norwood, NJ: Ablex Publishing.

Hunter, Sharon K. & John E. Richards. 2003. Peripheral stimulus localization by 5- to 14-week-old infants during phases of attention. *Infancy* 4. 1–25. doi:10.1207/S15327078IN0401_1.

Huttenlocher, Janellen, Wendy Haight, Anthony Bryk, Michael Seltzer & Thomas Lyons. 1991. Early Vocabulary Growth: Relation to Language Input and Gender. *Developmental Psychology* 27(2). 236–248. doi:10.1037/0012-1649.27.2.236.

Hwang, Heeju & Elsi Kaiser. 2009. The effects of lexical vs. perceptual primes on sentence production in Korean: An on-line investigation of event apprehension and sentence formulation. Talk presented at the 22nd CUNY conference on sentence processing. Davis, CA.

Ibbotson, Paul, Vsevolod Salnikov & Richard Walker. 2019. A dynamic network analysis of emergent grammar. *First Language* 39(6). 652–680. doi:10.1177/0142723719869562.

Ibbotson, Paul. 2013a. The role of semantics, pre-emption and skew in linguistic distributions: The case of the un-construction. *Frontiers in Psychology* 4. 989. doi:10.3389/fpsyg.2013.00989.

Ibbotson, Paul. 2013b. The scope of usage-based theory. *Frontiers in Psychology* 4. 255. doi:10.3389/fpsyg.2013.00255.

Ibbotson, Paul, Rose M. Hartman & Kristina Nilsson Björkenstam. 2018. Frequency filter: an open access tool for analysing language development. *Language, Cognition and Neuroscience* 33(10). 1325–1339. doi:10.1080/23273798.2018.1480788.

Ibbotson, Paul & Jennifer Kearvell-White. 2015. Inhibitory control predicts grammatical ability. *PLoS ONE* 10(12). e0145030. doi:10.1371/journal.pone.0145030.

Ibbotson, Paul, Elena Lieven & Michael Tomasello. 2014. The communicative contexts of grammatical aspect use in English. *Journal of Child Language* 41(3). 705–23. doi:10.1017/S0305000913000135.

Ibbotson, Paul, Elena V. M. Lieven & Michael Tomasello. 2013. The attention-grammar interface: Eye-gaze cues structural choice in children and adults. *Cognitive Linguistics* 24, 3. 457–481. doi:10.1515/cog-2013-0020.

Ibbotson, Paul, Diana G. López & Alan J. McKane. 2018. Goldilocks forgetting in cross-situational learning. *Frontiers in Psychology* 9. 1301. doi:10.3389/fpsyg.2018.01301.

Ibbotson, Paul, Anna Theakston, Elena Lieven & Mike Tomasello. 2010. The role of pronoun frames in early comprehension of transitive constructions in English. *Language Learning and Development* 7(1). 24–39. doi:10.1080/15475441003732914.

Ibbotson, Paul, Anna L. Theakston, Elena V. M. Lieven & Michael Tomasello. 2012. Semantics of the Transitive Construction: Prototype Effects and Developmental Comparisons. *Cognitive Science* 36. 1268–1288. doi:10.1111/j.1551-6709.2012.01249.x.

Ibbotson, Paul & Michael Tomasello. 2009. Prototype constructions in early language acquisition. *Language and Cognition* 1(1). 59–85. doi:10.1515/LANGCOG.2009.004.

Ido, Junichi, Yoshio Matsumoto, Tsukasa Ogasawara & Ryuichi Nisimura. 2006. Humanoid with interaction ability using vision and speech information. *2006 IEEE/RSJ International Conference on Intelligent Robots and Systems*. 1316–1321. doi:10.1109/IROS.2006.281896.

Imuta, Kana, Damian Scarf & Harlene Hayne. 2013. The effect of verbal reminders on memory reactivation in 2-, 3-, and 4-year-old children. *Developmental Psychology* 49(6). 1058–1065. doi:10.1037/a0029432.

Iverson, Jana M. & Mary K. Fagan. 2004. Infant vocal-motor coordination: Precursor to the gesture-speech system? *Child Development* 75. 1053–1066. doi:10.1111/j.1467-8624.2004.00725.x.

Iverson, Jana M. & Susan Goldin-Meadow. 2005. Gesture paves the way for language development. *Psychological Science* 6(5). 367–371. doi:10.1111/j.0956-7976.2005.01542.x.

Jackendoff, Ray. 1983. *Semantics and cognition*. Cambridge, MA: MIT Press.

Jackson-Maldonado, Donna, Donna Thal, Virginia Marchman, Elizabeth Bates & Vera Gutierrez-Clellen. 1993. Early lexical development in Spanish-speaking infants and toddlers. *Journal of Child Language* 20(3). 523–549. doi:10.1017/S0305000900008461.

Jaffe, Joseph, Beatrice Beebe, Stanley Feldstein, Cynthia L. Crown, Michael D. Jasnow, Philippe Rochat & Daniel N. Stern. 2001. Rhythms of dialogue in infancy: coordinated timing and social development. *Monographs of the Society for Research in Child Development* (66) (2), i-149. Washington, DC.

Jarvis, Helen L. & Susan E. Gathercole. 2003. Verbal and non-verbal working memory and achievements on National Curriculum tests at 11 and 14 years of age. *Educational and Child Psychology* 20(3). 123–140.

Johnson, Mark H. 2001. Functional brain development in humans. *Nature Reviews Neuroscience* 2. 475–483. doi:10.1038/35081509.

Johnson, Scott P., Dima Amso & Jonathan A. Slemmer. 2003. Development of object concepts in infancy: Evidence for early learning in an eye-tracking paradigm. *Proceedings of the National Academy of Sciences* 100(18). 10568–10573. doi:10.1073/pnas.1630655100.

Johnston, Timothy D. & Laura Edwards. 2002. Genes, interactions, and the development of behavior. *Psychological Review* 109(1). 26–34. doi:10.1037/0033-295X.109.1.26.

Kan, Irene P. & Sharon L. Thompson-Schill. 2004. Effect of name agreement on prefrontal activity during overt and covert picture naming. *Cognitive, Affective and Behavioral Neuroscience* 4. 43–57. doi:10.3758/CABN.4.1.43.

Kanemaru, Nao, Hama Watanabe & Gentaro Taga. 2012. Increasing selectivity of interlimb coordination during spontaneous movements in 2- to 4-month-old infants. *Experimental Brain Research* 218. 49–61. doi:10.1007/s00221-012-3001-3.

Kannass, Kathleen N. & Lisa M. Oakes. 2008. The development of attention and its relations to language in infancy and toddlerhood. *Journal of Cognition and Development* 9(2). 222–246. doi:10.1080/15248370802022696.

Kappes, Juliane, Annette Baumgaertner, Claudia Peschke & Wolfram Ziegler. 2009. Unintended imitation in nonword repetition. *Brain and Language* 111(3). 140–51. doi:10.1016/j.bandl.2009.08.008.

Karasik, Lana B., Catherine S. Tamis-LeMonda & Karen E. Adolph. 2016. Decisions at the brink: Locomotor experience affects infants' use of social information on an adjustable drop-off. *Frontiers in Psychology* 7. 797. doi:10.3389/fpsyg.2016.00797.

Karmiloff-Smith, Annette. 1986. From meta-processes to conscious access: Evidence from children's metalinguistic and repair data. *Cognition* 23(2). 95–147. doi:10.1016/0010-0277(86)90040-5.

Kawamoto, A. H. & J. McClelland. 1987. Mechanisms of sentence processing: Assigning roles to constituents of sentences. In James L. McClelland, David E. Rumelhart & PDP Research Group (eds.), *Parallel distributed processing. Vol. 2: Psychological and biological models*, 195–248. Lawrence Erlbaum Associates.

Kaye, Kenneth & Rosalind Charney. 1980. How mothers maintain "dialogue" with two-year-olds. In David R. Olson (ed.), *The Social Foundations of Language and Thought*, 211–30. New York, Norton.

Keenan, Edward. 1976. Towards a universal definition of "subject". In Charles N. Li (ed.) *Subject and Topic*, 303–333. New York: Academic Press

Keller, Heidi, Arnold Lohaus, Susanne Völker, Martina Cappenberg & Athanasios Chasiotis. 1999. Temporal contingency as an independent component of parenting behavior. *Child Development* 70. 474–485. doi:10.1111/1467-8624.00034.

Kelly, David J., Paul C. Quinn, Alan M. Slater, Kang Lee, Liezhong Ge & Olivier Pascalis. 2007. The other-race effect develops during infancy: Evidence of perceptual narrowing. *Psychological Science* 18(12). 1084–1089. doi:10.1111/j.1467-9280.2007.02029.x.

Kemmer, Suzanne. 2003. Human cognition and the elaboration of events: Some universal conceptual categories. In Michael Tomasello (ed.), *The New Psychology of Language, Volume II,* 89–118. Mahwah, NJ: Lawrence Erlbaum Associates.

Kibrik, Alexandr E. 1985. Toward a typology of ergativity. In. Johanna Nichols & Anthony Woodbury (eds.), *Grammar Inside and Outside the Clause,* 268–324. Cambridge: Cambridge University Press.

Kidd, Celeste, Katherine S. White & Richard N. Aslin. 2011. Toddlers use speech disfluencies to predict speakers' referential intentions. *Developmental Science* 14. 925–934. doi:10.1111/j.1467-7687.2011.01049.x.

Kidd, Evan. 2012. Implicit statistical learning is directly associated with the acquisition of syntax. *Developmental Psychology* 48(1). 171–184. doi:10.1037/a0025405.

Kidd, Evan, Seamus Donnelly & Morten H. Christiansen. 2018. Individual Differences in Language Acquisition and Processing. *Trends in Cognitive Sciences* 22(2). 154–169. doi:10.1016/j.tics.2017.11.006.

Kim, Mikyong, Karla K. McGregor & Cynthia K. Thompson. 2000. Early lexical development in English- and Korean-speaking children: Language-general and language-specific patterns. *Journal of Child Language* 27(2). 225–254. doi:10.1017/S0305000900004104.

King, Jonathan & Marcel Adam Just. 1991. Individual differences in syntactic processing: The role of working memory. *Journal of Memory and Language* 30(5). 580–602. doi:10.1016/0749-596X(91)90027-H.

Kinzler, Katherine D., Kristin Shutts, Jasmine DeJesus & Elizabeth S. Spelke. 2009. Accent Trumps Race in Guiding Children's Social Preferences. *Social Cognition* 27(4). 623–634. doi:10.1521/soco.2009.27.4.623.

Kirby, Simon. 1998. Fitness and the selective adaptation of language. In James R. Hurford, Michael Studdert-Kennedy & Chris Knight (eds.), *Approaches to the evolution of language: Social and cognitive bases,* 359–383. Cambridge: Cambridge University Press.

Kirby, Simon. 1999. *Function, selection and innateness: The emergence of language universals.* New York: Oxford University Press.

Kirjavainen, Minna, Anna Theakston & Elena Lieven. 2009. Can input explain children's me-for-I errors? *Journal of Child Language* 36(5). 1091–1114. doi:10.1017/s0305000909009350.

Kirkham, Natasha Z., Jonathan A. Slemmer & Scott P. Johnson. 2002. Visual statistical learning in infancy: Evidence for a domain general learning mechanism. *Cognition* 83(2). B35–B42. doi:10.1016/S0010-0277(02)00004-5.

Klatt, Dennis H. 1989. Review of selected models of speech perception. In William Marslen-Wilson (ed.), *Lexical representation and process,* 169–226. Cambridge, MA: MIT Press.

Klein, Dan & Christopher D. Manning. 2005. Natural language grammar induction with a generative constituent-context model. *Pattern Recognition* 38(9). 1407–1419. doi:10.1016/j.patcog.2004.03.023.

Knoeferle, Pia, Boukje Habets, Matthew W. Crocker & Thomas F. Münte. 2008. Visual scenes trigger immediate syntactic reanalysis: Evidence from ERPs during situated spoken comprehension. *Cerebral Cortex* 18(4). 789–795. doi:10.1093/cercor/bhm121.

Kobayashi, H. & S. Kohshima. 1997. Unique morphology of the human eye. *Nature* 387, 767–768. doi:10.1038/42842.

Kodama, K. 2004. The English Caused-Motion Construction Revisited–A Cognitive Perspective. *Papers in Linguistic Science* 10, 41–54. doi:10.14989/66977

Kolb, Bryan & Robbin Gibb. 2011. Brain Plasticity and Behaviour in the Developing Brain. *Journal of the Canadian Academy of Child and Adolescent Psychiatry* 20(4), 265–276.

Konishi, Haruka, Aimee E. Stahl, Roberta Michnick Golinkoff & Kathy Hirsh-Pasek. 2016. Individual differences in nonlinguistic event categorization predict later motion verb comprehension. *Journal of Experimental Child Psychology* 151, 18–32. doi:10.1016/j.jecp.2016.03.012.

Kopp, Claire B. 1982. Antecedents of self-regulation: A developmental perspective. *Developmental Psychology* 18(2). 199–214. doi:10.1037/0012-1649.18.2.199.

Koski, Sonja E. & Elisabeth H. M. Sterck. 2007. Triadic postconflict affiliation in captive chimpanzees: does consolation console? *Animal Behaviour* 73(1). 133–142. doi:10.1016/j.anbehav.2006.04.009.

Koski, Sonja E. & Elisabeth H. M. Sterck. 2009. Post-conflict third-party affiliation in chimpanzees: What's in it for the third party? *American Journal of Primatology* 71. 409–418. doi:10.1002/ajp.20668.

Kretch, Kari S. & Karen E. Adolph. 2013. Cliff or Step? Posture-Specific Learning at the Edge of a Drop-Off. *Child Development* 84(1). 226–240. doi:10.1111/j.1467-8624.2012.01842.x.

Krupenye, Christopher, Fumihiro Kano, Satoshi Hirata, Josep Call & Michael Tomasello. 2016. Great apes anticipate that other individuals will act according to false beliefs. *Science* 354 (6308). 110–113. doi:10.1126/science.aaf8110.

Kuhl, Patricia K. 2000. A new view of language acquisition. *Proceedings of the National Academy of Sciences of the United States of America* 97(22). 11850. doi: 10.1073/pnas.97.22.11850

Kuhl, Patricia K. 2004. Early language acquisition: Cracking the speech code. *Nature Reviews Neuroscience* 5(11). 831–841. doi:10.1038/nrn1533.

Kuhl, Patricia K. & James D. Miller. 1975. Speech perception by the chinchilla: Voiced-voiceless distinction in alveolar plosive consonants. *Science* 90(4209). 69–72. doi:10.1126/science.1166301.

Kuhl, Patricia K., Erica Stevens, Akiko Hayashi, Toshisada Deguchi, Shigeru Kiritani & Paul Iverson. 2006. Infants show a facilitation effect for native language phonetic perception between 6 and 12 months. *Developmental Science* 9(2). F13–F21. doi:10.1111/j.1467-7687.2006.00468.x.

Kulick, Don. 1992. *Language Shift and Cultural Reproduction: Socialization, Self, and Syncretism in a Papua New Guinean Village*. Cambridge: Cambridge University Press.

Labov, William & Joshua Waletzky. 1967. Narrative analysis: oral versions of personal experience. In June Helm (ed.), *Essays in the Verbal and Visual Arts*, 12–44. Seattle, WA: University of Washington Press.

LaFrance, Marianne & Maida Broadbent. 1976. Group Rapport: Posture Sharing as a Nonverbal Indicator. *Group & Organization Management* 1(3). 328–333. doi:10.1177/105960117600100307.

Lakin, Jessica L. & Tanya L. Chartrand. 2003. Using nonconscious behavioral mimicry to create affiliation and rapport. *Psychological Science* 14(4). 334–339. doi:10.1111/1467-9280.14481.

Lakoff, George. 1987. Cognitive models and prototype theory. In Ulric Neisser (ed.), *Concepts and conceptual development*, 63–100. Cambridge: Cambridge University Press.

Lakoff, George & Mark Johnson. 1999. Primary Metaphor and Subjective Experience. *Philosophy in the Flesh: The Embodied Mind and Its Challenge to Western Thought*. New York: Basic Books. doi:10.1590/S0102-44502001000100008.

Lakusta, Laura, Danielle Spinelli & Kathryn Garcia. 2017. The relationship between pre-verbal event representations and semantic structures: The case of goal and source paths. *Cognition* 164.174–187. doi:10.1016/j.cognition.2017.04.003.

Lakusta, Laura, Laura Wagner, Kirsten O'Hearn & Barbara Landau. 2011. Conceptual Foundations of Spatial Language: Evidence for a Goal Bias in Infants. *Language Learning and Development* 3(3). 179–197. doi:10.1080/15475440701360168.

Lambrecht, Knud. 2012. *Information Structure and Sentence Form. Information Structure and Sentence Form*. Cambridge: Cambridge University Press. doi:10.1017/cbo9780511620607.

Landau, Barbara & Ray Jackendoff. 1993. "What" and "where" in spatial language and spatial cognition. *Behavioral and Brain Sciences* 16(2). 217–265. doi:10.1017/S0140525X00029733.

Langacker, Ronald W. 1987. *Foundations of Cognitive Grammar, Vol. 1: Theoretical Prerequisites. Foundations of cognitive grammar Theoretical Prerequisites*.

Langacker, Ronald W. 1991. *Foundations of cognitive grammar. Vol. 2: Descriptive application*. Stanford: Stanford University Press.

Langergraber, Kevin E., Kay Prüfer, Carolyn Rowney, Christophe Boesch, Catherine Crockford, Katie Fawcett, Eiji Inoue, Miho Inoue-Muruyama, John C. Mitani, Martin N. Muller, Martha M. Robbins, Grit Schubert, Tara S. Stoinski, Bence Viola, David Watts, Roman M. Wittig, Richard W. Wrangham, Klaus Zuberbühler, Svante Pääbo, and Linda Vigilant 2012. Generation times in wild chimpanzees and gorillas suggest earlier divergence times in great ape and human evolution. *Proceedings of the National Academy of Sciences* 109(39). 15716–15721. doi:10.1073/pnas.1211740109.

Larkin, Willard & David Burns. 1977. Sentence comprehension and memory for embedded structure. *Memory & Cognition* 5. 17–22. doi:10.3758/BF03209186.

Lasnik, Howard & Juan Uriagereka. 1988. *A course in GB syntax : lectures on binding and empty categories*. Current studies in linguistics series. Cambridge, MA: MIT Press.

Lass, Norman J., Karen R. Hughes, Melanie D. Bowyer, Lucille T. Waters & Victoria T. Bourne. 1976. Speaker sex identification from voiced, whispered, and filtered isolated vowels. *The Journal of the Acoustical Society of America* 59. 675. doi:10.1121/1.380917.

Laws, Glynis & Dorothy V.M. Bishop. 2004. Pragmatic language impairment and social deficits in Williams syndrome: A comparison with Down's syndrome and specific language impairment. *International Journal of Language and Communication Disorders* 39(1). 45–64. doi:10.1080/13682820310001615797.

Leclercq, Anne Lise & Steve Majerus. 2010. Serial-Order Short-Term Memory Predicts Vocabulary Development: Evidence From a Longitudinal Study. *Developmental Psychology* 46(2). 417–427. doi:10.1037/a0018540.

Lee, Kang, Michelle Eskritt, Lawrence A. Symons & Darwin Muir. 1998. Children's use of triadic eye gaze information for "mind reading". *Developmental Psychology* 34(3). 525–539. doi:10.1037/0012-1649.34.3.525.

Leon-Carrion, Jose, Javier García-Orza & Francisco Javier Pérez-Santamaría. 2004. Development of the inhibitory component of the executive functions in children and adolescents. *International Journal of Neuroscience* 114(10). 1291–1311. doi:10.1080/00207450490476066.

Leon-Carrion, Jose, Javier Garcia-Orza, Francisco Perez-Santamaria. 2004. Development of the inhibitory component of the executive functions in children and adolescents. International Journal of Neuroscience, 114, 1291–1311.

Lev-Ari, Shiri & Boaz Keysar. 2010. Why don't we believe non-native speakers? The influence of accent on credibility. *Journal of Experimental Social Psychology* 46(6). 1093–1096. doi:10.1016/j.jesp.2010.05.025.

Levinson, Stephen C. 1996. Relativity in Spatial Conception and Description. In John Gumperz & Stephen Levinson (eds.), *Rethinking linguistic relativity*, 177–202. Cambridge: Cambridge University Press.

Levitin, Daniel J. & Ursula Bellugi. 1998. Musical abilities in people with Williams Syndrome. *Music Perception* 15(4). 357–389. doi:10.2307/40300863.

Lew-Williams, Casey & Anne Fernald. 2007. Young children learning spanish make rapid use of grammatical gender in spoken word recognition. *Psychological Science* 18(3). 193–198. doi:10.1111/j.1467-9280.2007.01871.x.

Lewis, Marc D., Alex V. Lamey & Lori Douglas. 1999. A new dynamic systems method for the analysis of early socioemotional development. *Developmental Science* 2(4). 457–475. doi:10.1111/1467-7687.00090.

Lewis, Terri L. & Daphne Maurer. 1992. The development of the temporal and nasal visual fields during infancy. *Vision Research* 32(5). 903–911. doi:10.1016/0042-6989(92)90033-F.

Lewkowicz, David J. & Asif A. Ghazanfar. 2006. The decline of cross-species intersensory perception in human infants. *Proceedings of the National Academy of Sciences of the United States of America* 103(17). 6771–6774. doi:10.1073/pnas.0602027103.

Lewkowicz, David J. & Asif A. Ghazanfar. 2009. The emergence of multisensory systems through perceptual narrowing. *Trends in Cognitive Sciences* 3(11). 470–478. doi:10.1016/j.tics.2009.08.004.

Libertus, Klaus, Jennifer Gibson, Nadia Z. Hidayatallah, Jane Hirtle, R. Alison Adcock & Amy Needham. 2013. Size matters: How age and reaching experiences shape infants' preferences for different sized objects. *Infant Behavior and Development* 36(2). 189–98. doi:10.1016/j.infbeh.2013.01.006.

Lieven, Elena, Julian Pine & Gillian Baldwin. 1997. Lexically-based learning and early grammatical development. *Journal of Child Language* 24(1). 187–219. doi:10.1017/S0305000996002930.

Lieven, Elena, Heike Behrens, Jennifer Speares & Michael Tomasello. 2003. Early syntactic creativity: A usage-based approach. *Journal of Child Language* 30(2). 333–370. doi:10.1017/S0305000903005592.

Lieven, Elena, Dorothé Salomo & Michael Tomasello. 2009. Two-year-old children's production of multiword utterances: A usage-based analysis. *Cognitive Linguistics* 20(3). 481–507. doi:10.1515/COGL.2009.022.

Logan, Gordon D. 1988. Toward an instance theory of automatization. *Psychological Review* 95(4). 492–527. doi:10.1037/0033-295X.95.4.492.

Lopes, Luís Seabra & Tony Belpaeme. 2008. Beyond the individual: New insights on language, cognition and robots. *Connection Science* 20(4). 231–237. doi:10.1080/09540090802518661.

Loucks, Jeff & Jessica Sommerville. 2018. Developmental Change in Action Perception: Is Motor Experience the Cause? *Infancy* 23(4). 519–537. doi:10.1111/infa.12231

Löwel, Siegrid and Wolf Singer. 1992. Selection of intrinsic horizontal connections in the visual cortex by correlated neuronal activity. *Science* 255, 209–212. doi:10.1126/science.1372754.

Löwel, Siegrid & Wolf Singer. 1992. Selection of intrinsic horizontal connections in the visual cortex by correlated neuronal activity. *Science* 255(5041). 209–212. doi:10.1126/science.1372754.

Lukyanenko, Cynthia & Cynthia Fisher. 2016. Where are the cookies? Two- and three-year-olds use number-marked verbs to anticipate upcoming nouns. *Cognition* 146. 349–70. doi:10.1016/j.cognition.2015.10.012.

Lum, Jarrad A. G., Gina Conti-Ramsden, Debra Page & Michael T. Ullman. 2012. Working, declarative and procedural memory in specific language impairment. *Cortex* 48(9). 1138–54. doi:10.1016/j.cortex.2011.06.001.

Lupyan, Gary & Andy Clark. 2015. Words and the World: Predictive Coding and the Language-Perception-Cognition Interface. *Current Directions in Psychological Science* 24(4). 279–284. doi:10.1177/0963721415570732.

Lyons, Derek E., Andrew G. Young & Frank C. Keil. 2007. The hidden structure of overimitation. *Proceedings of the National Academy of Sciences* 104(50). 19751–19756. doi:10.1073/pnas.0704452104.

Mark H. Johnson & John Morton. 1991. *Biology and cognitive development: the case of face recognition*. Oxford: Blackwell.

Maas, Han L. J. Van der & Peter C. M. Molenaar. 1992. Stagewise cognitive development: An application of catastrophe theory. *Psychological Review* 99(3). 395–417. doi:10.1037/0033-295X.99.3.395.

Macchi Cassia, Viola, Francesca Simion & Carlo Umiltà. 2001. Face preference at birth: The role of an orienting mechanism. *Developmental Science* 4(1). 101–108. doi:10.1111/1467-7687.00154.

MacWhinney, Brian. 1977. Starting points. *Language* 53(1). 152–168. doi:10.2307/413059

MacWhinney, Brian. 1979. The Acquisition of Morphophonology. *Monographs of the Society for Research in Child Development* 43(1/2). 1–123. doi:10.2307/1166047.

MacWhinney, Brian. 2000. *The Childes Project*. New York: Psychology Press. doi:10.4324/9781315805641.

MacWhinney, Brian. 2005. The emergence of linguistic form in time. *Connection Science* 17(3–4). 191–211. doi:10.1080/09540090500177687.

MacWhinney, Brian & Elizabeth Bates. 1978. Sentential devices for conveying givenness and newness: A cross-cultural developmental study. *Journal of Verbal Learning and Verbal Behavior* 17(5). 539–558. doi:10.1016/S0022-5371(78)90326-2.

Maess, Burkhard, Stefan Koelsch, Thomas C. Gunter & Angela D. Friederici. 2001. Musical syntax is processed in Broca's area: An MEG study. *Nature Neuroscience* 4. 540–545. doi:10.1038/87502.

Maguire, Mandy J. & Guy O. Dove. 2008. Speaking of events: Event word learning and event representation. In Thomas F. Shipley & Jeffrey M. Zacks (eds.), *Understanding events: From perception to action*, 193–218. New York: Oxford University Press.

Maguire, Mandy J., Kathryn A. Hirsh-Pasek & Roberta M. Golinkoff. 2010. A Unified Theory of Word Learning: Putting Verb Acquisition in Context. In Kathryn Hirsh-Pasek & Roberta M. Golinkoff (eds.), *Action Meets Word: How Children Learn Verbs*, 364–391. New York: Oxford University Press. doi:10.1093/acprof:oso/9780195170009.003.0015.

Malaia, Evie. 2004. *Event structure and telicity in Russian: an event-based analysis for telicity puzzle in Slavic languages*. Ohio State University Working Papers in Slavic Studies 4. 87–98.

Malaia, Evie & Debarchana Basu. 2013. Verb-verb predicates in Bangla and Russian: morpho-semantic event structure analysis. NINJAL International Conference on V-V complexes in Asian languages, Tokyo, Japan.

Mallinson, Graham & Barry Blake. 1981. *Language Typology: Cross-Cultural Studies in Syntax.* Amsterdam: North-Holland.

Mandler, Jean. 1992. How to build a baby: II. Conceptual primitives. *Psychological Review* 99(4). 587–604. doi:10.1037/0033-295X.99.4.587.

Mandler, Jean. 2007. *Foundations of Mind: Origins of Conceptual Thought.* New York: Oxford University Press. doi:10.1093/acprof:oso/9780195311839.001.0001.

Mandler, Jean M. 2010. Actions Organize the Infant's World. In Kathryn Hirsh-Pasek & Roberta M. Golinkoff (eds.), *Action meets word: How children learn verbs*, 111–133. New York: Oxford University Press. doi:10.1093/acprof:oso/9780195170009.003.0005.

Mani, Nivedita & Falk Huettig. 2012. Prediction during language processing is a piece of cake–But only for skilled producers. *Journal of Experimental Psychology: Human Perception and Performance* 38(4). 843–847. doi:10.1037/a0029284.

Marchman, Virginia A. 1997. Children's productivity in the English past tense: The role of frequency, phonology, and neighborhood structure. *Cognitive Science* 21. 283–304. doi:10.1207/s15516709cog2103_2.

Marchman, Virginia A. & Elizabeth Bates. 1994. Continuity in lexical and morphological development: a test of the critical mass hypothesis. *Journal of Child Language* 21(2). 339–366. doi:10.1017/s0305000900009302.

Mareschal, Denis & Paul C. Quinn. 2001. Categorization in infancy. *Trends in Cognitive Sciences* 5(10). 443–450. doi:10.1016/S1364-6613(00)01752-6.

Mariën, Peter, Herman Ackermann, Michael Adamaszek, Caroline H.S. Barwood, Alan Beaton, John Desmond, Elke De Witte, Angela J. Fawcett, Ingo Hertrich, Michael Küper, Maria Leggio, Cherie Marvel, Marco Molinari, Bruce E. Murdoch, Roderick I. Nicolson, Jeremy D. Schmahmann, Catherine J. Stoodley, Markus Thürling, Dagmar Timmann, Ellen Wouters & Wolfram Ziegler. 2014. Consensus paper: Language and the cerebellum: An ongoing enigma. *Cerebellum* 13. 386–410. doi:10.1007/s12311-013-0540-5.

Markman, Ellen M. 1992. Constraints on word learning: Speculation about their nature, origins, and domain specificity. In Megan R. Gunnar & Michael Maratsos (eds.), *The Minnesota symposia on child psychology, Vol. 25. Modularity and constraints in language and cognition*, 59–101. Hillsdale NJ: Lawrence Erlbaum Associates.

Markman, Ellen M. 1994. Constraints on word meaning in early language acquisition. *Lingua* 92. 199–227. doi:10.1016/0024-3841(94)90342-5.

Markov, Nikola T. & Henry Kennedy. 2013. The importance of being hierarchical. *Current Opinion in Neurobiology* 23(2). 187–94. doi:10.1016/j.conb.2012.12.008.

Martens, Marilee A., Sarah J. Wilson & David C. Reutens. 2008. Research Review: Williams syndrome: A critical review of the cognitive, behavioral, and neuroanatomical phenotype. *Journal of Child Psychology and Psychiatry and Allied Disciplines* 49. 576–608. doi:10.1111/j.1469-7610.2008.01887.x.

Martin-Rhee, Michelle M. & Ellen Bialystok. 2008. The development of two types of inhibitory control in monolingual and bilingual children. *Bilingualism* 11(1). 81–93. doi:10.1017/S1366728907003227.

Massey, Christine & Rochel Gelman. 1988. Preschoolers decide whether pictured unfamiliar objects can move themselves. *Developmental Psychology* 24(3). 307–17. doi:10.1037/0012-1649.24.3.307

Masson, Michael & Jo Miller. 1983. Working memory and individual differences in comprehension and memory of text. *Journal of Educational Psychology* 75(2). 314–318. doi:10.1037/0022-0663.75.2.314.

Matthews, Alexandra, Ann E. Ellis & Charles A. Nelson. 1996. Development of Preterm and Full-Term Infant Ability on AB, Recall Memory, Transparent Barrier Detour, and Means-End Tasks. *Child Development* 67(6). 2658–2676. doi:10.1111/j.1467-8624.1996.tb01881.x.

Matthews, Danielle & Colin Bannard. 2010. Children's production of unfamiliar word sequences is predicted by positional variability and latent classes in a large sample of child-directed speech. *Cognitive Science* 34(3). 465–488. doi:10.1111/j.1551-6709.2009.01091.x.

Maurer, Daphne. and Janet Werker. 2014. Perceptual narrowing during infancy: A comparison of language and faces. Dev Psychobiol, 56 (2). 154–178. doi:10.1002/dev.21177.

Maurits, Luke, Amy Perfors & Dan Navarro. 2010. Why are some word orders more common than others? A uniform information density account. Annual Conference on Neural Information Processing Systems, Lake Tahoe.

Mayberry, Marshall R., Matthew W. Crocker & Pia Knoeferle. 2009. Learning to attend: A connectionist model of situated language comprehension. *Cognitive Science* 33(3). 449–496. doi:10.1111/j.1551-6709.2009.01019.x.

McCabe, Allyssa & Carole Peterson. 1991. *Developing Narrative Structure*. Hillsdale, NJ, Lawrence Erlbaum Associates.

McCall, Robert B. & Clay W. Mash. 1995. Infant cognition and its relation to mature intelligence. In Ross Vasta (ed.), *Annals of Child Development* 10, 27–56.

McCauley, Stewart M. & Morten H. Christiansen. 2019. Language learning as language use: A cross-linguistic model of child language development. *Psychological Review* 126(1), 1–51. doi:10.1037/rev0000126

McClelland, James L. & David E. Rumelhart. 1988. *Explorations in parallel distributed processing : a handbook of models, programs, and exercises*. Cambridge, MA: MIT Press.

McDonald, Janet L. 2008a. Differences in the cognitive demands of word order, plural, and subject-verb agreement constructions. *Psychonomic Bulletin and Review* 15. 980–984. doi:10.3758/PBR.15.5.980.

McDonald, Janet L. 2008b. Grammaticality judgments in children: The role of age, working memory and phonological ability. *Journal of Child Language* 35(2). 247–268. doi:10.1017/S0305000907008367.

McDonough, Laraine, Soonja Choi & Jean M. Mandler. 2003. Understanding spatial relations: Flexible infants, lexical adults. *Cognitive Psychology* 46(3). 229–259. doi:10.1016/S0010-0285(02)00514-5.

McTear, Michael. 1985. *Children's Conversation*. Oxford: Blackwell.

Meer, Audrey L.H. van der, Marte Ramstad & F. R. (Ruud) van der Weel. 2008. Choosing the shortest way to mum: Auditory guided rotation in 6- to 9-month-old infants. *Infant Behavior and Development* 31(2). 207–216. doi:10.1016/j.infbeh.2007.10.007.

Mehler, Jacques, Peter Jusczyk, Ghislaine Lambertz, Nilofar Halsted, Josiane Bertoncini & Claudine Amiel-Tison. 1988. A precursor of language acquisition in young infants. *Cognition* 29(2). 143–178. doi:10.1016/0010-0277(88)90035-2.

Melby-Lervåg, Monica, Thomas S. Redick & Charles Hulme. 2016. Working Memory Training Does Not Improve Performance on Measures of Intelligence or Other Measures of "Far Transfer": Evidence From a Meta-Analytic Review. *Perspectives on Psychological Science* 11(4). 512–534. doi:10.1177/1745691616635612.

Meltzoff, Andrew N. 2005. Imitation and other minds: The "like me" hypothesis. In Susan Hurley & Nick Chater (eds.), *Perspectives on imitation: From neuroscience to social science: Vol. 2. Imitation, human development, and culture*, 55–77. Cambridge, MA: MIT Press.

Menard, Karen R. 2005. *Means-end search for hidden objects by 6.5-month-old infants: Examination of an experiential limitation hypothesis*. Waterloo, Canada: University of Waterloo.

Menzel, Emil W. 1973. Chimpanzee Spatial Memory Organization. *Science* 182(4115). 943–945. doi:10.1126/science.182.4115.943.

Mervis, Carolyn B. & Eleanor Rosch. 2003. Categorization of Natural Objects. *Annual Review of Psychology* 32. 89–115. doi:10.1146/annurev.ps.32.020181.000513.

Metsala, Jamie L. 1999. Young children's phonological awareness and nonword repetition as a function of vocabulary development. *Journal of Educational Psychology* 91(1). 3–19. doi:10.1037/0022-0663.91.1.3.

Meulenbroek, Ruud G. J. & Gerard P. van Galen. 1988. The Acquisition of Skilled Handwriting: Discontinuous Trends in Kinematic Variables. In Ann M. Colley & John R. Beech (eds.), *Advances in psychology, 55. Cognition and action in skilled behaviour*, 273–281. Amsterdam: North-Holland. doi:10.1016/S0166-4115(08)60627-5.

Miall, Rowland C., Jennifer Stanley, S. Todhunter, C. Levick, S. Lindo & J. D. Miall. 2006. Performing hand actions assists the visual discrimination of similar hand postures. *Neuropsychologia* 44(6). 966–976. doi:10.1016/j.neuropsychologia.2005.09.006.

Miller, George A. 1956. The magical number seven, plus or minus two: some limits on our capacity for processing information. *Psychological Review* 63(2). 81–97. doi:10.1037/h0043158.

Miller, George A., Eugene Galanter & Karl H. Pribram. 1960. *Plans and the structure of behavior*. New York: Holt, Rinehart & Winston.

Mintz, Toben H. 2002. Category induction from distributional cues in an artificial language. *Memory & Cognition* 30(5). 678–686. doi:10.3758/BF03196424.

Mintz, Toben H. 2003. Frequent frames as a cue for grammatical categories in child directed speech. *Cognition* 90(1). 91–117. doi:10.1016/S0010-0277(03)00140-9.

Mintz, Toben H., Elissa L. Newport & Thomas G. Bever. 2002. The distributional structure of grammatical categories in speech to young children. *Cognitive Science* 26(4). 393–424. doi:10.1207/s15516709cog2604_1.

Mitani, John C. & David P. Watts. 2001. Why do chimpanzees hunt and share meat? *Animal Behaviour* 61(5). 915–924. doi:10.1006/anbe.2000.1681.

Mitchener, Garrett & Misha Becker. 2011. A computational model of learning the raising-control distinction. *Research on Language & Computation* 8(2). 167–207. doi:10/1007/s11168-011-9073-6.

Miyake, Akira, Marcel Adam Just & Patricia A. Carpenter. 1994. Working Memory Constraints on the Resolution of Lexical Ambiguity: Maintaining Multiple Interpretations in Neutral Contexts. *Journal of Memory and Language* 33(2). 175–202. doi:10.1006/jmla.1994.1009.

Moffitt, Terrie E., Louise Arseneault, Daniel Belsky, Nigel Dickson, Robert J. Hancox, HonaLee Harrington, Renate Houts, Richie Poulton, Brent W. Roberts, Stephen Ross, Malcolm R. Sears, W. Murray Thomson, and Avshalom Caspi. 2011. A gradient of childhood self-control predicts health, wealth, and public safety. *Proceedings of the National Academy of Sciences* 108(7). 2693–2698. doi:10.1073/pnas.1010076108.

Molenaar, Peter C.M., Dorret I. Boomsma & Conor V. Dolan. 1993. A third source of developmental differences. *Behavior Genetics* 23. 519–524. doi:10.1007/BF01068142.

Monaghan, Padraic & Morten H. Christiansen. 2010. Words in puddles of sound: Modelling psycholinguistic effects in speech segmentation. *Journal of Child Language* 37(3). 545–64. doi:10.1017/S0305000909990511.

Moore, Chris & Valerie Corkum. 1994. Social understanding at the end of the first year of life. *Developmental Review* 14(4). 349–372. doi:10.1006/drev.1994.1014.

Moore, Roger K. 2005. Results from a survey of attendees at ASRU 1997 and 2003. *Proceedings of the INTERSPEECH 2005, Lisbon, Portugal*, 117–120.

Morales, Michael, Peter Mundy, Christine E. F. Delgado, Marygrace Yale, Rebecca Neal & Heidi K. Schwartz. 2000. Gaze following, temperament, and language development in 6-month-olds: A replication and extension. *Infant Behavior and Development* 23(2). 231–236. doi:10.1016/S0163-6383(01)00038-8.

Morales, Michael, Peter Mundy & Jennifer Rojas. 1998. Following the direction of gaze and language development in 6-month-olds. *Infant Behavior and Development* 21(2). 373–377. doi:10.1016/S0163-6383(98)90014-5.

Morgan-Short, Kara, Mandy Faretta-Stutenberg, Katherine A. Brill-Schuetz, Helen Carpenter & Patrick C. M. Wong. 2014. Declarative and procedural memory as individual differences in second language acquisition. *Bilingualism* 17(1). 56–72. doi:10.1017/S1366728912000715.

Morgan, Kirstie & Harlene Hayne. 2006. The effect of encoding time on retention by infants and young children. *Infant Behavior and Development* 29(4). 599–602. doi:10.1016/j.infbeh.2006.07.009.

Morgan, Thomas J. H. & Thomas L. Griffiths. 2015. What the Baldwin Effect affects. *Proceedings of the 37th Annual Conference of the Cognitive Science Society*. 1643–1648. Austin, TX: Cognitive Science Society.

Mullally, Sinéad L. & Eleanor A. Maguire. 2014. Counterfactual thinking in patients with amnesia. *Hippocampus* 24(11). 1261–1266. doi:10.1002/hipo.22323.

Mumme, Donna, Emily Bushnell, Jennifer DiCorcia & Lesley Lariviere. 2007. Infants' use of gaze cues to interpret others' actions and emotional reactions. In Ross Flom, Kang Lee & Darwin Muir (eds.), *Gaze-following: Its development and significance*, 143–170. Mahwah NJ: Lawrence Erlbaum Associates.

Munakata, Yuko & James L. McClelland. 2003. Connectionist models of development. *Developmental Science* 6(4). 413–429. doi:10.1111/1467-7687.00296.

Munakata, Yuko, James L. McClelland, Mark H. Johnson & Robert S. Siegler. 1997. Rethinking Infant Knowledge: Toward an Adaptive Process Account of Successes and Failures in Object Permanence Tasks. *Psychological Review* 104(4). 686–713. doi:10.1037/0033-295X.104.4.686.

Muratori, Lisa M., Eric M. Lamberg, Lori Quinn & Susan V. Duff. 2013. Applying principles of motor learning and control to upper extremity rehabilitation. *Journal of Hand Therapy* 26(2). 94–102. doi:10.1016/j.jht.2012.12.007.

Murdock, Bennet B. Jr. 1962. The serial position effect of free recall. *Journal of Experimental Psychology* 64(5). 482–488. doi:10.1037/h0045106.

Murphy, Gregory. 2018. *The Big Book of Concepts*. Cambridge, MA: MIT Press. doi:10.7551/mitpress/1602.001.0001.

Myachykov, Andriy & Russell S Tomlin. 2008. Perceptual priming and structural choice in Russian sentence production. *Journal of Cognitive Science* 9. 31–48. doi: 10.17791/jcs.2008.9.1.31.

Myachykov, Andriy, Simon Garrod & Christoph Scheepers. 2010. Perceptual priming of structural choice during English and Finnish sentence production. In Ramesh K. Mishra & Narayanan Srinivasan (eds.), *Language & Cognition: State of the art*, 54–72. Munich: Lincom Europa.

Myachykov, Andriy, Dominic Thompson, Christoph Scheepers & Simon Garrod. 2011. Visual Attention and Structural Choice in Sentence Production Across Languages. *Linguistics and Language Compass* 5(2). 95–107. doi:10.1111/j.1749-818X.2010.00265.x.

Naess, Åshild. 2007. *Prototypical Transitivity*. Typological Studies in Language 72. Amsterdam: John Benjamins Publishing Company.

Naigles, Letitia. 1990. Children Use Syntax To Learn Verb Meanings. *Journal of Child Language* 17(2). 357–374. doi:10.1017/S0305000900013817.

Naigles, Letitia R. & Erika Hoff-Ginsberg. 1998. Why are some verbs learned before other verbs? Effects of input frequency and structure on children's early verb use. *Journal of Child Language* 25(1). 95–120. doi:10.1017/S0305000997003358.

Nappa, Rebecca, Allison Wessel, Katherine L. McEldoon, Lila R. Gleitman & John C. Trueswell. 2009. Use of Speaker's Gaze and Syntax in Verb Learning. *Language Learning and Development* 5(4). 203–234. doi:10.1080/15475440903167528.

Narasimhan, Bhuvana & Marianne Gullberg. 2011. The role of input frequency and semantic transparency in the acquisition of verb meaning: Evidence from placement verbs in Tamil and Dutch. *Journal of Child Language* 38(3). 504–532. doi:10.1017/S0305000910000164.

Nastase, Samuel, Vittorio Iacovella & Uri Hasson. 2014. Uncertainty in visual and auditory series is coded by modality-general and modality-specific neural systems. *Human Brain Mapping* 35(4). 1111–1128. doi:10.1002/hbm.22238.

Neisser, Ulric, Gwyneth Boodoo, Thomas J. Bouchard, A. Wade Boykin, Nathan Brody, Stephen J. Ceci, Diane F. Halpern, John C. Loehlin, Robert Perloff, Robert J. Sternberg & Susana Urbina. 1996. Intelligence: Knowns and unknowns. *American Psychologist* 51. 77–101.

Nelson, Charles A. 2001. The Development and Neural Bases of Face Recognition. *Infant and Child Development* 10(1–2). 3–18. doi:10.1002/icd.239.

Nelson, Katherine. 1974. Concept, word, and sentence: Interrelations in acquisition and development. *Psychological Review* 81(4). 267–285. doi:10.1037/h0036592.

Nelson, Katherine. 1985. *Making sense: The acquisition of shared meaning*. New York: Academic Press.

Nelson, Katherine. 1996. *Language in cognitive development*. New York: Cambridge University Press.

Newell, Allen & Paul S. Rosenbloom. 1981. Mechanisms of skill acquisition and the law of practice. In John R. Anderson (ed.), *Cognitive skills and their acquisition*, 1–55. Hillsdale, NJ: Lawrence Erlbaum Associates.

Newell, Kari M. 1986. Constraints on the Development of Coordination. In Michael G. Wade and H. T. A. (John) Whiting (eds.), *Motor Development in Children: Aspects of Coordination and Control*, 341–360. Martinus Nijhoff Publishers, Dordrecht. doi:10.1007/978-94-009-4460-2_19.

Newman, Mark, Albert-László Barabási & Duncan Watts. 2006. *The structure and dynamics of networks*. Princeton and Oxford: Princeton University Press.

Newport, Elissa L. 1988. Constraints on learning and their role in language acquisition: Studies of the acquisition of American sign language. *Language Sciences* 10(1). 147–172. doi:10.1016/0388-0001(88)90010-1.

Newport, Elissa L. 1990. Maturational constraints on language learning. *Cognitive Science* 14(1). 11–28. doi:10.1016/0364-0213(90)90024-Q.

Nielsen, Mark & Keyan Tomaselli. 2010. Overimitation in kalahari bushman children and the origins of human cultural cognition. *Psychological Science* 21(5). 729–36. doi:10.1177/0956797610368808.

Novick, Jared M., John C. Trueswell & Sharon L. Thompson-Schill. 2005. Cognitive control and parsing: Reexamining the role of Broca's area in sentence comprehension. *Cognitive, Affective and Behavioral Neuroscience* 5(3). 263–281. doi:10.3758/CABN.5.3.263.

Oakes, Lisa M. & Thomas L. Spalding. 1997. The role of exemplar distribution in infants' differentiation of categories. *Infant Behavior and Development* 20(4). 457–475. doi:10.1016/S0163-6383(97)90036-9.

Oakes, Lisa M. & Donald J. Tellinghuisen. 1994. Examining in infancy: Does it reflect active processing? *Developmental Psychology* 30(5). 748–756. doi:10.1037/0012-1649.30.5.748.

Ogiela, Diane A., Cristina Schmitt & Michael W. Casby. 2014. Interpretation of Verb Phrase Telicity: Sensitivity to Verb Type and Determiner Type. *Journal of Speech, Language and Hearing Research* 57(3). 865–875. doi:10.1044/2013_JSLHR-L-12-0271.

Onis, Mercedes De. 2006. WHO Motor Development Study: Windows of achievement for six gross motor development milestones. *Acta Paediatrica, International Journal of Paediatrics* 95(S450). 86–95. doi:10.1080/08035320500495563.

Osgood, Charles E. & J. Kathryn Bock. 1977. Salience and Sentencing: Some Production Principles. In Sheldon Rosenberg (ed.) *Sentence Production: Developments in Research and Theory*, 89–140. Hillsdale, NJ: Lawrence Erlbaum Associates.

Over, Harriet. 2018. The influence of group membership on young children's prosociality. *Current Opinion in Psychology* 20. 17–20.

Pantos, Andrew J. & Andrew W. Perkins. 2013. Measuring Implicit and Explicit Attitudes Toward Foreign Accented Speech. *Journal of Language and Social Psychology* 32(1). 3–20. doi:10.1177/0261927X12463005.

Papafragou, Anna. 2010. Source-Goal Asymmetries in Motion Representation: Implications for Language Production and Comprehension. *Cognitive Science* 34(6). 1064–1092. doi:10.1111/j.1551-6709.2010.01107.x.

Papafragou, Anna, Kimberly Cassidy & Lila Gleitman. 2007. When we think about thinking: The acquisition of belief verbs. *Cognition* 105(1). 125–165. doi:10.1016/j.cognition.2006.09.008.

Papafragou, Anna, Justin Hulbert & John Trueswell. 2008. Does language guide event perception? Evidence from eye movements. *Cognition* 108(1). 155–84. doi:10.1016/j.cognition.2008.02.007.

Papathanassiou, Dimitri, Olivier Etard, Emmanuel Mellet, Laure Zago, Bernard Mazoyer & Nathalie Tzourio-Mazoyer. 2000. A common language network for comprehension and production: A contribution to the definition of language epicenters with PET. *NeuroImage* 11(4). 347–357. doi:10.1006/nimg.2000.0546.

Pardo, Jennifer S., Rachel Gibbons, Alexandra Suppes & Robert M. Krauss. 2012. Phonetic convergence in college roommates. *Journal of Phonetics* 40(1). 190–197. doi:10.1016/j.wocn.2011.10.001.

Pardo, Jennifer S., Isabel Cajori Jay & Robert M. Krauss. 2010. Conversational role influences speech imitation. *Attention, Perception, and Psychophysics* 72. 2254–2264. doi:10.3758/BF03196699.

Parisien, Christopher, Afsaneh Fazly & Suzanne Stevenson. 2010. An incremental bayesian model for learning syntactic categories. *CoNLL '08: Proceedings of the Twelfth Conference on Computational Natural Language Learning*. 89–96. doi:10.3115/1596324.1596340.

Parsell, M. 2010. Williams syndrome: Dissociation and mental structure. In Wayne Christensen, Elizabeth Schier, & John Sutton (eds.), *ASCS09: Proceedings of the 9th conference of the Australasian society for cognitive science*, 277–284. Sydney: Macquarie Centre for Cognitive Science.

Pascalis, Olivier, Michelle De Haan & Charles A. Nelson. 2002. Is face processing species-specific during the first year of life? *Science* 296(5571). 1321–1323. doi:10.1126/science.1070223.

Pascalis, Olivier, Lisa S. Scott, David J. Kelly, Robert W. Shannon, Ellen Nicholson, Mike Coleman & Charles A. Nelson. 2005. Plasticity of face processing in infancy. *Proceedings of the National Academy of Sciences of the United States of America* 102(14). 5297–5300. doi:10.1073/pnas.0406627102.

Passolunghi, Maria Chiara & Hiwet Mariam Costa. 2016. Working memory and early numeracy training in preschool children. *Child Neuropsychology* 22(1). 81–98. doi:10.1080/09297049.2014.971726.

Patterson, Nick, Daniel J. Richter, Sante Gnerre, Eric S. Lander & David Reich. 2006. Genetic evidence for complex speciation of humans and chimpanzees. *Nature* 441(7097). 1103–1108. doi:10.1038/nature04789.

Pearson, Barbara Z. and Ciolli, Lois. 2004. Distinguishing dialect and development from disorder: case studies. *Seminars in Speech and Language* 25(1). 101–112.

Pellicano, Elizabeth & Gillian Rhodes. 2003. The role of eye-gaze in understanding other minds. *British Journal of Developmental Psychology* 21(1). 33–43. doi:10.1348/026151003321164609.

Pelphrey, Kevin A., J. Steven Reznick, Barbara Davis Goldman, Noah Sasson, Judy Morrow, Andrea Donahoe & Katharine Hodgson. 2004. Development of visuospatial short-term memory in the second half of the 1st year. *Developmental Psychology* 40(5). 836–851. doi:10.1037/0012-1649.40.5.836.

Perfors, Amy, Joshua B. Tenenbaum & Elizabeth Wonnacott. 2010. Variability, negative evidence, and the acquisition of verb argument constructions. *Journal of Child Language* 37(3). 607–642. doi:10.1017/S0305000910000012.

Perlovsky, Leonid. 2007. Modeling Field Theory of Higher Cognitive Functions. In Angelo Loula, Ricardo Gudwin & João Queiroz (eds.), *Artificial Cognition Systems*, 64–105. Hershey, PA: IGI Global. doi:978-1-59904-111-7.ch003.

Perner, Josef, Manuel Sprung, Petra Zauner & Hubert Haider. 2003. Want That is Understood Well before Say That, Think That, and False Belief: A Test of de Villiers's Linguistic Determinism on German-Speaking Children. *Child Development* 74(1). 179–188. doi:10.1111/1467-8624.t01-1-00529.

Perrett, David I. & Amanda J. Mistlin. 1990. Perception of facial characteristics by monkeys. In William C. Stebbins & Mark A. Berkley (eds.), *Comparative perception. Vol. 2. Complex signals*, 187–215. New York: Wiley.

Peterson, Candida C. & Michael Siegal. 1995. Deafness, conversation and theory of mind. *Journal of Child Psychology and Psychiatry* 36(3). 459–474. doi:10.1111/j.1469-7610.1995.tb01303.x

Peterson, Carole. 1990. The Who, When and Where of Early Narratives. *Journal of Child Language* 17(2). 433–455. doi:10.1017/S0305000900013854.

Pham, Andy V. & Ramzi M. Hasson. 2014. Verbal and visuospatial working memory as predictors of children's reading ability. *Archives of Clinical Neuropsychology* 29(5). 467–477. doi:10.1093/arclin/acu024.

Piaget, Jean. 1952. When thinking begins. *The origins of intelligence in children*, 25–36. New York: International Universities Press. doi: 10.1037/11494-000.

Piaget, Jean. 2007. *The language and thought of the child*. Goldberg Press.
Piattelli-Palmarini, Massimo. 1994. Ever since language and learning: afterthoughts on the Piaget-Chomsky debate. *Cognition* 50(1–3). 315–346. doi:10.1016/0010-0277(94)90034-5.
Pickering, Martin J. & Simon Garrod. 2004. Toward a mechanistic psychology of dialogue. *Behavioral and Brain Sciences* 27(2). 169–226. doi:10.1017/S0140525X04000056.
Pickering, Martin J. & Simon Garrod. 2013. An integrated theory of language production and comprehension. *Behavioral and Brain Sciences* 36(4). 329–47. doi:10.1017/s0140525x12001495.
Pine, Julian M., Caroline F. Rowland, Elena V. M. Lieven & Anna L. Theakston. 2005. Testing the agreement/tense omission model: Why the data on children's use of non-nominative 3psg subjects count against the ATOM. *Journal of Child Language* 32(2). 269–289.
Pine, Julian M., Daniel Freudenthal, Grzegorz Krajewski & Fernand Gobet. 2013. Do young children have adult-like syntactic categories? Zipf's law and the case of the determiner. *Cognition* 127(3). 345–360. doi:10.1016/j.cognition.2013.02.006.
Pinker, Steven. 1979. Formal models of language learning. *Cognition* 7(3). 217–283. doi:10.1016/0010-0277(79)90001-5.
Pinker, Steven. 1984. The semantic bootstrapping hypothesis. *Language Learnability & Language Development*, 39–47. Cambridge, MA: Harvard University Press.
Pinker, Steven. 1989. *Learnability and cognition. The acquisition of verb-argument structure*. Cambridge, MA: MIT Press/Bradford Books.
Pinker, Steven. 1994. *The Language Instinct. How the Mind Creates Language*. Penguin Books.
Pinker, Steven. 1999. *Words and Rules*. London: Weidenfeld & Nicolson.
Pinker, Steven. 2001. Talk of genetics and vice versa. *Nature* 413. 465–466. doi:10.1038/35097173.
Pinker, Steven. 2003. Language as an adaptation to the cognitive niche. In Simon Kirby & Morten H. Christiansen (eds.), *Language evolution: States of the art*, 16–37. New York: Oxford University Press.
Pinker, Steven. 2010. Language as an Adaptation to the Cognitive Niche. In Simon Kirby & Morten H. Christiansen (eds.), *Language evolution: States of the art*, 16–37. Oxford Scholarship Online. doi:10.1093/acprof:oso/9780199244843.003.0002.
Pinker, Steven & Paul Bloom. 1990. Natural language and natural selection. *Behavioral and Brain Sciences* 13(4). 707–784. doi:10.1017/s0140525x00081061.
Pinker, Steven & Ray Jackendoff. 2005. The faculty of language: What's special about it? *Cognition* 95(2). 201–236. doi:10.1016/j.cognition.2004.08.004.
Pinker, Steven, David S. Lebeaux & Loren Ann Frost. 1987. Productivity and constraints in the acquisition of the passive. *Cognition* 26(3). 195–267. doi:10.1016/S0010-0277(87)80001-X.
Plomin, Robert. 2018. *Blueprint: How DNA makes us who we are*. UK: Penguin Random House.
Plumert, Jodie M. & John P. Spencer. 2007. *The Emerging Spatial Mind*. Oxford: Oxford University Press. doi:10.1093/acprof:oso/9780195189223.001.0001.
Plunkett, Kim & Virginia Marchman. 1993. From rote learning to system building: acquiring verb morphology in children and connectionist nets. *Cognition* 48(1). 21–69. doi:10.1016/0010-0277(93)90057-3.
Poldrack, Russell A. & Mark G. Packard. 2003. Competition among multiple memory systems: Converging evidence from animal and human brain studies. *Neuropsychologia* 41(3). 245–251. doi:10.1016/S0028-3932(02)00157-4.
Pons, Ferran, David J. Lewkowicz, Salvador Soto-Faraco & Núria Sebastián-Gallés. 2009. Narrowing of intersensory speech perception in infancy. *Proceedings of the National*

Academy of Sciences of the United States of America 106(26). 10598–10602. doi:10.1073/pnas.0904134106.

Posner, Michael I. 1980. Orienting of attention. *The Quarterly Journal of Experimental Psychology* 32(1). 3–25. doi:10.1080/00335558008248231.

Posner, Michael I. & Steven W. Keele. 1968. On The Genesis of Abstract Ideas. *Journal of Experimental Psychology* 77(3-1). 353–363. doi:10.1037/h0025953.

Poulin-Dubois, Diane & James N. Forbes. 2002. Toddlers' attention to intentions-in-action in learning novel action words. *Developmental Psychology* 38(1). 104–114. doi:10.1037/0012-1649.38.1.104.

Poulin-Dubois, Diane & James N. Forbes. 2006. Word, intention, and action: A two-tiered model of action word learning. In Kathryn Hirsh-Pasek & Roberta M. Golinkoff (eds.), *Action meets word: How children learn verbs*, 262–285. New York: Oxford University Press.

Poulin-Dubois, Diane, Anouk Lepage & Doreen Ferland. 1996. Infants' concept of animacy. *Cognitive Development* 11(1). 19–36. doi:10.1016/S0885-2014(96)90026-X.

Prat-Sala, Mercè & Holly P. Branigan. 2000. Discourse Constraints on Syntactic Processing in Language Production: A Cross-Linguistic Study in English and Spanish. *Journal of Memory and Language* 42(2). 168–182. doi:10.1006/jmla.1999.2668.

Prentice, Joan L. 1967. Effects of cuing actor vs cuing object on word order in sentence production. *Psychonomic Science* 8(4). 163–164. doi:10.3758/BF03331600.

Price, Cathy J. 2010. The anatomy of language: A review of 100 fMRI studies published in 2009. *Annals of the New York Academy of Sciences* 1191. 62–88. doi:10.1111/j.1749-6632.2010.05444.x.

Prinz, Jesse. 2006. Is the mind really modular? In Robert J. Stainton (ed.), *Contemporary debates in cognitive science*, 22–36. Malden, MA: Blackwell Publishing.

Prinz, Wolfgang. 1997. Perception and Action Planning. *European Journal of Cognitive Psychology* 9(2). 129–154. doi:10.1080/713752551.

Prinz, Wolfgang. 1990. A common coding approach to perception and action. In Odmar Neumann & Wolfgang Prinz (eds.), *Relationships between perception and action*, 167–201. Berlin: Springer-Verlag. doi:10.1007/978-3-642-75348-0.

Pruden, Shannon M., Tilbe Göksun, Sarah Roseberry, Kathy Hirsh-Pasek & Roberta M. Golinkoff. 2012. Find Your Manners: How Do Infants Detect the Invariant Manner of Motion in Dynamic Events? *Child Development* 83(3). 977–991. doi:10.1111/j.1467-8624.2012.01737.x.

Pruden, Shannon M., Sarah Roseberry, Tilbe Göksun, Kathy Hirsh-Pasek & Roberta M. Golinkoff. 2013. Infant Categorization of Path Relations During Dynamic Events. *Child Development* 84(1). 331–345. doi:10.1111/j.1467-8624.2012.01843.x.

Pulverman, Rachel, Roberta Michnick Golinkoff, Kathy Hirsh-Pasek & Jennifer Sootsman Buresh. 2008. Infants discriminate manners and paths in non-linguistic dynamic events. *Cognition* 108(3). 825–830. doi:10.1016/j.cognition.2008.04.009.

Pulverman, Rachel, Lulu Song, Kathy Hirsh-Pasek, Shannon M. Pruden & Roberta M. Golinkoff. 2013. Preverbal Infants' Attention to Manner and Path: Foundations for Learning Relational Terms. *Child Development* 84(1). 241–252. doi:10.1111/cdev.12030.

Pye, Clifton & Pedro Poz. 1988. Precocious passives (and antipassives) in Quiché Mayan. *Papers and Reports on Child Language Development* 27. 71–80.

Quinn, Paul C. 1987. The categorical representation of visual pattern information by young infants. *Cognition* 27(2). 145–179. doi:10.1016/0010-0277(87)90017-5.

Quinn, Paul C. & Peter D. Eimas. 1996. Perceptual organization and categorization in young infants. In Carolyn Rovee-Collier & Lewis P. Lipsitt (eds.), *Advances in Infancy Research* 10, 1–36. Norwood, NJ: Ablex Publishing.

Raffaelli, Marcela, Lisa J. Crockett & Yuh Ling Shen. 2005. Developmental stability and change in self-regulation from childhood to adolescence. *Journal of Genetic Psychology* 166(1). 54–75. doi:10.3200/GNTP.166.1.54-76.

Rakison, David H. & George E. Butterworth. 1998. Infants' use of object parts in early categorization. *Developmental psychology* 34(1),49–62. doi:10.1037/0012-1649.34.1.49.

Rakison, David H. & Diane Poulin-Dubois. 2001. Developmental Origin of the Animate-Inanimate Distinction. *Psychological Bulletin* 27(2). 209–228. doi:10.1037/0033-2909.127.2.209.

Ramscar, Michael, Melody Dye & Stewart M. McCauley. 2014. Error and expectation in language learning: The curious absence of mouses in adult speech. *Language* 89(4). 760–793. doi:10.1353/lan.2013.0068.

Rao, Rajesh P. N. & Dana H. Ballard. 1997. Dynamic model of visual recognition predicts neural response properties in the visual cortex. *Neural Computation* 9(4). 721–763. doi:10.1162/neco.1997.9.4.721.

Rao, Rajesh P. N. & Dana H. Ballard. 1999. Predictive coding in the visual cortex: A functional interpretation of some extra-classical receptive-field effects. *Nature Neuroscience* 2. 79–87. doi:10.1038/4580.

Reali, Florencia & Morten H. Christiansen. 2009. Sequential learning and the interaction between biological and linguistic adaptation in language evolution. *Interaction Studies* 10(1). 5–30. doi:10.1075/is.10.1.02rea.

Redington, Martin, Nick Chater & Steven Finch. 1998. Distributional information: A powerful cue for acquiring syntactic categories. *Cognitive Science* 22(4). 425–469. doi:10.1207/s15516709cog2204_2.

Reeder, Patricia A., Elissa L. Newport & Richard N. Aslin. 2013. From shared contexts to syntactic categories: The role of distributional information in learning linguistic form-classes. *Cognitive Psychology* 66(1). 30–54. doi:10.1016/j.cogpsych.2012.09.001.

Repp, Bruno H. & Günther Knoblich. 2007. Action can affect auditory perception: Short report. *Psychological Science* 18(1). 6–7. doi:10.1111/j.1467-9280.2007.01839.x.

Reuter, Tracy, Lauren Emberson, Alexa Romberg & Casey Lew-Williams. 2018. Individual differences in nonverbal prediction and vocabulary size in infancy. *Cognition* 176. 215–219. doi:10.1016/j.cognition.2018.03.006.

Reynolds, Greg D. & John E. Richards. 2007. Infant heart rate: A developmental psychophysiological perspective. In Louis Schmidt & Sidney Segalowitz (eds.), *Developmental Psychophysiology: Theory, Systems, and Methods*, 173–212. Cambridge: Cambridge University Press. doi:10.1017/CBO9780511499791.009.

Reynolds, Greg D., Mary L. Courage & John E. Richards. 2011. The Development of Attention. *Oxford Handbook of Cognitive Psychology*. New York: Oxford University Press.

Richards, John E. 1997. Peripheral Stimulus Localization by Infants: Attention, Age, and Individual Differences in Heart Rate Variability. *Journal of Experimental Psychology: Human Perception and Performance* 23(3). 667–680. doi:10.1037/0096-1523.23.3.667.

Richards, John E. 2003. Attention affects the recognition of briefly presented visual stimuli in infants: An ERP study. *Developmental Science* 6(3). 312–328. doi:10.1111/1467-7687.00287.

Richmond, Lauren L., David A. Gold & Jeffrey M. Zacks. 2017. Event perception: Translations and applications. *Journal of Applied Research in Memory and Cognition*. 6(2),111–20. doi:10.1016/j.jarmac.2016.11.002.

Rijntjes, Michel, Cornelius Weiller, Tobias Bormann & Mariacristina Musso. 2012. The dual loop model: Its relation to language and other modalities. *Frontiers in Evolutionary Neuroscience* 4. 9. doi:10.3389/fnevo.2012.00009.

Rispoli, Matthew. 1991. The mosaic acquisition of grammatical relations. *Journal of Child Language* 18(3). 517–551. doi:10.1017/S0305000900011235.

Roberts, John R. 1998. Give in Amele. In John Newman (ed.), *The Linguistics of Giving*, 1–33. Typological Studies in Language, 36th ed. Amsterdam: John Benjamins Publishing Company.

Robinson, Byron, Carolyn Mervis & Bronwyn Robinson. 2003. The Roles of Verbal Short-Term Memory and Working Memory in the Acquisition of Grammar by Children With Williams Syndrome. *Developmental Neuropsychology* 23(1–2). 13–31. doi:10.1207/S15326942DN231&2_2.

Rochat Philippe & Tricia Striano. 1999. Social cognitive development in the first year. In Philippe Rochat (ed.), *Early Social Cognition*, 3–34. Hillsdale, NJ: Lawrence Erlbaum Associates.

Rohr, Claudia Rudolf von, Judith M. Burkart & Carel P. van Schaik. 2011. Evolutionary precursors of social norms in chimpanzees: A new approach. *Biology and Philosophy* 26. 1–30. doi:10.1007/s10539-010-9240-4.

Rosch, Eleanor. 1983. Prototype classification and logical classification: The two systems. In Ellin Scholnick (ed.), *New trends in conceptual representation: Challenges to Piaget's theory?* 73–86. Hillsdale, NJ: Lawrence Erlbaum Associates.

Rose, Susan A. & Judith F. Feldman. 1995. Prediction of IQ and Specific Cognitive Abilities at 11 Years From Infancy Measures. *Developmental Psychology* 31(4),685–696. doi:10.1037/0012-1649.31.4.685.

Rose, Susan A. & Judith F. Feldman. 1997. Memory and Speed: Their Role in the Relation of Infant Information Processing to Later IQ. *Child Development* 68(4). 630–641. doi:10.1111/j.1467-8624.1997.tb04226.x.

Rothbart, Mary K. & John E. Bates. 2006. Temperament. In Nancy Eisenberg, William Damon & Richard M. Lerner (eds.), *Handbook of child psychology: Social, emotional, and personality development*, 99–166. Hoboken, NJ: John Wiley & Sons.

Rovee-Collier, Carolyn. 1996. Shifting the focus from what to why. *Infant Behavior and Development* 19(4). 385–400. doi:10.1016/S0163-6383(96)90001-6.

Rovee-Collier, Carolyn, and Kimberley Cuevas. 2009. Multiple memory systems are unnecessary to account for infant memory development: an ecological model. *Dev. Psychol.* 45, 160–174. doi:10.1037/a0014538.

Rovee-Collier, Carolyn & Kimberly Cuevas. 2009a. Multiple Memory Systems Are Unnecessary to Account for Infant Memory Development: An Ecological Model. *Developmental Psychology* 45(1). 160–174. doi:10.1037/a0014538.

Rovee-Collier, Carolyn & Kimberly Cuevas. 2009b. The development of infant memory. In Mary Courage & Nelson Cowan (eds.), *The development of memory in infancy and childhood*, 11–41. Hove, UK: Psychology Press.

Rowland, Caroline F. & Julian M. Pine. 2000. Subject-auxiliary inversion errors and wh-question acquisition: "What children do know?" *Journal of Child Language* 27(1). 157–181. doi:10.1017/S0305000999004055.

Rowland, Caroline F., Julian M. Pine, Elena V. Lieven & Anna L. Theakston. 2003. Determinants of acquisition order in wh-questions: re-evaluating the role of caregiver speech. *Journal of Child Language* 30(3). 609–635. doi:10.1017/s0305000903005695.

Roy, Brandon C., Michael C. Frank, Philip DeCamp, Matthew Miller & Deb Roy. 2015. Predicting the birth of a spoken word. *Proceedings of the National Academy of Sciences* 112(41). 12663–12668. doi:10.1073/pnas.1419773112.

Ruff, Holly A. & Mary C. Capozzoli. 2003. Development of Attention and Distractibility in the First 4 Years of Life. *Developmental Psychology* 39(5). 877–890. doi:10.1037/0012-1649.39.5.877.

Ruff, Holly A. & Mary K. Rothbart. 1996. *Attention in early development*. New York : Oxford University Press.

Ruff, Holly A. & Lisa M. Saltarelli. 1993. Exploratory play with objects: Basic cognitive processes and individual differences. *New Directions for Child and Adolescent Development* 1993(59). 5–16. doi:10.1002/cd.23219935903.

Ryan, Ellen Bouchard. 1983. Social Psychological Mechanisms Underlying Native Speaker Evaluations of Non-Native Speech. *Studies in Second Language Acquisition* 5(2). 148–159. doi:10.1017/S0272263100004824.

Sabbagh, Mark A. & Dare A. Baldwin. 2001. Learning Words from Knowledgeable versus Ignorant Speakers: Links between Preschoolers' Theory of Mind and Semantic Development. *Child Development* 72(4). 1054–1070. doi:10.1111/1467-8624.00334.

Saffran, Jenny R., Elissa L. Newport & Richard N. Aslin. 1996. Word segmentation: The role of distributional cues. *Journal of Memory and Language* 35(4). 606–621. doi:10.1006/jmla.1996.0032.

Salomo, Dorothé, Elena Lieven & Michael Tomasello. 2010. Young children's sensitivity to new and given information when answering predicate-focus questions. *Applied Psycholinguistics* 31(1). 101–115. doi:10.1017/S014271640999018X.

Santos, Laurie R., Aaron G. Nissen & Jonathan A. Ferrugia. 2006. Rhesus monkeys, Macaca mulatta, know what others can and cannot hear. *Animal Behaviour* 71(5). 1175–1181. doi:10.1016/j.anbehav.2005.10.007.

Sapir, Edward. 1921. *Language: An introduction to the study of speech*. New York: Harcourt, Brace and company.

Saur, Dorothee, Björn W. Kreher, Susanne Schnell, Dorothee Kümmerer, Philipp Kellmeyer, Magnus-Sebastian Vry, Roza Umarova, Mariacristina Musso, Volkmar Glauche, Stefanie Abel, Walter Huber, Michel Rijntjes, Jürgen Hennig, and Cornelius Weiller. 2008. Ventral and dorsal pathways for language. *Proceedings of the National Academy of Sciences* 105 (46) 18035–18040. doi:10.1073/pnas.0805234105.

Schank, Roger & Robert Abelson. 1977. *Scripts, Plans Goals and Understanding: An Inquiry Into Human Knowledge Structures*. Hillsdale, NJ: Lawrence Erlbaum Associates.

Schlesinger, Matthew & Jonas Langer. 1999. Infants' developing expectations of possible and impossible tool-use events between ages 8 and 12 months. *Developmental Science* 2(2). 195–205. doi:10.1111/1467-7687.00068.

Schneider, Wofgang, Hans Gruber, Andreas Gold, & Klaus Opwis. 1993. Chess expertise and memory for chess positions in children and adults. Journal of Experimental Child Psychology 56, 328–349.

Scholz, John P. 1990. Dynamic pattern theory – Some implications for therapeutics. *Physical Therapy* 70(12). 827–843. doi:10.1093/ptj/70.12.827.

Schöner, Gregor. 2009. Development as Change of System Dynamics: Stability, Instability, and Emergence. In John P. Spencer, Michael S. C. Thomas & James L. McClelland (eds.), *Toward a Unified Theory of Development Connectionism and Dynamic System Theory Re-Considered*, 25–47. New York: Oxford University Press. doi:10.1093/acprof:oso/9780195300598.003.0002.

Schreiweis, Christiane, Ulrich Bornschein, Eric Burguière, Cemil Kerimoglu, Sven Schreiter, Michael Dannemann, Shubhi Goyal, Ellis Rea, Catherine A. French, Rathi Puliyadi, Matthias Groszer, View ORCID ProfileSimon E. Fisher, Roger Mundry, Christine Winter, Wulf Hevers, Svante Pääbo, Wolfgang Enard & Ann M. Graybiel. 2014. Humanized Foxp2 accelerates learning by enhancing transitions from declarative to procedural performance. *Proceedings of the National Academy of Sciences* 111(39). 14253–14258. doi:10.1073/pnas.1414542111.

Schubö, Anna, Gisa Aschersleben & Wolfgang Prinz. 2001. Interactions between perception and action in a reaction task with overlapping S-R assignments. *Psychological Research* 65(3). 145–157. doi:10.1007/s004260100061.

Schulze, Katrin, Faraneh Vargha-Khadem & Mortimer Mishkin. 2018. Phonological working memory and FOXP2. *Neuropsychologia* 108. 147–152. doi:10.1016/j.neuropsychologia.2017.11.027.

Schütze, Hinrich. 1993. Part-of-speech induction from scratch. *Proceedings of the 31st annual meeting on Association for Computational Linguistics*, 251–258. doi:10.3115/981574.981608.

Scott, Lisa S., Olivier Pascalis & Charles A. Nelson. 2007. A domain-general theory of the development of perceptual discrimination. *Current Directions in Psychological Science* 16(4). 197–201. doi:10.1111/j.1467-8721.2007.00503.x.

Scott, Rose M. & Cynthia Fisher. 2009. Two-year-olds use distributional cues to interpret transitivity-alternating verbs. *Language and Cognitive Processes* 24(6). 777–803. doi:10.1080/01690960802573236.

Seligman, Martin E. P. 1975. *Helplessness: On depression, development, and death.* San Francisco, CA: W. H. Freeman.

Shannon, Claude E. 1951. Prediction and Entropy of Printed English. *Bell System Technical Journal* 30. 50–64. doi:10.1002/j.1538-7305.1951.tb01366.x.

Shiffrin, Richard M. & Walter Schneider. 1977a. Controlled and automatic human information processing: I. detection, search, and attention. *Psychological Review* 84(1). 1–66. doi:10.1037/0033-295X.84.1.1.

Shiffrin, Richard M. & Walter Schneider. 1977b. Controlled and automatic human information processing: II. Perceptual learning, automatic attending and a general theory. *Psychological Review* 84(2). 127–190. doi:10.1037/0033-295X.84.2.127.

Shirai, Yasuhiro & Roger W. Andersen. 2006. The Acquisition of Tense-Aspect Morphology: A Prototype Account. *Language* 1(4). 743–762. doi:10.2307/415743.

Shneidman, Laura A. & Susan Goldin-Meadow. 2012. Language input and acquisition in a Mayan village: How important is directed speech? *Developmental Science* 15(5). 659–673. doi:10.1111/j.1467-7687.2012.01168.x.

Shutt, Kathryn, Ann MacLarnon, Michael Heistermann & Stuart Semple. 2007. Grooming in Barbary macaques: Better to give than to receive? *Biology Letters* 3(3). 231–233. doi:10.1098/rsbl.2007.0052.

Skinner, Burrhus F. 1957. *Verbal behavior.* New York: Appleton.

Slater, A. 1995. Visual perception and memory at birth. In Carolyn Rovee-Collier & Lewis P. Lipsitt (eds.), *Advances in Infancy Research 9*, 107–162. Norwood, NJ: Ablex Publishing.

Slobin, Dan. 1996. Two ways to travel: Verbs of motion in English and Spanish. In: Sandra A. Thompson and Masayoshi Shibatani (eds.), Grammatical Constructions: Their Form and Meaning, 195–217. Oxford: Oxford University Press.

Slobin, Dan I. 1996a. Two ways to travel: Verbs of motion in English and Spanish. In Masayoshi Shibatani & Sandra Thompson (eds.), *Grammatical constructions: Their form and meaning*, 195–220. Oxford: Clarendon Press.

Slobin, Dan I. 1996b. From '"thought and language"' to '"thinking for speaking"'. In John Gumperz & Stephen C. Levinson (eds.), *Rethinking Linguistic Relativity*, 70–96. Cambridge, MA: Cambridge University Press.

Sloutsky, Vladimir M. 2003. The role of similarity in the development of categorization. *Trends in Cognitive Sciences* 7(6). 246–251. doi:10.1016/S1364-6613(03)00109-8.

Smith, Linda B. 2005. Cognition as a dynamic system: Principles from embodiment. *Developmental Review* 25(3-4). 278–298. doi:10.1016/j.dr.2005.11.001.

Smith, Linda B. & Esther Thelen. 2003. Development as a dynamic system. *Trends in Cognitive Sciences* 7(8). 343–348. doi:10.1016/S1364-6613(03)00156-6.

Smith, Nathaniel J., Noah Goodman & Michael Frank. 2013. Learning and using language via recursive pragmatic reasoning about other agents. *Advances in Neural Information Processing Systems* 26. 3039–3047.

Solomon, Sarah H., Nicholas C. Hindy, Gerry T. M. Altmann & Sharon L. Thompson-Schill. 2015. Competition between mutually exclusive object states in event comprehension. *Journal of Cognitive Neuroscience* 27(12). 2324–2338. doi:10.1162/jocn_a_00866.

Sommerville, Jessica A. & Amanda L. Woodward. 2005. Infant's sensitivity to the casual features of means-end support sequences in action and perception. *Infancy* 8(2). 119–145. doi:10.1207/s15327078in0802_2.

Son, Minjeong & Peter Cole. 2008. An Event-Based Account of -kan Constructions in Standard Indonesian. *Language* 84(1).120–60. doi:10.1353/lan.2008.0045.

Song, Jae Jung. 2001. *Linguistic Typology: Morphology and Syntax*. Harlow: Longman.

Soska, Kasey C., Karen E. Adolph & Scott P. Johnson. 2010. Systems in Development: Motor Skill Acquisition Facilitates Three-Dimensional Object Completion. *Developmental Psychology* 46(1). 129–138. doi:10.1037/a0014618.

Souza, André L., Krista Byers-Heinlein & Diane Poulin-Dubois. 2013. Bilingual and monolingual children prefer native-accented speakers. *Frontiers in Psychology* 4. 953. doi:10.3389/fpsyg.2013.00953.

Spencer, John P., Mark S. Blumberg, Bob Mcmurray, Scott R. Robinson, Larissa K. Samuelson & J. Bruce Tomblin. 2009. Short arms and talking eggs: Why we should no longer abide the nativist-empiricist debate. *Child Development Perspectives* 3(2),79–87. doi:10.1111/j.1750-8606.2009.00081.x.

Spencer, John P. & Sammy Perone. 2008. Defending qualitative change: The view from dynamical systems theory. *Child Development* 79(6),1639–1647. doi:10.1111/j.1467-8624.2008.01214.x.

Spencer, John P., Sammy Perone & Aaron T. Buss. 2011. Twenty years and going strong: A dynamic systems revolution in motor and cognitive development. *Child Development Perspectives* 5(4). 260–266. doi:10.1111/j.1750-8606.2011.00194.x.

Sperber, Dan & Deirdre Wilson. 1986. *Relevance: Communication and cognition*. Cambridge, MA: Harvard University Press.

Sperber, Dan. 2002. In defense of massive modularity. In Emmanuel Dupoux (ed.), *Language, brain, and cognitive development: Essays in honor of Jacques Mehler*, 47–57. Cambridge, MA: MIT Press.

Spinozzi, Giovanna. 1996. Categorization in monkeys and chimpanzees. *Behavioural Brain Research* 74(1-2). 17–24. doi:10.1016/0166-4328(95)00030-5.

Sporns, Olaf. 2002. Network analysis, complexity, and brain function. *Complexity* 8(1). 56–60. doi:10.1002/cplx.10047.

Squire, Larry R. & John T. Wixted. 2011. The Cognitive Neuroscience of Human Memory Since H.M. *Annual Review of Neuroscience* 34. 259–88. doi:10.1146/annurev-neuro-061010-113720.

Steele, Claude M. 1988. The Psychology of Self-Affirmation: Sustaining the Integrity of the Self. *Advances in Experimental Social Psychology* 21. 261–302. doi:10.1016/S0065-2601(08)60229-4.

Steels, Luc & Tony Belpaeme. 2005. Coordinating perceptually grounded categories through language: A case study for colour. *Behavioral and Brain Sciences* 28(4). 469–489. doi:10.1017/S0140525X05000087.

Steiper, Michael E. & Erik R. Seiffert. 2012. Evidence for a convergent slowdown in primate molecular rates and its implications for the timing of early primate evolution. *Proceedings of the National Academy of Sciences* 109(16). 6006–6011. doi:10.1073/pnas.1119506109.

Stel, Marielle & Roos Vonk. 2010. Mimicry in social interaction: Benefits for mimickers, mimickees, and their interaction. *British Journal of Psychology* 101(2). 311–323. doi:10.1348/000712609X465424.

Stevens, Jeffrey R. 2004. The selfish nature of generosity: Harassment and food sharing in primates. *Proceedings of the Royal Society B: Biological Sciences* 271(1538). 451–456. doi:10.1098/rspb.2003.2625.

Steyvers, Mark & Joshua B. Tenenbaum. 2005. The large-scale structure of semantic networks. *Cognitive Science* 29(1). 41–78. doi:10.1207/s15516709cog2901_3

Stiefelhagen, Rainer, Christian Fugen, Petra Gieselmann, Hartwig Holzapfel, Kai Nickel & Alex Waibel. 2004. Natural human-robot interaction using speech, head pose and gestures. *2004 IEEE/RSJ International Conference on Intelligent Robots and Systems (IROS)* 3. 2422–2427.

Stojanovik, Vesna. 2006. Social interaction deficits and conversational inadequacy in Williams syndrome. *Journal of Neurolinguistics* 19(2). 157–173. doi:10.1016/j.jneuroling.2005.11.005.

Stojanovik, Vesna & Lizet van Ewijk. 2008. Do children with Williams syndrome have unusual vocabularies? *Journal of Neurolinguistics* 21(1). 18–34. doi:10.1016/j.jneuroling.2007.06.003.

Stojanovik, Vesna, Mick Perkins & Sara Howard. 2004. Williams syndrome and specific language impairment do not support claims for developmental double dissociations and innate modularity. *Journal of Neurolinguistics* 17(6). 403–424. doi:10.1016/j.trim.2013.10.008.

Stojanovik, Vesna, Mick Perkins & Sara Howard. 2001. Language and conversational abilities in Williams syndrome: how good is good? *International Journal of Language & Communication Disorders* 36(sup1). 234–239. DOI: 10.3109/13682820109177890

Strauss, Mark S. 1979. Abstraction of prototypical information by adults and 10-month-old infants. *Journal of Experimental Psychology: Human Learning and Memory* 5(6). 618–632. doi:10.1037/0278-7393.5.6.618.

Striano, Tricia & Evelin Bertin. 2005a. Coordinated affect with mothers and strangers: A longitudinal analysis of joint engagement between 5 and 9 months of age. *Cognition and Emotion* 19(5). 781–790. doi:10.1080/02699930541000002.

Striano, Tricia & Evelin Bertin. 2005b. Social-cognitive skills between 5 and 10 months of age. *British Journal of Developmental Psychology* 23(4). 559–568. doi:10.1348/026151005X26282.

Striano, Tricia, Anne Henning & Daniel Stahl. 2005. Sensitivity to social contingencies between 1 and 3 months of age. *Developmental Science* 8(6). 509–518. doi:10.1111/j.1467-7687.2005.00442.x.

Striano, Tricia & Vincent M. Reid. 2006. Social cognition in the first year. *Trends in Cognitive Sciences* 10(10). 471–476. doi:10.1016/j.tics.2006.08.006.

Strid, Karin, Tomas Tjus, Lars Smith, Andrew N. Meltzoff & Mikael Heimann. 2006. Infant recall memory and communication predicts later cognitive development. *Infant Behavior and Development* 29(4). 545–553. doi:10.1016/j.infbeh.2006.07.002.

Stürmer, Birgit, Gisa Aschersleben & Wolfgang Prinz. 2000. Correspondence Effects with Manual Gestures and Postures: A Study of Imitation. *Journal of Experimental Psychology: Human Perception and Performance* 26(6). 1746–1759. doi:10.1037/0096-1523.26.6.1746.

Sundqvist, Annette, Emelie Nordqvist, Felix Sebastian Koch & Mikael Heimann. 2016. Early declarative memory predicts productive language: A longitudinal study of deferred imitation and communication at 9 and 16 months. *Journal of Experimental Child Psychology* 151.109–19. doi:10.1016/j.jecp.2016.01.015.

Suzman, Susan. 1985. Learning the passive in Zulu. *Papers and Reports on Child Language Development* 24. 131–137.

Swanson, H. Lee. 1996. Individual and age-related differences in children's working memory. *Memory & Cognition* 24(1). 70–82. doi:10.3758/BF03197273.

Swingley, Daniel, John P. Pinto & Anne Fernald. 1999. Continuous processing in word recognition at 24 months. *Cognition* 71(2). 73–108. doi:10.1016/S0010-0277(99)00021-9.

Symons, Lawrence A. 1998. Look at me: Five-month-old infants' sensitivity to very small deviations in eye-gaze during social interactions. *Infant Behavior and Development* 21(3). 531–536. doi:10.1016/S0163-6383(98)90026-1.

Számadó, Szabolcs & Eörs Szathmáry. 2012. Evolutionary biological foundations of the origin of language: the co-evolution of language and brain. In Kathleen R. Gibson and Maggie Tallerman (eds.), *The Oxford Handbook of Language Evolution*, 157–167. Oxford: Oxford University Press.

Tager-Flusberg, Helen, Jenea Boshart & Simon Baron-Cohen. 1998. Reading the windows to the soul: Evidence of domain-specific sparing in Williams syndrome. *Journal of Cognitive Neuroscience* 10(5). 631–639. doi:10.1162/089892998563031.

Takac, Martin & Alistair Knott. 2016. Mechanisms for storing and accessing event representations in episodic memory, and their expression in language: a neural network model. *Proceedings of the 38th Annual Meeting of the Cognitive Science Society*, 532–537.

Takac, Martin, Lubica Benuskova & Alistair Knott. 2012. Mapping sensorimotor sequences to word sequences: A connectionist model of language acquisition and sentence generation. *Cognition* 125(2). 288–308. doi:10.1016/j.cognition.2012.06.006.

Talmy, Leonard. 1985. Lexicalization patterns: Semantic Structure in Lexical Forms. In Timothy Shopen (ed.), *Language Typology and Syntactic Description. Vol. 3: Grammatical Categories and the Lexicon*, 57–149. Cambridge: Cambridge University Press.]

Talmy, Leonard. 1988. Force dynamics in language and cognition. *Cognitive Science* 12(1). 49–100. doi:10.1016/0364-0213(88)90008-0.
Talmy, Leonard. 2000. Lexicalization patterns. In *Toward a cognitive semantics: Typology and process in concept structuring*, 21–146. Cambridge, MA: MIT Press.
Talmy, Leonard. 2007. Attention phenomena. In Dirk Geeraerts & Hubert Cuyckens (eds.), *Oxford Handbook of Cognitive Linguistics*, 264–293. Oxford: Oxford University Press.
Talmy, Leonard. 2012. Attention Phenomena. In Dirk Geeraerts & Hubert Cuyckens (eds.), *Oxford Handbook of Cognitive Linguistics*, 264–293. Oxford: Oxford University Press, online publication. doi:10.1093/oxfordhb/9780199738632.013.0011.
Tardif, Twila. 1996. Nouns are not always learned before verbs: Evidence from Mandarin speakers' early vocabularies. *Developmental Psychology* 32(3). 492–504. doi:10.1037/0012-1649.32.3.492.
Tardif, Twila, Susan A. Gelman & Fan Xu. 1999. Putting the "noun bias" in context: A comparison of English and Mandarin. *Child Development* 70(3),620–635. doi:10.1111/1467-8624.00045.
Tardif, Twila, Marilyn Shatz & Letitia Naigles. 1997. Caregiver speech and children's use of nouns versus verbs: A comparison of English, Italian, and Mandarin. *Journal of Child Language* 24(3). 535–565. doi:10.1017/S030500099700319X.
Taylor, Gemma., & Jane Herbert. 2014. Infant and adult visual attention during an imitation demonstration. Developmental Psychobiology: 56., (4), 770–782. http://dx.doi.org/10.1002/dev.21147.
Tennie, Claudio, Josep Call & Michael Tomasello. 2009. Ratcheting up the ratchet: On the evolution of cumulative culture. *Philosophical Transactions of the Royal Society B: Biological Sciences* 364(1528). 2405–2415. doi:10.1098/rstb.2009.0052.
Tennie, Claudio, Keith Jensen & Josep Call. 2016. The nature of prosociality in chimpanzees. *Nature Communications* 7. 13915. doi:10.1038/ncomms13915.
Theakston, Anna L., Elena V. M. Lieven, Julian M. Pine & Caroline F. Rowland. 2001. The role of performance limitations in the acquisition of verb-argument structure: An alternative account. *Journal of Child Language* 28(1),127–152. doi:10.1017/S0305000900004608.
Thelen, Esther. 1992. Development as a dynamic system. *Current Directions in Psychological Science* 1(6). 189–193. doi: 10.1111/1467-8721.ep10770402.
Thelen, Esther & Linda B. Smith. 1994. *A dynamic systems approach to the development of cognition and action*. Cambridge, MA: MIT Press.
Thelen, Esther, Donna M. Fisher & Robyn Ridley-Johnson. 1984. The relationship between physical growth and a newborn reflex. *Infant Behavior and Development* 25(1),72–85. doi:10.1016/S0163-6383(02)00091-7.
Thelen, Esther, Beverly D. Ulrich & Peter H. Wolff. 1991. Hidden Skills: A Dynamic Systems Analysis of Treadmill Stepping during the First Year. *Monographs of the Society for Research in Child Development* 56(1). 104. doi:10.2307/1166099.
Thibaut, Jean Pierre & Lucette Toussaint. 2010. Developing motor planning over ages. *Journal of Experimental Child Psychology* 105(1-2). 116–129. doi:10.1016/j.jecp.2009.10.003.
Thomas, Michael S. C. & Annette Karmiloff-Smith. 2003. Modeling Language Acquisition in Atypical Phenotypes. *Psychological Review* 110(4). 647–682. doi:10.1037/0033-295X.110.4.647.
Thompson, Susan P. & Elissa L. Newport. 2007. Statistical Learning of Syntax: The Role of Transitional Probability. *Language Learning and Development* 3(1). 1–42. doi:10.1207/s15473341lld0301_1.

Thorell, Lisa B., Sofia Lindqvist, Sissela Bergman Nutley, Gunilla Bohlin & Torkel Klingberg. 2009. Training and transfer effects of executive functions in preschool children. *Developmental Science* 12(1).106–113. doi:10.1111/j.1467-7687.2008.00745.x.

Tomasello, Michael. 1995. Joint attention as social cognition. In Chris Moore & Philip J. Dunham (eds.), *Joint attention: Its origins and role in development*, 103–130. Hillsdale, NJ: Lawrence Erlbaum Associates.

Tomasello, Michael. 2003. *Constructing a language. A usage-based theory of language acquisition*. Cambridge, MA: Harvard University Press.

Tomasello, Michael. 2008. *Origins of human communication*. Cambridge, MA: MIT Press.

Tomasello, Michael. 2018. How children come to understand false beliefs: A shared intentionality account. *Proceedings of the National Academy of Sciences* 115(34). 8491–8498. doi:10.1073/pnas.1804761115.

Tomasello, Michael & Michael J. Farrar. 1986. Joint attention and early language. *Child Development* 57(6). 1454–1463. doi:10.2307/1130423

Tomasello, Michael, Ann C. Kruger & Hilary H. Ratner. 1993. Cultural learning. *Behavioral and Brain Sciences* 16(3). 495–511. doi:10.1017/S0140525X0003123X.

Tomasello, Michael & Michelle Barton. 1994. Learning Words in Nonostensive Contexts. *Developmental Psychology* 30(5). 639–650. doi:10.1037/0012-1649.30.5.639.

Tomasello, Michael, Michael Jeffrey Farrar & Jennifer Dines. 1984. Children's Speech Revisions for a Familiar and an Unfamiliar Adult. *Journal of Speech, Language, and Hearing Research* 27(3). 359–363. doi:10.1044/jshr.2703.359.

Tomasello, Michael & Katharina Haberl. 2003. Understanding Attention: 12- and 18-Month-Olds Know What Is New for Other Persons. *Developmental Psychology* 39(5). 906–912. doi:10.1037/0012-1649.39.5.906.

Tomasello, Michael & Ann Cale Kruger. 1992. Joint Attention On Actions Acquiring Verbs In Ostensive And Non-Ostensive Contexts. *Journal of Child Language* 19(2). 311–333. doi:10.1017/S0305000900011430.

Tomasello, Michael, Alicia P Melis, Claudio Tennie, Emily Wyman & Esther Herrmann. 2012. Two Key Steps in the Evolution of Human Cooperation: The Interdependence Hypothesis. *Current Anthropology* 53(6). 673–692. doi:10.1086/668207.

Tomasello, Michael & Hannes Rakoczy. 2003. What makes human cognition unique? From individual to shared to collective intentionality. *Mind and Language* 18(2). 121–147. doi:10.1111/1468-0017.00217.

Tomlin, Russell S. 1986. *Basic Word Order: Functional Principles*. London: Croom Helm.

Tomlin, Russell. 1995. Focal attention, voice, and word order: an experimental, cross-linguistic study. In Pamela Downing & Michael Noonan (eds.), *Word order in discourse*, 517–554. Amsterdam: John Benjamins Publishing Company.

Tomlin, Russell. 1997. Mapping conceptual representations into linguistic representations: The role of attention in grammar. In Jan Nuyts & Eric Pederson (eds.), *Language and conceptualization*, 162–189. Cambridge: Cambridge University Press.

Tononi, Giulio, Gerald M. Edelman & Olaf Sporns. 1998. Complexity and coherency: Integrating information in the brain. *Trends in Cognitive Sciences* 2(12). 474–484. doi:10.1016/S1364-6613(98)01259-5.

Toppino, Thomas C. & Emilie Gerbier. 2014. About practice. Repetition, spacing, and abstraction. *Psychology of Learning and Motivation* 60. 113–189. doi:10.1016/B978-0-12-800090-8.00004-4.

Toptsis, Ioannis, Alex Haasch, Sonja Hüwel, Jannick Fritsch & Gernot Fink. 2005. Modality Integration and Dialog Management for a Robotic Assistant. *Proceedings of the INTERSPEECH 2005, Lisbon, Portugal*. 837–840.

Trabasso, Tom & Philip Rodkin. 1994. Knowledge of goal/plans: a conceptual basis for narrating Frog, where are you? In Dan I. Berman & Ruth A. Slobin (eds.), *Relating Events in Narrative: A Crosslinguistic Developmental Study*, 85–106. Hillsdale, NJ: Lawrence Erlbaum Associates.

Tranel, Daniel, Christine G. Logan, Randall J. Frank & Antonio R. Damasio. 1997. Explaining category-related effects in the retrieval of conceptual and lexical knowledge for concrete entities: Operationalization and analysis of factors. *Neuropsychologia* 35(10). 1329–1339. doi:10.1016/S0028-3932(97)00086-9.

Traxler, Matthew. 2012. *Introduction to Psycholinguistics: Understanding Language Science*. Chichester: Wiley-Blackwell.

Tremblay, Pascale, Marco Baroni & Uri Hasson. 2013. Processing of speech and non-speech sounds in the supratemporal plane: Auditory input preference does not predict sensitivity to statistical structure. *NeuroImage* 66. 318–332. doi:10.1016/j.neuroimage.2012.10.055.

Tremblay, Pascale & Anthony Steven Dick. 2016. Broca and Wernicke are dead, or moving past the classic model of language neurobiology. *Brain and Language* 162. 60–71. doi:10.1016/j.bandl.2016.08.004.

Trueswell, John C., Irina Sekerina, Nicole M. Hill & Marian L. Logrip. 1999. The kindergarten-path effect: Studying on-line sentence processing in young children. *Cognition* 73(2). 89–134. doi:10.1016/S0010-0277(99)00032-3.

Trueswell, John C. & Michael K. Tanenhaus. 2005. *Approaches to studying world-situated language use. Bridging the language-as-product and language-as-action traditions*. Cambridge, MA: MIT Press.

Tulving, Endel. 1983. *Elements of Episodic Memory*. Oxford: Clarendon Press.

Turkewitz, Gerald & Patricia A. Kenny. 1982. Limitations on input as a basis for neural organization and perceptual development: A preliminary theoretical statement. *Developmental Psychobiology* 15(4). 357–368. doi:10.1002/dev.420150408.

Turner, Elizabeth Ann & Ragnar Rommetveit. 1968. Focus of attention in recall of active and passive sentences. *Journal of Verbal Learning and Verbal Behavior*. 7(2). 543–548. doi:10.1016/S0022-5371(68)80047-7.

Turner, Marilyn L. & Randall W. Engle. 1989. Is working memory capacity task dependent? *Journal of Memory and Language* 28(2). 127–154. doi:10.1016/0749-596X(89)90040-5.

Tversky, Amos. 1977. Features of similarity. *Psychological Review* 84(4). 327–352. doi:10.1037/0033-295X.84.4.327.

Ullman, Michael. 2004. Contributions of memory circuits to language: The declarative/procedural model. *Cognition* 92(1-2), 231–270. doi:10.1016/j.cognition.2003.10.008.

Ullman, Michael. 2016. The Declarative/Procedural Model: A Neurobiological Model of Language Learning, Knowledge, and Use. In Gregory Hickok & Steven L. Small (eds.), *Neurobiology of Language*, 953–968. San Diego, CA: Elsevier. doi:10.1016/B978-0-12-407794-2.00076-6.

Ullman, Michael & Myrna Gopnik. 1999. Inflectional morphology in a family with inherited specific language impairment. *Applied Psycholinguistics* 20(1). 51–117. doi:10.1017/S0142716499001034.

Ullman, Michael & Elizabeth Pierpont. 2005. Specific language impairment is not specific to language: The procedural deficit hypothesis. *Cortex* 41(3). 399–433. doi:10.1016/S0010-9452(08)70276-4.

Van der Maas, Han and Peter Molenaar. 1992. Stagewise cognitive development: an application of catastrophe theory. Psychological Review. 99(3), 395–417.

van Heuven, Walter, Kathy Conklin, Emily Coderre, Taomei Guo, Ton Dijkstra. 2011. The Influence of Cross-Language Similarity on within- and between-Language Stroop Effects in Trilinguals. *Frontiers in psychology*, 2, 374. https://doi.org/10.3389/fpsyg.2011.00374

Verba, Mina. 1994. The Beginnings of Collaboration in Peer Interaction. *Human Development* 37. 125–139. doi:10.1159/000278249.

Vihman, Marilyn M. & Virve-Anneli Vihman. 2011. From first words to segments: A case study in phonological development. In Inbal Arnon & Eve V. Clark (eds.), *Experience, variation, and generalization: Learning a first language*, 109–133. Amsterdam: John Benjamins Publishing Company.

Villiers, Jill G. de. 2005. Can Language Acquisition Give Children a Point of View? In Jodie Baird & Janet Astington (eds.), *Why Language Matters for Theory of Mind*, 186–219. Oxford University Press; New York: doi:10.1093/acprof:oso/9780195159912.003.0010.

Villiers, Jill G. de & Peter A. de Villiers. 2000. Linguistic determinism and the understanding of false beliefs. In Peter Mitchell & Kevin J. Riggs (Eds.), *Children's reasoning and the mind*, 191–228. Hove: Psychology Press.

Vlach, Haley. 2014. The spacing effect in children's generalization of knowledge: Allowing children time to forget promotes their ability to learn. *Child Development Perspectives* 8(3). 163–168. doi:10.1111/cdep.12079.

Vlach, Haley, Amber Ankowski & Catherine Sandhofer. 2012. At the same time or apart in time? the role of presentation timing and retrieval dynamics in generalization. *Journal of Experimental Psychology: Learning, Memory, and Cognition* 38(1). 246–254. doi:10.1037/a0025260.

Vlach, Haley & Catherine Sandhofer. 2012. Fast Mapping Across Time: Memory Processes Support Children's Retention of Learned Words. *Frontiers in Psychology* 3. 46. doi:10.3389/fpsyg.2012.00046.

Vlach, Haley, Catherine Sandhofer & Nate Kornell. 2008. The spacing effect in children's memory and category induction. *Cognition* 109(1). 163–167. doi:10.1016/j.cognition.2008.07.013.

Waddington, Conrad H. 1957. *The strategy of the genes. A discussion of some aspects of theoretical biology. With an appendix by H. Kacser*. London: George Allen & Unwin.

Watanabe, Hama & Gentaro Taga. 2009. Flexibility in infant actions during arm- and leg-based learning in a mobile paradigm. *Infant Behavior and Development* 32(1). 79–90. doi:10.1016/j.infbeh.2008.10.003.

Watts, Duncan J. & Steven H. Strogatz. 2002. Collective dynamics of 'small-world' networks. *Nature* 393(6684). 440–442. doi:10.1038/30918.

Webb, Andrew, Alistair Knott & Michael R. MacAskill. 2010. Eye movements during transitive action observation have sequential structure. *Acta Psychologica* 133(1). 51–56. doi:10.1016/j.actpsy.2009.09.001.

Weikum, Whitney M., Athena Vouloumanos, Jordi Navarra, Salvador Soto-Faraco, Núria Sebastián-Gallés & Janet F. Werker. 2007. Visual language discrimination in infancy. *Science* 316(5828). 1159. doi:10.1126/science.1137686.

Weiller, Cornelius, Tobias Bormann, Dorothee Saur, Mariachristina Musso & Michel Rijntjes. 2011. How the ventral pathway got lost – and what its recovery might mean. *Brain and Language* 118(1-2). 29–39. doi:10.1016/j.bandl.2011.01.005.

Weisleder, Adriana & Anne Fernald. 2013. Talking to children matters: early language experience strengthens processing and builds vocabulary. *Psychological Science* 24(11). 2143–2152. doi:10.1177/0956797613488145.

Weismer, Susan E., Meghan M. Davidson, Ishanti Gangopadhyay, Heidi Sindberg, Hettie Roebuck & Margarita Kaushanskaya. 2017. The role of nonverbal working memory in morphosyntactic processing by children with specific language impairment and autism spectrum disorders. *Journal of Neurodevelopmental Disorders* 9. 28. doi:10.1186/s11689-017-9209-6.

Wells, Gordon. 1981. *Learning through interaction: The study of language development.* Cambridge: Cambridge University Press.

Welsh, Marilyn C., Sarah L. Friedman & Susan J. Spieker. 2006. Executive functions in developing children: Current conceptualizations and questions for the future. In Kathleen McCartney & Deborah Phillips (eds.), *Blackwell handbook of early childhood development*, 167–187. Malden: Blackwell Publishing.

Werker, Janet F. & Richard C. Tees. 1984. Cross-language speech perception: Evidence for perceptual reorganization during the first year of life. *Infant Behavior and Development* 7(1). 49–63. doi:10.1016/S0163-6383(84)80022-3.

Werker, Janet F. & Richard C. Tees. 2005. Speech perception as a window for understanding plasticity and commitment in language systems of the brain. *Developmental Psychobiology* 46(3). 233–251. doi:10.1002/dev.20060.

Werner, Heinz & Bernard Kaplan. 1963. *Symbol Formation: an organismic-developmental approach to language and the expression of thought.* New York: Wiley.

Whiten, Andrew, Nicola McGuigan, Sarah Marshall-Pescini & Lydia M. Hopper. 2009. Emulation, imitation, over-imitation and the scope of culture for child and chimpanzee. *Philosophical Transactions of the Royal Society B: Biological Sciences* 364(1528). 2417–2428. doi:10.1098/rstb.2009.0069.

Whorf, Benjamin L. 1956. *Language, Thought, and Reality: Selected Writings of Benjamin Lee Whorf.* (Edited by John B. Carroll). Cambridge, MA: MIT Press.

Wilbur, Ronnie B. 2003. Representation of telicity in ASL. *Chicago Linguistic Society* 39. 354–368.

Willatts, Peter. 1999. Development of means-end behavior in young infants: pulling a support to retrieve a distant object. *Developmental Psychology* 35(3). 651–667. doi:10.1037/0012-1649.35.3.651.

Willatts, Peter. & Karen Rosie. 1989. Planning by 12-month-old infants. Paper presented at the Biennial Meeting of the Society for Research in Child Development, Kansas City, MO.

Williams, Kipling D. 2009. Ostracism: A temporal need-threat model. In Mark P. Zanna (ed.), *Advances in Experimental Social Psychology* 41, 275–314. San Diego, CA: Elsevier Academic Press. doi:10.1016/S0065-2601(08)00406-1.

Williams, Kipling D. & Steve A. Nida. 2011. Ostracism: Consequences and coping. *Current Directions in Psychological Science* 20(2). 71–75. doi:10.1177/0963721411402480.

Wilson, Margaret. 2002. Six views of embodied cognition. *Psychonomic Bulletin and Review* 9(4). 625–636. doi:10.3758/BF03196322.

Winawer, Jonathan, Nathan Witthoft, Michael C. Frank, Lisa Wu, Alex R. Wade & Lera Boroditsky. 2007. Russian blues reveal effects of language on color discrimination.

Proceedings of the National Academy of Sciences 104(19). 7780–7785. doi:10.1073/pnas.0701644104.
Wolff, Phillip. 2007. Representing causation. *Journal of Experimental Psychology: General* 136(1). 82–111. doi:10.1037/0096-3445.136.1.82.
Wolff, Phillip & Kevin J. Holmes. 2011. Linguistic relativity. *Wiley Interdisciplinary Reviews: Cognitive Science* 2(3). 253–265. doi:10.1002/wcs.104.
Wolpert, Daniel M., Zoubin Ghahramani & J Randall Flanagan. 2001. Perspectives and problems in motor learning. *Trends in Cognitive Sciences* 5(11). 4878–494. doi:10.1016/S1364-6613(00)01773-3.
Woltering, Joost M., Daan Noordermeer, Marion Leleu & Denis Duboule. 2014. Conservation and Divergence of Regulatory Strategies at Hox Loci and the Origin of Tetrapod Digits. *PLoS Biology* 12(1). e1001773. doi:10.1371/journal.pbio.1001773.
Wong, Patrick C. M., Marc Ettlinger & Jing Zheng. 2013. Linguistic Grammar Learning and DRD2-TAQ-IA Polymorphism. *PLoS ONE* 8(5). e64983. doi:10.1371/journal.pone.0064983.
Woodward, Amanda L. 2009. Infants' grasp of others' intentions. *Current Directions in Psychological Science* 18(1). 53–57. doi:10.1111/j.1467-8721.2009.01605.x.
Woodward, Amanda, Ann Phillips & Elizabeth Spelke. 1993. Infants' expectations about the motion of animate versus inanimate objects. *Proceedings of the Fifteenth Annual Meeting of the Cognitive Science Society, Boulder, CO.*, 1087–1091. Hillsdale, NJ: Lawrence Erlbaum Associates.
Woodward, Amanda L. & Jessica A. Sommerville. 2000. Twelve-month-old infants interpret action in context. *Psychological Science* 11(1). 73–77. doi:10.1111/1467-9280.00218.
Woodard, Kristina, Lucia Pozzan & John C. Trueswell. 2016. Taking your own path: Individual differences in executive function and language processing skills in child learners. *Journal of Experimental Child Psychology* 141.187–209. doi:10.1016/j.jecp.2015.08.005.
Woolfe, Tyron, Stephen C. Want & Michael Siegal. 2002. Signposts to development: Theory of mind in deaf children. *Child Development* 73(3). 768–778. doi:10.1111/1467-8624.00437.
Wühr, Peter & Jochen Müsseler. 2001. Time course of the blindness to response-compatible stimuli. *Journal of Experimental Psychology: Human Perception and Performance* 27(5). 1260–1270. doi:10.1037/0096-1523.27.5.1260.
Wulfeck, Beverly. 1993. A Reaction Time Study of Grammaticality Judgments in Children. *Journal of Speech Language and Hearing Research* 36(6). 1208–1215. doi:10.1044/jshr.3606.1208.
Wulfeck, Beverly & Elizabeth Bates. 1991. Differential sensitivity to errors of agreement and word order in Broca's aphasia. *Journal of Cognitive Neuroscience* 3(3). 258–272. doi:10.1162/jocn.1991.3.3.258.
Wunsch, Kathrin & Matthias Weigelt. 2016. A three-stage model for the acquisition of anticipatory planning skills for grip selection during object manipulation in young children. *Frontiers in Psychology* 7. 958. doi:10.3389/fpsyg.2016.00958.
Wynn Karen. 1995. Origins of numerical knowledge. *Mathematical Cognition* 1. 35–60.
Yang, Charles. 2013. Ontogeny and phylogeny of language. *Proceedings of the National Academy of Sciences* 110(16). 6324–6327. doi:10.1073/pnas.1216803110.
Younger, Barbara A. 1985. The segregation of items into categories by ten-month-old infants. *Child Development* 56(6). 1574–1583. doi:10.2307/1130476.
Younger, Barbara. 1990. Infants' Detection of Correlations among Feature Categories. *Child Development* 61(3). 614–620. doi:10.1111/j.1467-8624.1990.tb02806.x.

Younger, Barbara A. & Leslie B. Cohen. 1986. Developmental change in infants' perception of correlations among attributes. *Child Development* 57(3). 803–815. doi:10.2307/1130356.

Younger, Barbara A. & Dru D. Fearing. 1999. Parsing items into separate categories: Developmental change in infant categorization. *Child Development* 70(2). 291–303. doi:10.1111/1467-8624.00022.

Younger, Barbara & Sharon Gotlieb. 1988. Development of Categorization Skills: Changes in the Nature or Structure of Infant Form Categories? *Developmental Psychology* 24(5). 611–619. doi:10.1037/0012-1649.24.5.611.

Yuan, Sylvia & Cynthia Fisher. 2009. "Really? She blicked the baby?": Two-year-olds learn combinatorial facts about verbs by listening: Research article. *Psychological Science* 20(5). 619–26. doi:10.1111/j.1467-9280.2009.02341.x.

Yuile, Amanda & Sabbagh, Mark. In press. Inhibitory control and preschoolers' use of irregular past tense verbs. Journal of Child Language.

Zacks, Jeffrey M., Nicole K. Speer & Jeremy R. Reynolds. 2009. Segmentation in Reading and Film Comprehension. *Journal of Experimental Psychology: General* 138(2). 307–327. doi:10.1037/a0015305.

Zacks, Jeffrey M., Nicole K. Speer, Khena M. Swallow, Todd S. Braver & Jeremy R. Reynolds. 2007. Event perception: a mind/brain perspective. *Psychological Bulletin* 133(2). 273–293. doi:10.1037/0033-2909.133.2.273.

Zacks, Jeffrey M., Nicole K. Speer, Jean M. Vettel & Larry L. Jacoby. 2006. Event understanding and memory in healthy aging and dementia of the Alzheimer type. *Psychology and Aging* 21(3). 466–482. doi:10.1037/0882-7974.21.3.466.

Zacks, Jeffrey M. & Khena M. Swallow. 2007. Event segmentation. *Current Directions in Psychological Science* 16(2). 80–84. doi:10.1111/j.1467-8721.2007.00480.x.

Zacks, Jeffrey M. & Barbara Tversky. 2001. Event structure in perception and conception. *Psychological Bulletin* 127(1). 3–21. doi:10.1037/0033-2909.127.1.3.

Zacks, Jeffrey M., Barbara Tversky & Gowri Iyer. 2001. Perceiving, remembering, and communicating structure in events. *Journal of Experimental Psychology: General* 130(1). 29–58. doi:10.1037/0096-3445.130.1.29.

Zamma, Koichiro. 2002. Grooming site preferences determined by lice infection among Japanese Macaques in Arashiyama. *Primates* 43. 41–49. doi:10.1007/BF02629575.

Zelazo, Philip David & Stephanie M. Carlson. 2012. Hot and Cool Executive Function in Childhood and Adolescence: Development and Plasticity. *Child Development Perspectives* 6(4). 354–360. doi:10.1111/j.1750-8606.2012.00246.x.

Zipf, George K. 1935. *The psycho-biology of language.* New York: Houghton-Mifflin.

Index

Agrammatism 8
Analogy *See* Categorization
animacy 46–48, 63
A-not-B task 77, 79
Attention 76
– the development of 76

Baldwin Effect 15
Beliefs 99, 112, 157
Broca's area 8

Categorization 45
– Event cognition 58
– Segmentation 61
– the development of 48
Centre-embedding 30
Child Directed Speech 149
– over-represented 151
– under-represented 151
Classic Model of Neurolinguistics 10
Cognitive grammar 36
Cognitive robotics 16–18
Cognitive transfer 33, 158
Cognitive typology 66
Comparative Psychology 12–14, 94, 99
Complex Adaptive System 133, 147
Construal 49, 81, 113
Construction semantics 107
Containment 66
Cooperative behavior 99
Corpus analysis 134
Cortical complexity 12

Decision theory 43
Degrees of freedom 19, 39, 44, 87, 127
Developmental Language Disorder 7
Discourse 113
Distribution of items 54, 73, 150
Ditransitive construction 53
Double embedding 30
Dynamic Networks 131
– Community structure 134, 136
Dynamic Systems Theory 41, 96, 124

Ecological niche 26–27
Embodied Cognition 17, 60
Emergentism 138
Encoding Specificity Hypothesis 25
Entrenchment 106
Error-based models of learning 46
Exaptations 13
Eye gaze 84, 96

Figure 66
Forgetting 58
FOXP2 38
Frequency effects 147
– Frequency filter 150
Functional specialization 10
Functionalism 49

Gender agreement 111
Genetics 7, 78
Goal 66
Google Ngram 107
Ground 66

Habituation 38
Hebbian learning 10, 57, 143
Hierarchical organization 64

Image schemas 66
Imperfective 60
Informing 102
In-group 105, 109
Inhibition 76, 89
– Interference suppression 92
– Response inhibition 93
– the development of 76

Joint attention 149

Language as intention made public 101
Language differences and similarities 144
Left-branching 30
Linguistic relatively 156

Manner 59, 66
Maximally distinct argument
   hypothesis 52
Memory 25
– computational modelling of 39
– Declarative 35
– Forgetting 41
– Long-term 35, 62
– Primacy and recency 43
– Procedural 35
– the development of 25
– Working 28, 158
Modularity 3–4
Motor development 96, 124

Narrative 113
Neuronal Recycling Hypothesis 163
Non-linear development 26, 41, 100
Normative reasoning 105
Noun bias 152
Now-Or-Never bottleneck 28, 64

Optional infinitive errors 42
Overgeneralization errors 90, 106

Passives 63, 82
Past tense 89
Path 59, 66
Perceptual priming 81
Perfective 60
Pre-emption 107
Prototypes 50, 70

Raising constructions 47
Reference 113
Requesting 102

Semantic bootstrapping 69
Shared attention 98, 104
Sharing 102
Social Cognition 62, 68, 94
– and language development 103
– the development of 96
Social death 109
Source 66
Specific Language Impairment *See*
   Developmental Language Disorder
Subjacency 18
Subject 82
Superposition 29
Support 66
Syntactic bootstrapping 69

The file-drawer problem 129
Topic-comment 114
Tough constructions 47
Trace back 129
Transitive construction 51, 63
Triple negation 30

Wernicke's area 8
Williams Syndrome 7
Word order 83, 146
World-to-word mapping 152

Zipfian distribution 58, 149

www.ingramcontent.com/pod-product-compliance
Lightning Source LLC
Chambersburg PA
CBHW070802230426
43665CB00017B/2457